11.1

Mike East went out to meet the world after a spell of teaching in the Sudan. His globetrotting has taken him from the gunrunning towns of the North West Frontier to bandit country in the Horn of Africa. Seeking the quieter waters of the Caribbean, Mike's first writing covered the island of Barbados. He now divides his time between travel writing, historical research and teaching.

Whilst completing his studies to become a registered architect **Adrian Jones** accumulated a range of travel experiences. Whether being detained by the Albanian Secret Police or taken on a guided tour of a nuclear bunker in Beijing, the enjoyment of meeting other cultures has always been inspirational. In any spare time he gets Adrian also campaigns for a variety of Third World charities.

Dedication

To all SDSers - reach for the stars....
and
To those who have branched out and 'hit the road'

Acknowledgements

The authors would like to thank the following people who have greatly assisted in the preparation of this work: Angela Cleare, Velda Campbell, Juanita Carey all of the Bahamian Ministry of Tourism; Margaret Ansell and all the staff of the British High Commission, Nassau; Roy Davies, Keith Saunders and family, Richard Brown, Doctor Bob, Fenella Noble, Phil Sowden, Cynthia King and the crew of the Rogue Dog; Mrs J P Jones, Judith Taylor, Mr and Mrs East, John Armeson, Roy and Nigel Lindop, Fiona Inglesent, Sonia Kotarski, Bryn Thomas and Roger Lascelles.

Front cover: *A Cat Islander launches a model boat in a race to raise money for the Summer Regatta.*

Lascelles Caribbean Guides

BAHAMAS

A Traveller's Guide

Mike East and Adrian Jones

Roger Lascelles, Cartographic and Travel Publisher
47 York Road, Brentford, Middlesex TW8 OQP. Tel: 081-847 0935

Publication Data

Title	The Bahamas — Traveller's Guide
Typeface	Phototypeset in Compugraphic Times
Photographs	Front Cover: Pete Johnson
	Other Photographs by the Authors
Printing	Kelso Graphics, Kelso, Scotland.
ISBN	0 903909 92 8
Edition	First Aug 1991
Publisher	Roger Lascelles
	47 York Road, Brentford, Middlesex, TW8 0QP.
Copyright	Text: Mike East and Adrian Jones
	Front Cover: Pete Johnson, 1990

Distribution

Africa:	South Africa —	Faradawn, Box 17161, Hillbrow 2038
Americas:	Canada —	International Travel Maps & Books, P.O. Box 2290, Vancouver BC V6B 3W5
Asia:	India —	English Book Store, 17-L Connaught Circus/P.O. Box 328, New Delhi 110 001
	Singapore —	Graham Brash Pte Ltd., 36-C Prinsep St
Australasia:	Australia —	Rex Publications, 413 Pacific Highway, Artarmon NSW 2064. 428 3566
Europe:	Belgium —	Brussels - Peuples et Continents
	Germany —	Available through major booksellers with good foreign travel sections
	GB/Ireland —	Available through all booksellers with good foreign travel sections
	Italy —	Libreria dell'Automobile, Milano
	Netherlands —	Nilsson & Lamm BV, Weesp
	Denmark —	Copenhagen - Arnold Busck, G.E.C. Gad, Boghallen, G.E.C. Gad
	Finland —	Helsinki — Akateeminen Kirjakauppa
	Norway —	Oslo - Arne Gimnes/J.G. Tanum
	Sweden —	Stockholm/Esselte, Akademi Bokhandel, Fritzes, Hedengrens Gothenburg/Gumperts, Esselte Lund/Gleerupska
	Switzerland —	Basel/Bider: Berne/Atlas; Geneve/Artou; Lausanne/Artou: Zurich/Travel Bookshop

Getting the best out of this guidebook

Accommodation
We have calculated the cost of hotels from the basic rate for the room without meals (European Plan, EP), in the winter-high season (16th December to 21st April). Top ($161 plus), high ($121-$160), middle ($81-$120), moderate ($41-$80) and budget ($40 and under). 8% government resort levy and tax to be added on to all prices and sometimes a service or maid's gratuity on top. Enquire in advance as these surcharges are not usually quoted. On average prices tend to be between 20% and 60% less in the summer-low season.

If the charge includes meals we have noted it with the following symbols: AI = All Inclusive: meals rooms and facilities.
AP = American Plan: room with three meals.
CP = Continental Plan: room and breakfast.
MAP = Modified American Plan: room, breakfast and dinner.

Places to eat
With restaurants we have included the cost of a three course meal without drinks. The eating establishments on New Providence and Grand Bahama are divided into sections depicting the style of food served. They are in order of our recommendation. In the Family Islands (Out Islands), restaurants are arranged by cost.

Credit Cards
After each hotel and restaurant review, the credit cards that may be used therein are listed. Abbreviations: AMEX = American Express, MC = Mastercard, V = Visa.

Currency
The US and Bahamian dollars are of equal value.

Language
To avoid confusion between the different phraseology used in North America and Europe (e.g. gasoline/ petrol or liquor/ alcohol), Bahamian terms are used throughout.

Addresses
There is no door to door delivery service; all mail is collected from the Post Office. To contact any establishment mentioned in the text use the PO Box number and indicate clearly which island.

Contents

16 Freeport — Grand Bahama

Part 5: The Northern Family Islands

Part 6: The Southern Family Islands

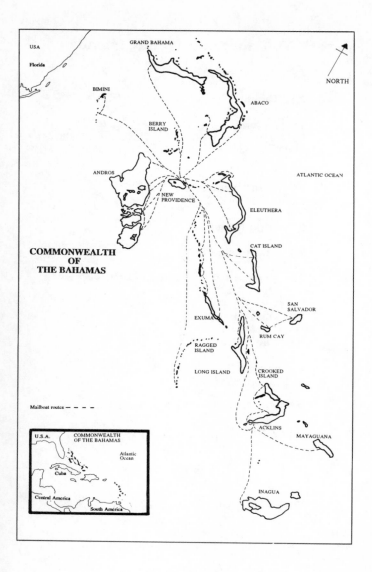

USA

Florida

GRAND BAHAMA

BIMINI

ABACO

BERRY
ISLAND

NORTH

ANDROS

ATLANTIC OCEAN

NEW
PROVIDENCE

ELEUTHERA

CAT ISLAND

COMMONWEALTH
OF
THE BAHAMAS

SAN
SALVADOR

EXUMA

RUM CAY

RAGGED
ISLAND

LONG ISLAND

CROOKED
ISLAND

Mailboat routes — — — —

ACKLINS

MAYAGUANA

INAGUA

COMMONWEALTH
OF THE BAHAMAS

U.S.A.

Atlantic
Ocean

Cuba

Central America

South America

ONE

Introducing the Bahamas

'Hey mon what's happ'nin?' is the archetypal Bahamian welcome. It sounds like a question but it is more of a greeting and perhaps a conversation starter. Walking down a Bahamian street you will see the faces of a people who live to enjoy life. They break into a smile easily, often calling greetings across the way.

The country's name derives from the 'Baja Mar', or shallow sea surrounding it. Tropical but not too hot, the Bahamas earned the appellation 'the isles of perpetual June' many years ago. The 700 islands and cays are totally dwarfed in size by the mighty land mass beside them. Only half an hour from Miami they may be, but proximity does not mean similarity.

The Bahamas are an enigma, neither part of the Caribbean nor of the North American continent. They are described as a developing country, yet they enjoy a good GNP and high standard of living. Although an island chain that contains elements of Caribbean culture, African heritage, a British colonial legacy and the latest American trends, the Bahamas still somehow manage to assert an individuality all of their own.

It would be easy to stand in the centre of Nassau and take the country's prosperity for granted, but this would be a gross misunderstanding. In earlier centuries Bahamians constantly searched for ways to make ends meet. Life was a struggle until a few decades ago when Bahamians realised their greatest gift was the natural beauty of their surroundings. The good news spread and now over three million visitors come every year.

There are over a quarter of a million Bahamians, a young people with over 65% under 30 years of age. Well over half of the workforce is employed in tourism, with significant numbers working in the international banking sector. Nassau contains well over half the population; and if you add to this those living in Freeport, this leaves less than 50,000 people on all the other islands combined.

The Bahamas: did you know?

Despite being a nation of 700 islands many Bahamians cannot swim.

The Bahamas have their own Loch Ness Monster called Lusca, who supposedly inhabits the coves and inlets of Andros and occasionally gobbles up a passing boat.

More Bahamians are hurt annually by falling coconuts than by shark attacks.

The most expensive hotel room in the world is the Galaxy Suite at Carnival's Crystal Palace. A mere snip a $25,000 a night.

Most people agree Columbus' landfall was on San Salvador but several other places, including Cat Island, Exuma and Samana Cay, claim this privilege.

Over 2,250,000 lobsters are exported to the United States every year, yet more are found each season, a seemingly inexhaustible supply.

The disappearance of Flight 19, one of the most famous cases in the mystery of the Bermuda triangle, occurred whilst the planes flew out to bomb the derelict 'Sapona' near Bimini.

At the height of the drugs war extravagant smugglers would fly from Bimini to Miami just to order a pizza.

During the Second World War scurrilous rumours circulated that a Nazi sympathiser was building a U-boat hideout on Paradise Island.

In the Bahamas entrants to beauty contests seek sponsorship, resulting in such unlikely names as Mrs Beefeater, Miss Phoenix Pest Control, Miss Jungle Juice and Miss Ooh La La.

The original Lucayan inhabitants of the Bahamas left one gift to posterity before they were wiped out, the hammock.

The largest passenger cruise ship in the world, the Fantasy, sails to the Bahamas twice a week. It has a capacity of 2600 passengers plus crew.

The thought of countless miles of pristine sand shaded by lines of casuarina trees and lapped by gin-clear waters is a vision of heaven to the worker in a snowbound northern city. Accessibility is problem for anywhere on the eastern seaboard of the USA is only about two and a half hours away. The West Coast and Canada are slightly further afield, and western Europe only several hours away. Sea lines are also numerous, especially from Florida.

For many years the Bahamas have held a certain allure to the rich and famous. It is a place where one can disappear for a while. With attractions including virtually no taxation and strictly secret banking laws, it is no surprise that some of the world's wealthiest people have homes here, or even their own private island.

With so many islands, which one should a prospective visitor choose? The most popular destination has always been New

Providence which boasts the capital Nassau and two of the most sophisticated casino-resort areas in the world: Paradise Island and the Bahamian Riviera. Nassau is a show-case of fine architecture from the bygone colonial era, and the magic of the ocean depths is on display at Coral World. New Providence prides itself on its fine selection of eating establishments.

Freeport on Grand Bahama is a forward looking modern town with many top class resorts and casinos. The International Bazaar and Lucayan Marketplace offer a host of duty free bargains. Sports fans are well catered for, with several 18-hole golf courses and the full range of water sports. There are beautiful gardens to explore or the natural wonders of the Lucayan National Park. You can spend the morning at the Dolphin Experience, a pioneering experiment that allows humans to interact with and learn about these intelligent and playful mammals, or perhaps take your first scuba course.

The outlying islands, known as the Family Islands because of their friendly atmosphere, are home to several exclusive hideaway resorts. It is a peaceful and uncluttered world of virgin beaches, shady palm trees and hospitable village communities ideal for the sun-seeker or civilised recluse to escape the pressure of a western lifestyle.

TWO

Before you go

When to go

The Bahamas 'perpetual June' weather is due to two moderating influences: warming by the Gulf Stream in the winter and cooling by the Trade Winds in the summer. On a practical level August is the hottest month, averaging 28°C (82°F); and January/February the coolest 21°C (70°F). In winter months (mid-November to mid-April) the afternoon temperature ranges from 16°C (60°F) to 26°C (78°F), though the northern isles, especially in the mornings, are cooler. Sea temperature is about 21°C (74°F). Summer temperatures average 26°C (78°F) at night and rarely more than 32°C (91°F) in the day, with the heat more intense further south. Water temperature will be about 27°C (82°F). Rainfall is more variable, usually coming in cloudbursts without a marked increase in windspeed and lasting approximately an hour, then quickly drying up. June and October are the wettest months (approximately 175mm/7ins rainfall).

Prices

Accommodation is generally between 20% and 60% cheaper in the summer. This is to do with the propensity of most North Americans (the main visitors) to take winter holidays to escape the cold, leading to a fall in demand in the summer.

The Government raises finance by import duties rather than by personal taxation. As virtually all goods are imported, usually from the USA, prices reflect both shipping costs and duties. For example there is a 35% duty on all imported foods. All toiletries are expensive (shampoo, suntan lotion etc.), so locals and expatriates prefer to travel to Miami for such items.

The average price for a restaurant meal is between $20 and $30 per person. Most places add a 15% service charge automatically for 'your convenience'. Hotels add a daily maid gratuity and government resort tax.

Hurricanes

Fortunately these are rare, rare appearing maybe once every ten years, their destructive powers can be immense. Cash in your insurance policy if you can make firm arrangements to leave. There is an efficient, modern warning system which will give approximately 24 hours notice.

The season for hurricanes and storms is from June until October. Storms or tropical depressions may hit once every three years. After the torrential rains and winds have ceased, the sun appears and within 24 hours life is back to normal.

Passports and visas

Passports are not required for entry by British or Canadian subjects for up to three weeks and by United States citizens for up to eight months, providing proof of citizenship (e.g. birth certificate) is available. Taking a passport avoids any difficulties upon returning to your home country. Visas are never required by United Kingdom, Canadian or other Commonwealth citizens, but a time limit, which can be extended, is given by Customs Officers upon entry.

Similarly passports but not visas are required by visitors from Belgium, Greece, Iceland, Italy, Luxembourg, Netherlands, Norway, Spain, Switzerland and Turkey. Three month stays with passport only, are permitted for citizens of Austria, France, Germany, Denmark, Finland, Sweden, Ireland, Israel and Japan. South American citizens may stay up to a fortnight with passports only. Longer stays require visas. Other nationals should contact the Bahamian consulate, or if this is not possible, the British Consulate.

Travel alternatives

Packages
By far the least expensive means of visiting the Bahamas is to purchase a package holiday. This will always include flight and accommodation and sometimes airport transfer transport and a host

of other extras as well. The cost is again usually cheaper in the low season from May to mid-December. Contact your nearest Bahamas Tourist Office for leaflets on cruise and tour packages:

Europe

Britain	Chesterfield Street, London W1X 8AH (tel. 071 629 5238).
France	9 Boulevard de la Madeleine, 75001 Paris (tel. 1 4261 30).
Italy	Foro Buonaparte 68, 21231 Milano (tel. 2 7202 3003).
Germany	6000 Frankfurt am Main, Poststrasse 2-4 (tel. 049 069 25 20 29).

North America

Miami	255 Alhambra Circle, Suite 425 Coral Gables, Florida 33134 (tel. 305 442 4860).
	Latin America, (tel. 305 447 9797).
Canada	Montreal (tel. 514 861 6796)
	Toronto (tel. 416 968 2990).

Independent

The Bahamas Reservations Service will make bookings free of charge for the independent traveller at any of the hotels in its register. They can be contacted via the above offices. If telephoning from the United States call toll free 800 327 0787 or in Florida (except Dale County) call toll free 800 432 5594. In Canada call Toronto 416 968 2999 or Montreal 514 861 6797.

The other possible saving is to take advantage of low air-fares on chartered or scheduled flights. Florida is usually the best gateway, taking advantage of the competition for passengers throughout North America or across the Atlantic and between the Bahamas and Florida itself. If visiting the Family Islands, Bahamasair have flight and hotel package deals offering considerable savings. Use your travel agent to explore these savings.

Tourism with a difference

As package tours and mass tourism spreads worldwide, there is now a counter movement which is steadily gaining in popularity. This is 'Intercultur', or social tourism, a new type of cultural exchange. In return for a small registration fee this organisation arranges a host person or family for visitors. Accommodation can vary widely with costs being kept to a minimum. As a guest you are expected to contribute about $40 per week to household costs.

The advantages are that this type of vacation is substantially cheaper than staying in a hotel. You are able to meet people from the country you are visiting and get a deeper understanding about them. It is a chance to make new friends. Even so normal precautions, such as travel and health insurance, should still be obtained.

As yet there is no scheme in the Bahamas though the UK branch, is currently seeking to establish one: Intercultur GB, c/o CRS Ltd. Political Committee, 78-102 The Broadway, Stratford, London E15 1NL (tel. 081 534 4201 ext. 271). Social Tourism was conceived by the German Young Friends of Nature: NFTG-Intercultur, Postfach 2157, Rosenstrasse 1, 4806 Werther, Germany. In North America there is the Center for Responsible Tourism, which seeks to educate people as to the effects of mass tourism: 2 Kensington Road, San Anselmo, CA 94960 (tel. USA 415 258 6594). Its general philosophy is similar to European Social Tourism.

Independent women travellers

Nassau and Freeport contain all the dangers inherent in any large conurbation. On the Family Islands everything is much more relaxed. The culture is very much male dominated (where is it not?), though you will find women in key positions, particularly in managerial and administrative posts. Working women on top of this are expected to cook the meals and do all the household chores as well.

Dress is conservative. Most people are used to all sorts of beachwear though wraps should be worn to and from the beach and changed before going into town. During daylight hours it is safe to walk around all the tourist areas by yourself. At night it is advisable to be in pairs (see section on crime and safety on page 41).

All night clubs will have an even mix of sexes. The Bahamians love to party. Bahamian men are informal and extroverted, to them dancing is a contact sport, whether it is with longstanding friends or a complete stranger. A firm 'no' is understood by all.

In built up areas, when driving a car, lock all doors. Use the air-conditioning rather than open the windows, especially if wearing snatchable jewellery. The Jitneys (minibuses) are a lively, friendly means of transport with the drivers and passengers being very helpful. Taxis, identifiable by white plates, are registered and any complaints will be dealt with. If you do have any problems, immediately contact the Ministry of Tourism who will be cooperative and friendly (staffed by women throughout its various levels). Private taxis hackers also exist, but you have less means of recourse.

Taking the children

A number of the big resort hotels offer 'camps' for children (listed below and in the accommodation section). They involve such activities as sandcastle building, seashell collecting, aerobics, finger painting etc., under proper supervision.

When travelling with very young children it is advisable to bring your own supply of disposable nappies, as these are very expensive in the Bahamas; similarly with baby foods, though duty will have to be paid on imports.

Club Med, Eleuthera. No extra costs: the Peti, Mini and Kids clubs, ages 2 to 11 years of age; 9.00-21.00.

Pirate's Cove, Holiday Inn, Paradise Island. Complimentary: Captain Kids Camp, ages 4 to 12, 9.00-12.00 and 14.00-16.00; extended over summer and holidays.

Sheraton Grand Hotel, Paradise Island. Complimentary: Camp Caribbean, ages 5 to 13 years, 10.00-1700; extended Thursday through Saturday. Open only during the summer, Easter and Christmas vacations.

Nassau Beach Hotel, Bahamian Riviera. Complimentary: Sand-pipers, ages 3 to 12 and Ambassadors for teenagers; 10.00-1700.

Crystal Palace. Camp Carnival, ages 5 to 12.

Travel for the disabled

The Bahamas Association for the Physically Disabled and its dedicated staff are doing their utmost to ensure that handicapped people can enjoy a vacation in the Bahamas, (Dolphin Drive, PO Box N4252, Nassau; tel. 322 2393). The Association does regular surveys of accommodation and facilities on New Providence and is hoping to widen its activities to other islands.

Nassau is regrettably the only place with good facilities for the handicapped. Freeport, more car-oriented, has few pavements and large steps.

A suggested hotel in the Family Islands is Hilton's Haven on

Eleuthera, which is managed by a retired nurse and allows wheelchair access.

On New Providence the Physically Disabled Association operates a minibus to cater for disabled tourists who cannot enter normal modes of transport. It can collect visitors from the airport and a guided tour of the island is offered . No fee is charged. although the Association seeks donations so that it can continue to offer this service. Ardastra Gardens and the casinos have ramp access.

Suggested hotels on New Providence:

Paradise Island. The Holiday Inn offers two specially adapted rooms and wheelchair access. Paradise Island Resort and Casino offer wheelchair access.

Bahamian Riviera. Carnival's Crystal Palace provide wheelchair access and grab bars in the bathrooms. The Wyndham Ambassador offers wheelchair access.

On balance, Holiday Inn probably offers the best facilities on the island. There is nowhere in Downtown Nassau which can be recommended at present.

Taking pets

Contact the Ministry of Agriculture, Trade and Industry (PO Box N-3028) for a permit, enclosing a $10 processing fee. Information required includes animal, breed, age, sex, country of embarkation and a copy of a Veterinary Health Certificate. The permit is valid for 90 days from date of issue.

Weddings and honeymoons

The lure of a tropical island is an irresistible temptation to most lovers and newly weds — the genesis of a lifelong romance. Arrangements can easily be made and a number of operators specialise in such packages (see section on 'Getting there'). The island authorities ensure that the paperwork is not a daunting proposition for a barefoot wedding down on the beach or amongst the elegance of lush gardens.

Marriage regulations

Minimum residency is 15 days (by either party), waived to three days upon advance notice. Contact the Registrar General's Office, East Hill Street, PO Box N-532, New Providence. The marriage licence costs $20. Original documents required are passports, birth certificates and a Decree Absolute (if one or both of the parties are divorcees). In the case of a widow/widower, a death certificate is advisable though not necessary, as your word will be acceptable. The minimum age without parental consent is 21. A blood test is not required. It is advisable to send only photocopies with postal enquiries.

If planning your own arrangements it is possible to organise the ceremony with a Magistrate or priest during the initial residency period. The 'People to People' programme will help in making this a particularly Bahamian affair. Please give the Ministry of Tourism advance notice.

Health and vaccinations

Travel insurance
Make sure you are covered for all medical needs. Emergency treatment is both excellent and expensive. Insurance must cover air ambulance — if a major accident or illness occurs you may be flown either to Nassau or out to Miami. Driving conditions in the Bahamas are bad; accidents do occur.

Vaccinations
Yellow fever jabs are only required from travellers coming from infected areas within the last seven days.

Water
It is safe to drink, though it could taste better. Bottled water is readily available; five gallons cost $3.

Sun
This is extremely strong and you could easily tan or burn even on the occasional overcast day. The sun's rays penetrate 2m (6ft) below the water's surface. Take plenty of the strongest sunblock, including the water-resistant kind, and aftersun lotions. Take it gradually at first and wrap up at other times.

Ear infection An infection can be caused by sea water becoming trapped in the ear, especially in small children. Take ear drops and talk to your family doctor before departure if you are concerned about this.

Medical kit
It is always sensible to take one, especially with small children. Bring your own supply of medicines if you are a diabetic or on a prescription. Most drugs are available but expensive. Also bring your prescription in case of emergencies.

Mosquitoes and poisonous animals
On some islands they can be a real problem. Use an insect repellent and talk to your doctor about anti-histamine tablets. Malaria has long been irradicated. **Poisonous animals** are unknown except on a few remote islands and then extremely rare.

Hospitals
The two principal government-run hospitals are Princess Margaret, Nassau and Rand Memorial, Freeport. There are over 50 government clinics located around the islands. It will cost a minimum of $30 a day to stay in hospital, plus all medical costs. Credit cards are accepted if your insurance policy relies on your paying out first and reclaiming the money. If possible get someone you know, to help sort out the details. If you are on your own, telephone the Ministry of Tourism for help. Also keep the address and telephone number of your consulate with you in case of a serious emergency.

Dentistry is expensive. (For example, if you are travelling from the United Kingdom and while on holiday a crown filling worked loose, it would be cheaper to fly back home than have it fixed in the Bahamas!). However the quality of workmanship is excellent. It is advisable to have a check-up before your holiday.

THREE

Getting there

By air

When purchasing your ticket the cost is often the most critical factor. The extensive rivalry for passengers in the skies over North America and across the Atlantic, makes most fares competitive. The next factor should be consideration of the number of connections or airplane changes. If your luggage is going to go astray this is the most likely reason. Similarly, transfer times can lead to long waits at airport terminals. Remaining with one airline is often the key to avoiding such problems.

With over 60 years of experience, Pan Am offer an extensive network across North America and the Atlantic being one of the largest airlines in the world. It is the number one carrier in the transatlantic market and the hassle of connections, transfer times and arrival of luggage safely can largely be avoided. With six daily flights out of Miami to Nassau and Freeport, plus direct flights from New York (Kennedy) to Nassau, the Bahamas are well served by this major airline.

To make reservations or to seek further information, contact your travel agents or telephone PanAm direct (UK 071 409 0688) or toll free USA 1 800 200 221 111. If possible have a list of alternative dates of departure, in case less expensive tickets are available.

A number of other world airlines fly directly into the Bahamas — Air Canada, Eastern, British Airways, Delta and Trans World Airlines. The national carrier, Bahamasair, have flights from a number of American cities. Miami is the busiest gateway and a list of commuter airlines that fly to the islands is given under the 'Arrival' section in each chapter.

Bahamasair links all the other islands with Nassau. It is proud to claim that it will never leave you stranded and will get you to your destination that day. When booking, always give the names of everybody in your party and confirm that all will fly name by name.

Reserve your seats when purchasing your ticket. In the summer, Goombay Packages offer discounted airfare and hotel rooms as a package. Ask your travel agent to check out details.

By sea

Cruise ship passage to the Bahamas

Once the preserve of the idle rich, the opportunity to cruise is now available to all. Part of the glamour is the pampered lifestyle cruising offers, whether it is a 2 day mini-cruise or a 7, 10 or 14 day jaunt across the seas.

The Bahamas attracts over a million cruise-ship passengers a year. Most journey to Nassau or Freeport and a few offer stops on the Family Isles (see lists in chapters on each island). The Bahamian government hopes to expand this operation to include other Family Island destinations.

There is a range of choices affecting cost and enjoyment. Cruises are more expensive around Christmas and Easter and of course the smaller cabins are the least expensive. The length of cruise and the number of ports to be visited will also affect cost.

For the first-time passenger or those wishing a short break, the two night mini-cruise by Crown Cruise offers a taste of ocean life at affordable prices. The Crown Del Mar is smaller than some ships and you will not become just another number! It departs Friday evenings at 17.00 from the Port of Palm Beach. A complimentary bottle of champagne and fruit basket will await you in your cabin. Each room is pleasantly decorated with double or twin beds, en-suite shower and toilet with complimentary array of fine toiletries, hand-held hair dryer and remote control colour television. Facilities on board include a casino, pool, sun deck, whirlpools, SeaFit instructor, masseur and saloon. Relax in the panoramic lounges, quicken the tempo on the dance floor of Club Tropicanna or enjoy the entertainment in the glittering cabaret show. The food, as befits an ocean liner, is excellent, from midnight buffets to eight course dinners. Shortly after daybreak the ship arrives in Nassau, giving you a full day for sightseeing, shopping and beachcombing. The homeward bound journey departs at approximately 18.00. Other cruise destinations and longer sea-going voyages are also available.

Similar itineraries and facilities are offered by other liners. Contact the Bahamian Tourist Board in your area for a list of cruise operators or use the services of your travel agent. The main companies include:

Admiral Cruise Line (USA tel. 305 374 1611). Three and four nights — Miami to Nassau, Little Stirrup Cay, Freeport.
Carnival Cruise Line (UK tel. 071 839 2383; USA tel. 305 599 2600). Three, four or seven nights — departing from Cape Canaveral, Fort Lauderdale or Miami to Nassau and Freeport.
Chandris Cruise Line (USA tel. 305 573 3140). Two nights — Miami to Nassau. Costa Line Cruises (UK tel. 071 436 9431; USA tel. 305 358 7325).
Seven nights — Fort Lauderdale to Nassau.
Crown Cruise Line (USA tel. 305 394 7450). Two nights — Palm Beach to Nassau.
Dolphin Cruise Line (UK tel. 071 235 0168; USA tel. 305 358 3005). Three, four, seven or fourteen nights - Miami to Nassau, Freeport and Salt Cay.
Norwegian Cruise Line (UK tel. 071 408 0046; USA tel. 305 358 6670).
Three, four or seven nights — Miami to Nassau, Freeport and Great Stirrup Cay.
Princess Voyages (UK tel. 071 831 1881). Nine or twelve nights — Miami to Nassau.
Premier Cruise Lines (UK tel. 071 839 5591; USA tel. 305 383 5061). Three or four nights — Fort Lauderdale to Nassau and Salt Cay; there are also cruises to Treasure Cay, Green Turtle Cay, Treasure Island and Man-O-War Cay.
Royal Caribbean Cruise Line (UK tel. 081 541 5044; USA tel. 305 379 2601).
Three or four nights — Miami to Nassau, Freeport and Little Stirrup Cay.
Sitmar Cruises (UK, Southern Worldwide tel. 0293 560777; USA tel. 305 592 3640). Twelve nights — Miami to Nassau.

Bareboat chartering
The term applies to a yacht rented with neither a captain nor crew. Sometimes a captain can be hired for about $90 to $120 a day. The boats are fully equipped and costs are lower, but only experienced sailors are allowed to rent. Rental prices vary with the size of boat, length of vacation and time of year. An essential guide on marinas, harbours and the surrounding seas is the Yachtsman's Guide to the Bahamas (Tropic Isle Publishers Inc, PO Box 340866, Miami, Florida 33134; tel. 305 893 4277). Operators are:
CSY Limited (Caribbean Sailing Yachts), PO Box 491, Tenafly, New Jersey 07670 (tel. 201 568 0390), which rents boats out of Marathon Key in the Florida Keys.

Fun in the Sun Yacht Charters Inc, 320 N Federal Highway, Dania, Florida 33004 (USA tel. toll free 800 327 0228), with rentals out of Fort Lauderdale and Marsh Harbour, Abaco.

Abaco Bahamas Charters Limited, 10905 Cowgill Place, Louisville. KY 40243 (tel. 502 245 9428); Hope Town, Abaco, Bahamas.

Package tours and travel agents

A whole range of options exists. There are specialist packages for tennis, golf, scuba and snorkeling holidays, plus honeymoon specials. Use your travel agent to find the best buys and options and to discover all the 'extras'. There are usually maid charges and government resort tax.

Most people choose package holidays for their convenience, cheapness and fixed advance price. Packages take advantage of mass volume and thereby reduce the price. Christmas and Easter vacations are usually more expensive. Nearly all are based on double occupancy so single travellers may have to pay a surcharge. Twin centred vacations between Florida and the Bahamas are alternative packages to consider and are becoming very popular. Your local Bahamian Tourism office will have a list of all operators with tours from your area. In the UK some of the leading operators are (those with a * have wedding and honeymoon specials):

Cosmosair plc, Tourama House, 17 Homesdale Road, Bromley, Kent, BR2 9LX.

Dream Island of the World*, 5 Chartherhouse Buildings, Goswell Road, London, EC1M 7AW.

Frontier Tours, 136 Devonshire Road, London, W4 2AW.

Harlequin Holidays, 124 Handsworth Road, Handsworth, Sheffield, Yorkshire S9 4AB.

Hayes and Jarvis*, 152 King Street, Hammersmith, London, W6 0QU.

Jetsave Limited, Sussex House, London Road, East Grinstead, West Sussex, RH19 1LD.

Jetset, Jetset House, 74 New Oxford Street, London, WC1A 1EU.

Kuoni Travel*, Kuoni House, Dorking, Surrey, RH5 4AZ.

New Beginnings*, Rawdon House, Victoria Way, High Street, Hoddesdon, Herts, EN11 8TE.

Pan Am Holidays, 14 Old Park Lane, London, W1Y 3LH.

Sol Golf Holidays, 48-50 Fore Street, Hertford, Herts, SG14 1AW.

Speedbird Holidays, Pacific House, Hazelwick Avenue, Three Bridges, Crawley, West Sussex, RH10 1NP.

The American Experience Belper Travel*, Meadow Court, South Normanton, Derbyshire, DE55 2BN.

Tradewinds Faraway Holidays, Station House, 81-83 Fulham High Street, London, SW6 3JP.

Virgin Holidays Limited*, 3rd Floor, Sussex House, High Street, Crawley, West Sussex, RH10 1BZ.

FOUR

What to take

Clothing

The emphasis is on the casual, so take shorts, T-shirts and light sportswear to wear during the day. Remember that beachwear is considered inappropriate in town, in restaurants, public buildings and the casinos. Some restaurants require men to wear a jacket and tie and women to be smartly attired, though this rule may be relaxed during summer. Dry cleaning is available on New Providence and Grand Bahama but you are unlikely to find this service in the Family Islands. For wet weather an umbrella is recommended; to keep the sun off your head a hat is advisable.

Money

The Bahamian dollar is on par with the US dollar and both currencies are legal tender and accepted everywhere. Denominations of Bahamian coins are one, five, ten and 25 cents, with notes available in 50 cents, $1, $3, $5, $10, $20, $50, $100, $1,000. It is recommended that all visitors to the Bahamas take US dollar travellers' cheques as these are easily convertible; other currencies are less readily exchanged. Most large hotels, restaurants and shops cash travellers' cheques and for very late banking the casinos are always open and commission free. American Express, Master Card and Visa are widely accepted in Nassau and Freeport. If you intend to visit the Family Islands ensure that you have sufficient cash and travellers' cheques for your stay.

Electrical adaptors

The Bahamian standard is 120V, 60 cycles, identical to the US and Canada. Visitors from elsewhere should bring adaptors.

Film and photography

X-ray equipment when present at airports in the Bahamas does not damage equipment. Fresh film can be easily obtained on all but the most remote Family Islands but is expensive. New Providence and Grand Bahama have a wide range of efficient developing services, though only 'Mr Photo' develops slides. 'Patricks Camera Specialists' (tel. 325 0851) off Bay Street, Nassau have a camera repair service.

Food and necessities

The Bahamas have a consumer society with a huge variety of goods available on the main islands. It is unlikely that anything will be unattainable though many items are expensive: for example 4 pint container of milk ($2.75); can coke ($1); 4 oz coffee ($6); and large sliced bread ($1.80).

Presents

If you are visiting a Bahamian friend or family a suggested present is something typically associated with your country of origin. Bahamians themselves often take cakes as presents when they go visiting others.

Reading matter

Books are noticeably more pricey than elsewhere so if you can, buy them at home. Several paperbacks have a Bahamian theme to them.

Ernest Hemingway's *Islands in the Stream* is partly autobiographical, with about one third of the book set on Bimini. It contains vivid descriptions of fishing trips in Hemingway's rough and ready style.

James Frew's *In the Wake of the Leopard* has a cardboard cutout hero who battles with a ruthless gang of Nazis in this entertaining adventure. A race against time involving a beautiful actress, the DEA, an arrogant British agent and numerous bad guys. It includes many interesting sidelines about the Bahamas.

Paul Albury's *The Story of the Bahamas* is a light and readable account of the main events and notable characters of the Bahamian, from the earliest times to independence.

James Leasor's *Who Killed Sir Harry Oakes?* is an entertaining if fanciful account of this famous murder, which was used as the basis for the television series Murder in Paradise.

Sidney Poitier's *This Life* is the autobiographical account of the star of such films as *Guess Who's Coming to Dinner* and *In the Heat of the Night*. The book deals mainly with his acting career, though the earlier chapters describe Poitier's childhood days on Cat Island.

Charles Highnam's *The Duchess of Windsor — the Secret Life* an intriguing expos of what the Duchess was really like, her motivation and ambition. The book contains two excellent chapters on the Bahamas. Highnam has thoroughly investigated the murder of Sir Harry Oakes and produces a convincing argument on the motives and identity of the real murderer. Furthermore he goes on to show the Duke of Windsor's shady dealings as governor and his attempts to doctor the evidence in the subsequent inquiry into Sir Harry Oakes' murder. This thoroughly researched book brings into full light the Windsor's infamous connections with Hitler and fascism. Highnam's assertions are backed up with abundant evidence, a fascinating read.

Paul Eddy, Hugo Sabogal and Sara Walden's *The Cocaine Wars* this is a detailed examination of the war against the drug smugglers. One quarter of the book relates to Carlos Lehder and his activities in the Bahamas. It is a compelling but disturbing piece of investigative journalism.

Desmond Bagley's *Bahamas Crisis* a thriller about personal tragedy and the disaster that befalls a hotel magnate. Very cleverly written it gives a good insight into the importance of tourism.

Evans Cottrell's *Out Island Doctor* is a fascinating insight into Bahamian life in the Family Islands before the advent of tourism and modern communications. Slip back in time and appreciate the wonders of a lifestyle that can be seen as romantic and endearing, yet frugal and hard.

Saundra Ridley's *Captain's Ladies* is a tale of romance set on the high seas and the island of Jamaica. The story of the Bahamian women pirates Anne Bonny and Mary Read, their lives and loves.

Herman Wouk's *Don't Stop the Carnival* is a light-hearted novel set on a mythical island somewhere in the Caribbean, that well could be the Bahamas. A Hollywood publicist buys an hotel and leaves the rat-race behind but finds that his troubles are only just beginning.

FIVE

Arrival and departure

Immigration and customs

Upon arrival all visitors must fill in a Bahamas Immigration Form. A duplicate copy is returned to you, which must be kept safely until departure when it is inspected and collected. An onward or return ticket is another entry requirement. Bahamas customs are able to take thousands of arrivals and departures per day so there is usually a minimum of delay if all documents are in order. At Nassau and Freeport International Airports United States Immigration and Customs also complete their necessary formalities at your departure.

There is a **departure tax** of $7 per person.

Customs and duty free allowances

An oral declaration is required and officials may take a cursory glance at luggage though generally entrance is unhindered. Visitors are allowed to bring unlimited amounts of foreign currency, 50 cigars, 200 cigarettes, one quart each of liquor and wine, and gifts up to a total of $25 in value. As elsewhere, firearms, animals and narcotics are prohibited.

The **duty free allowance** for US residents, provided your stay in the Bahamas has been more than 48 hours, is $400 in merchandise each. This may be pooled by family members. Those over 21 are allowed to include one litre of alcohol. All may carry 100 (non-Cuban) cigars and 200 cigarettes. Those staying for less than 48 hours may carry up to $25 of gifts including 10 (non-Cuban) cigars, 50 cigarettes, 4fl oz of alcohol (if over 21) and 4oz of perfume.

For Canadian residents the allowance varies depending on the time spent away and previous duty free claims. After 24 hours of absence $20 of goods may be carried excluding cigarettes or alcohol;

after 48 hours $100, including up to 50 cigars, 200 cigarettes, 2lbs of tobacco and 40fl oz of liquor; once every calender year after seven days abroad up to $300, of items including the same liquor quotas as for 48 hours. The legal age to import tobacco is 16; 18 for alcohol.

UK and EEC residents may bring out 200 cigarettes, 100 cigarillos, 50 cigars or 250 grammes of tobacco. The alcohol allowance is one litre if over 22% proof, or two litres if less than 22% proof of spirits or fortified or sparkling wine. Two litres of table wine may be added, provided the person is 17 or over. Fifty grammes of perfume (2fl oz) and nine fl oz of toilet water may be carried duty free.

UK residents are only allowed to bring in another £32 worth of goods.

Mailing gifts home duty free

For the USA each present must not exceed $50 in value and have 'unsolicited gift' written upon the package. It may not include tobacco, liquor or over $5 worth of perfume.

For **Canada** each gift must not be worth more than C$40 and not consist of alcohol, tobacco or advertising material.

For the UK regulations are vague, packages can only contain gifts of 'small value' (judge for yourselves what that means!) and no tobacco or alcohol. Other parcels of up to 22lbs, marked 'gift' and not more than £5 in value, containing foodstuffs, soap, well-worn clothing and consumable medical supplies will escape duty.

Facilities at airports and harbours

Airports
Nassau International and Freeport International airports contain duty-free shops, international telephones, banks, car hire offices, taxi ranks, newsagents, restaurants, bars, airline offices, tourist information desks and United States Customs and Immigration. They are not connected to the island's public bus routes.

Family Island airports typically consist of a waiting room, customs office and a checking in desk. Taxis wait outside to meet incoming flights. There is often a public telephone and usually a snack bar.

Harbours

Nassau Harbour is located Downtown, all necessary facilities are available in the town's centre.

Freeport Harbour is located a few kilometres out of town and has only customs and immigration offices. Taxis will take visitors to Downtown or Port Lucaya. There is no public bus service.

Family Island harbours offer few facilities, often consisting of only a wharf with a shop or snack bar nearby. The ports built to receive cruise liners are more sophisticated with customs and immigration facilities, public telephones and taxis to meet incoming boats.

Movies

Not only is the Bahamas a tourist mecca but it is also a favoured location for the film industry. Perhaps the most persistent visitor to these isles has been James Bond, that master sleuth of Her Majesty's Government. Agent 007 first visited these islands in 1965 for *Thunderball*. Locations used included Cafe Martinique, Thunderball Reef in the Exumas and an underwater site off New Providence, where a vulcan bomber was sunk especially for filming. A later visit made for *Never Say Never Again* saw one scene shot at the beach bar of the British Colonial Hotel.

Footage for the underwater sequences of *20,000 Leagues under the Sea, Cocoon, Wet Gold* and *Splash* were also obtained here. One of the many *Jaws* sequels was filmed here. In contrast *Murder in Paradise,* made for a TV series about the Oakes murder (see separate inset), had to be made in Jamaica to avoid hurting local sensibilities.

SIX

Where to stay

Accommodation in the guidebook is listed by price in five categories. It is based on the winter-high season rack rate (cost of a room hired on the spot) for a double room (price per person) with no meals, European Plan (EP). Package holidays offer substantial financial savings on these prices. If you are making your own hotel arrangements prefix the hotel telephone numbers given by 809 (international dialing code).

Types of accommodation

The choice is huge , from the most expensive suite in the world, Carnival's Galactic Suite at Crystal Palace ($25,000 per day), to family-run guest houses. Typical facilities in a hotel guest-room include two queen-sized beds, a private bathroom and usually a television, balcony or terrace. Most establishments contain a restaurant and bar.

Resort complexes offer a variety of accommodation and facilities (sometimes inclusive) catering for most needs on site. Most guests leave them only to go sightseeing or shopping (e.g. Carnival's Crystal Palace, Nassau).

Country retreats emphasise relaxation and are much smaller in scale they offer personal touches in elegant surroundings (e.g. Green Turtle Club, Green Turtle Cay, Abaco).

Activity centres offer all-inclusive facilities, usually including water sports and land-based activities; great value if you want to keep 'on the go' (e.g. Paradise Paradise, Nassau).

Smaller resorts are usually in the moderate price range and give a friendly, personal service in informal surroundings. Trips and other activities are usually family run and easily arranged (e.g. Orange Hill Beach Resort and Inn, Nassau).

Guesthouses offer the cheapest accommodation. They are often very basic with spartan furnishings, cooled by ceiling fans, shared bathrooms and sometimes a kitchen; usually clean, but much depends on the manager. They offer an opportunity to meet the locals away from tourist centres and can be very convivial places. It should be remembered that they are often located away from beaches (e.g. Diplomatic Inn, Nassau).

Camping is prohibited in the Bahamas as is sleeping on the beach. (It could be possible to camp on the remote Family Islands for a short time, but such attempts would be frowned upon). There are no Youth Hostels, YMCAs or YWCAs with accommodation.

Rental apartments

Self catering is one of the least expensive methods of visiting the Bahamas. It is let on a weekly or monthly basis and is ideal for a longer stay for a family or group of friends staying together. Details of apartments and self-catering units are described in the accommodation sections.

The level of accommodation and facilities compare favourably to most 'standard' hotels. The units vary in size and facilities. Apartments that cater for the visiting business person or vacationer often include in the price a daily maid service. Some have their own swimming pool or tennis court. They are fully furnished, including bed linen. Most have satellite television and some have telephones. Although a few hotel apartments will not have kitchens, all others come fully equipped. Laundries are usually available if no washing machine is provided. Air-conditioning is standard, but check clarify whether electricity is inclusive, as it is very expensive. (In summer it is worth considering renting an apartment, even if slightly more expensive, that includes the electricity in the rate, as an average monthly bill is $100 for a two person unit.)

Timeshare and interval ownership

Both types are available. Timeshare is less popular these days because of the bad publicity associated with the selling techniques, but in theory still offer attractive accommodation below the price of hotel resorts; an opportunity to buy your own place in the sun for a fixed week or fortnight every year.

Interval ownership has developed this concept further. Instead of actually buying a share in a property you buy a slot of a week or more in a first class resort for a 20 year period. Vacations can be taken through certain months, dependent on the classification bought. Through a worldwide network of interval-ownership resorts it is possible to exchange your time-slot for a stay in a similar establishment elsewhere. To ensure your choice you book as early as possible. Other permutations exist, including combining two years' vacation weeks together.

In both timeshare and interval ownership you pay up front for the accommodation with a maintenance charge paid annually. Various promotional deals or free gifts will be used to gain your attention. The pressure is on to sell, but 'no' will be accepted as an answer. There is also a 15-day cooling off period on all timeshare agreements in the Bahamas.

Property and estate agents

As part of the government drive to 'Bahamanise' the economy, all foreigners are required to obtain a permit under the Immovable Property (Acquisition by Foreign Persons) Act of 1981 before the purchase or leasing of land. Application should be made to the Foreign Investment Board for a handling charge of $5. The permit costs $20. One of the aims is to ensure that no small businesses started would compete directly with similar Bahamian enterprises. Domestic property can be purchased from a property already owned by a foreign national, but only the leasehold can be bought when purchasing from a Bahamian.

The commission charged by real estate agents for the sale of developed properties is 6% of the price paid on undeveloped property it is 10%. There is also a government Stamp Tax ranging from 1½% to 11% for $100,000 or over. Lawyer's fees are usually 2½% of sale price. Agents and lawyers are listed in the Bahamian telephone directory.

SEVEN

Getting about in the Bahamas

Driving in the Bahamas

If you intend to drive in the Bahamas make sure you bring your license with you. Care should be taken initially even if you are used to driving on the left. In most cars the steering wheel is also located on the lefthand side. This restricts the driver's visibility and minor bumps or 'fenderbenders' are common. The speed limited is 35mph in most parts of the island.

Special care should be taken at roundabouts as there is no fixed rule over who has the right of way. Traffic infractions bring heavy fines in Nassau and Freeport. On New Providence, Nassau should be avoided during the rush hour if possible. On the Family Islands traffic congestion is not a problem, however the state of the roads is. Watch out for deep potholes that could catapult you through the sunroof. Seatbelts are advisable but not mandatory.

A selection of road maps can be purchased from the Land and Survey Office, Bay Street, Nassau.

Self drive car hire

Avis, Budget, Hertz and National all have offices on New Providence and Grand Bahama. Cars may be hired by the day or week. Typical rates are $50 to $100 per day, with slightly cheaper weekly rates. All companies offer insurance at $10 per day and it is strongly recommended that drivers take advantage of this. The rental includes unlimited mileage but not gasoline. Local agencies offering cheaper models exist. Most firms insist on a deposit of up to $200.

Cars are also obtainable on most of the Family Islands but you may have to ask around to find one. They are rented out by hotels, gas stations or individuals. Rates may be negotiable and the condition of vehicles could vary considerably.

Mopeds and bicycles

These are often available at $25 to $30 for mopeds (possibly more with two riders), and $10 for bicycles. Motorbike riders are required by law to ride with crash helmets which the rental agency must supply to you.

Taxis

A plentiful supply of cabs operate on New Providence, Grand Bahama and Eleuthera. On other islands taxis usually meet incoming flights and cruise ships. All cabs should be metered, if not you should negotiate the fare before heading off. Ensure that the meter is switched on — otherwise the driver will feel free to 'estimate' the fare when he or she arrives. The meter rate is set by the government and is based on two person occupancy; add an extra $2 for each extra person in the car.

The power of the Taxi Union has prevented the government from installing a regular bus service from Nassau or Freeport International Airports. You will therefore require the services of a cab to take you to your hotel unless your hotel operates a complimentary bus service. Most drivers are friendly and knowledgeable as they are encouraged to take part in courses organised by the Ministry of Tourism.

Buses

A regular 'Jitney' service is operated on New Providence, Grand Bahama and Eleuthera. On most routes the fare is 75 cents, paid when you get off. Most buses stop operating at approximately 19.00. If you intend to travel after this time you will probably require a taxi. In Freeport there are regular stopping places, elsewhere the Jitney stops when a passenger calls 'bus stop'. Several large hotels on New Providence operate complimentary bus services for their guests.

Inter-island travel

Bahamasair provides a comprehensive inter-island service from Nassau. There are three flights a day to Freeport; daily flights to Andros, Eleuthera, and Abaco; six flights weekly to Exuma and

Long Island; receive six flights weekly. whilst Cat Island, and two flights weekly to Mayaguana, Inagua, Crooked Island and Acklins. (See the route map for more details.)

Bahamasair links up the Family Island resorts with international flights. Except for the slow moving mailboats, the airline offers the cheapest and quickest way to visit the Family Islands from Nassau.

For reservations and information call 305 5913 1910 (Miami), 1-800 222 4262 (USA), 071 437 8766 (London), 071 327 8511 Nassau or 352 8341 for Freeport.

Chalks Airlines offer the only regular service to Bimini (tel. 363 2845 for details). **Taino Air Service** run a small service from Freeport to Bimini and Abaco (tel. 352 8885 for details). In addition, several resorts operate scheduled flights to bring their guests straight to their hotel. For the real individualist charter flights are available from $500 to $800 round trip. This becomes quite reasonable when shared between a group of four to six people.

The **mailboat service** is the only regular seabourne transport to the Family Isles; Nassau is used as the hub. For details of the service see below under the individual island or contact the Potters Cay office on 393 1064. A typical fare is $30 oneway and most trips take the best part of a day to complete. This mode of transport is used frequently by islanders but seeing a tourist on board is still quite a bit of a novelty.

EIGHT

Streetwise in the Bahamas

Crime and safety

Nassau is a big sprawling place and as such has its problems with crime, like any other western city. After dark care should be taken if you leave the Downtown Bay Street area. It you intend to visit Delancy Street, East Bay Street or any area 'Over-the-Hill', call a taxi. Women should not go out unescorted after nightfall. Do not leave valuables lying around on the beach or in your hotel room; and lock your car. Hotels often provide safety deposit boxes free of charge. In Freeport similar precautions should be taken.

Out in the Family Islands people are proud that they do not have the problems associated with Nassau. People are very honest and crime is virtually unknown but it is still wise to take sensible precautions so do not leave your valuables unattended.

Reporting a theft

If an item is stolen you may wish to notify the police. This will ease considerably any insurance claim you may wish to make. The Bahamian police do not issue reports detailing the circumstances of the incident. They do give you the case number and the name of the officer dealing with it. Most Bahamian police are polite and helpful. See under individual island sections for the location of police stations and the correct numbers to call.

Saving money

In a pricey place such as the Bahamas it is always handy to know there are ways to cut down your costs. Here are some tips to follow:

- Use the complimentary transport laid on by casinos or your hotel to save on taxi fares.
- On New Providence a pink coupon is available from the Tourist Office and your hotel. It contains a variety of special offers including a complimentary drink and glass at Crystal Palace, reductions for shopping, complimentary drinks with meals at restaurants and a host of other things. To get to know Nassau take the complimentary tour offered by the Ministry of Tourism.
- If you plan to go nightclubbing in Nassau obtain the complimentary tickets available at selected stores (see nightclub section for details).
- If staying in the larger resorts take advantage of their 'Dine-Around Plans'. Even though they do not include the gratuity or drinks they are excellent value.

NINE

Food and drink

Using the bars

As befitting an exotic location all manner of spirits and liqueurs are available. the local beers are commonly served in bottles. The more luxurious the surroundings the greater the expense. A number of bars will keep a tab going through the evening. When the bill is eventually settled, a tip (15%) is expected. With waiter and waitress service a tip is also the norm with every round of drinks. Some bars will add 15% automatically — if so this will be stated on the check received.

In 'native' bars drinks can be half the price or even less than in the resort and hotel bars. Again, if settling in for an evening a tip would be expected as time progresses. These bars tend to be simple huts, usually with satellite television. It is virtually unknown to see a woman drinking in these places unless they are part of some social gathering.

Drinks
The Bahamians brew a locally bottled lager beer, Kalik costing $1.25-$1.50 from liquor stores, to $2 in most bars and more in the big hotels.

There is also a propensity to drink rum in all its brands and all mixes, from coke to coconut milk. There are no half measures and when it comes to pouring the golden liquor, the greater the tip, usually the greater the measure.

Spirits start from $3 per measure.

Tropical drinks
Bahama Mama: Coconut rum, rum, Nassau Royale, pineapple juice, orange juice and Grenadine.
Pina Colada: White rum, milk, coconut rum and pineapple rum.
Yellow Bird: Rum Galliano, banana liqueur and orange juice.

Goombay Smash: Rum, coconut rum, Galliano, pineapple juice and lemon juice.

Using cafes and restaurants

As everywhere there are cheap and expensive places to eat. Prices are generally 30% to 40% higher than in the State of Florida. This is mainly due to the shipping costs and the government import duty on all food items. (See 'Places to eat' for costs and descriptions of various cafes and restaurants.)

Service
This can range from excellent to appalling, though staff in the more exclusive restaurants tend to be more attentive. As most people are on vacation there is no pressing need to rush a meal and this is certainly the attitude of the staff. A service charge of 15% is commonly added, whatever the service. Where this is not the case, 15% is expected as a tip and you can always give more.

Dress
In cafes and fast food outlets T-shirts, shorts and beach wraps are acceptable. Bare feet or torso are not. As the prices increase, so do the dress requirements. At the exclusive establishments one's attire is expected to match the elegant setting. The only rule as such is for men to wear jackets and ties, but in the summer this is relaxed to jackets only.

Tipping
This is expected virtually everywhere, and 15% is often automatically added to the bill in bars, cafes and restaurants. Remember to account for it in your budget plans. All meal prices quoted in this book are inclusive of the service charge.

Food, glorious food

Bahamian cooking
An added experience and pleasure to any trip abroad is to try the local cooking and delicacies. Sauce usually tomato-based lightly spiced with herbs and peppers, is the essence of Bahamian cooking. **Peas n' rice** is the staple dish of the nation — tiny black pigeon peas cooked with white rice, pork fat and the chef's own sauce with herbs and spices. A dash of hot sauce is a favourite addition.

Fried chicken is first marinated in a tomato and pepper sauce, covered in flour and then deep fried.

Conch (pronounced 'konk') competes with peas 'n rice as the kernel of all Bahamian foods. The firm white meat of the 'snail of the sea' is both tasteless and tough, but when tenderised, pounded flat and spiced, it is served in a variety of tasty fashions.

Bahamian lobster known locally as crawfish, is one of the more expensive items menus. Only the tail is eaten. It is available fresh August to April, but otherwise frozen. Much depends on the chef, as this delicacy becomes tough, dry and chewy if broiled too long.

Grouper is a mild-flavoured white meat fish commonly served throughout the archipelago. Much depends on the sauce it is cooked or served in: steamed in a spicy sauce (native style), poached in a white wine sauce or deep fried.

Souse and boiled fish Souse is a broth or clear soup spiced with all manner of herbs, onions, lime and other juices, with either a meat of fowl dish as the main ingredient. Chicken souse is a popular favourite. Boiled fish, eaten at breakfast is similarly prepared. All are usually served with Jonnycake.

Jonnycake consisting of butter, milk, flour, sugar, salt and baking powder is a pan-cooked bread and similar in taste to an English scone.

Guava duff is a paste made from the guava fruit, sugar, cinnamon and nutmeg. It is spread over a rolled, flat, plain dough which is rolled together like a 'Swiss roll'. It can be baked, steamed or boiled. It is served hot with sauce which melts and blends together. This dessert is a Bahamian speciality, but takes an age to make.

Other dishes include seafish such as snapper, grunt and jack. Meat dishes are usually curried in native restaurants. There is not an abundance of tropical fruit and what is on offer tends to be expensive. Typical Bahamian snacks include chicken and fries, and western-style burgers.

International cuisine A worldwide selection of culinary delights from Mexican to Italian or grill house to vegetarianism is available. Away from New Providence and Grand Bahama the choice is much more limited. (See 'Places to eat' section.)

Fast food Several fast food chains exist on New Providence and Grand Bahama, but only one in the Family Islands (Kentucky Fried Chicken in Marsh Harbour, Abaco). 'Cheap eats' are covered in our restaurant reviews from buffet dining to local cafes. Elsewhere native dishes are some of the best value buys.

The magic of the conch

A local staple food, the waters of the Bahamas abound with millions of these creatures. The humble conch spends its days sifting for food along the bottom of the seabed. Unlike a grouper or a snapper it cannot run when the sharp eyed Bahamian fishermen come by. Docksides piled high with the shells of these creatures are a testament to the countless numbers caught each year. A sharp blow on the shell and the conch is 'jewked' or prised out into oblivion and the kitchen pot.

Conch is a versatile, if not a gourmet dish. It can be served as a spicy chowder soup, raw, steamed, scorched, fried or, best of all, as fritters. Its popularity is assured because of its reputation as an aphrodisiac, though you cannot blame conch alone for the high Bahamian birth rate.

Conch had a brief 'walk on part' in the James Bond movie *Thunderball*. With his continual habit of mixing work and pleasure, the super-spy was dining with a beautiful lady at an exclusive restaurant. The old smoothie offered his companion some conch chowder, however she was all too aware of its properties as an aphrodisiac and politely declined his offer.

Buying food

The supermarkets on the main islands are well stocked. Prices are higher than in the USA because of import duties. The agricultural shops and warehouses controlled by the government (check the telephone directory in each locality) are the best places to buy fresh fruit and fish. The selection depends on what is in season. If buying from a street stall in the main centres, make a note of the prices in the supermarkets and aim for at least a 20% saving.

In the Family Islands shops may be well stocked or merely the front room of a Bahamian home. Beers and sodas are universally sold. Bread is made locally, and sold to members of the community. Locals will know which days are baking days.

TEN

Leisure activities

For the sport enthusiasts a number of hotels offer specialist holidays which are guaranteed to allow you to indulge in your chosen field, we provide some recommendations for the specialist.

Fishing

Bimini, Andros and the Berry islands have earned a name as 'fishing capitals of the world'. In reality fishing is good off every island in the Bahamas, see the fishing guides published by the Ministry of Tourism for specific details.

Golf

The most acclaimed course is at the Cotton Bay Club (tel. 334, 6106), on Eleuthera. However, the best choice is at Freeport. Here there is a different club for almost every day of the week. The Princes Hotel and Casino (tel. 352 6721) and the Atlantic Beach Hotel (tel. 373 1444) both offer special golf packages. On New Providence Crystal Palace (tel. 327 6200) Divi Beach Resort (tel. 362 4391) and Paradise Island Resort and Casino (tel. 363 2000) each maintains its own course and offers packages for players. On Abaco the Treasure Cay Beach Hotel (tel. 367 2570) offers an 18-hole course.

Scuba

Most islands offer facilities for scuba divers. The following is a selection of different, and sometimes unique, dives offered in particular areas or by certain operators.

New Providence has several offshore photogenic wrecks and reefs used as film locations. UNEXSO (tel. 373 1244), on Grand Bahama offer a pair of unique divis inside the largest charted cave system in the world; and free-swimming with dolphins. Amongst the full range of activities is the possibility to pose beside the life-sized shark replicas chained to the seabed.

Stella Maris Inn (tel. 336 2106) has been running a shark dive for several years where divers get the opportunity to observe sharks being fed at close quarters, whilst perched safely on a portion of reef.

Andros has the 6,000ft drop to the 'Tongue of the Ocean' and the third largest reef in the world, with many exciting dives. Bimini has near by what is claimed to be the remains of the Lost City of Atlantis, several plane and ship wrecks and the Bimini wall with its black coral formations.

Eleuthera. At 'Current Cut' the force of the incoming tide water can propel a diver along at five to seven knots, through a gap between two points of land.

Exuma is the home of the 'Iron Curtain', a series of black coral caves; and 'Thunderball Grotto', a location for the Bond movie of the same name.

Living aboard. Three operators currently offer diving cruises around the Bahamas Family Isles. For exact details on itinerary and cost contact the individual organisations:

Blackbeard Cruises have three 20 metre boats, with single or double bunks. (tel. USA 1 800 327 9600 or write to PO Box 66-1091 Miami Springs, Florida 33266.)

Sea Fever Diving Cruises offer diving vacations on board a 30-metre vessel which can accommodate up to 22 divers. (tel. USA 1 800 44 FEVER or write to PO Box 39-8276, Miami Beach, Florida 33139).

Bottom Time Adventures operate boats. (tel. 1 800 345 DIVE or write to PO Box 11919, Fort Lauderdale, Florida 33339).

Squash
Clubs exist on New Providence and Grand Bahama islands.

Tennis
Most large and medium sized resorts have tennis court facilities for their guests. These are usually lit for night play and complimentary to guests. Lessons are usually available.

Windsurfing
The Atlantic Beach Hotel (tel. 373 1444), has a windsurfing school where a wide range of courses are taught leading to certification in a variety of skills.

ELEVEN

A to Z information

Banks and bureau de change

On New Providence and Grand Bahama the banks are open Monday to Thursday 9.30 - 15.00 remaining open until 17.00 on Friday. Long queues can develop on Friday afternoons as pay cheques are cashed. Days of the week as well as hours vary widely on the Family Islands (read the 'Basics' section under each island. Government tax on each travellers cheque ranges from 10 - 60 cents depending on the outlet. Hotels and casinos do not charge for this service.

Casinos and gambling

The legal age to enter a casino is 18. Casual wear but not swimwear or bare feet, is permissible. Craps, roulette, blackjack, baccarat and big six tables are available along with a huge array of slot machines.

Churches

Bahamians are very religious people. There are a wide range of denominations of Christian churches as well as followers of the Baha'i, Jewish and Moslem faiths. For details of addresses, telephone numbers and times of services see under the relevant island section. For further information the Ministry of Tourism publishes a helpful booklet entitled 'Bahamas places of worship'.

Embassies

British High Commission, BITCO Building (3rd floor), East Street, PO Box N7516, Nassau (tel. 325 7471).

United States Embassy, Queen Street, PO Box N-8197, Nassau (tel. 322 4753).

Canadian Consulate, Out Island Traders Building (Ground Floor), East Bay Street, PO Box SS-6371, Nassau (tel. 323 2123).

Emergency services

Police stations exist on all the inhabited islands. On the smaller ones a police sergeant is sent from Nassau who then appoints local constables. A fire fighting service, ambulances and modern hospitals furnish the islands of New Providence and Grand Bahama, whilst smaller clinics exist on the Family Islands. In an emergency patients are flown to Nassau or Miami. The Bahamas Air Sea Rescue (BASRA), operates out of Nassau and Freeport. For telephone numbers see the sections on the island you will be visiting.

Hairdressing

A real native haircut is to have your hair beaded in an Afro-Caribbean style for $1 a bead. If that is not what you have in mind most of the resort hotels on New Providence and Grand Bahama have beauty salons and barber shops. Local salons downtown charge $15 for males and $20 for females. On Family Islands enquire at your hotel.

Laundry and dry cleaning

Most hotels will take laundry or dry clean items for a few dollars per item and return them that day if deposited before mid-morning. One or two large hotels have coin-operated laundrettes. Most apartments have laundrettes and some small hotels will allow you to use their own machines. Laundrettes and dry cleaners can always be found in urban areas.

Away from the main centres facilities are patchy and some places non-existent. It is a case of enquiring at your hotel and coming to some arrangement for someone to do your laundry.

Philately

At the main post offices in Nassau and Freeport there are special desks to cater for stamp collectors. Stamps are also stocked in specialist stores such as 'Coin of the Realm'.

Postage rates

Postcards cost 40 cents wherever their destination abroad, and 10 cents internally. Letters cost 45 cents to the USA, Canada and West Indies, 50 cents to Europe and Latin America; 60 cents to Africa, Asia, Australia and the Pacific; and 15 cents within the Bahamas.

Post restante

Mail should be directed to the person c/o The Main Post Office, Nassau, Bahamas and 'to be collected from the General Delivery desk'. All correspondence is retained for three weeks.

Public holidays

There are ten each year: New Years Day, 1 January; Good Friday and Easter Monday in mid-April; Labour Day, first Friday in June, Whit Monday, seven weeks after Easter; Independence Day, 10 July; Emancipation Day, first Monday in August; Discovery Day, 12 October; Christmas and Boxing Days, 25 and 26 December. Shops and banks are closed on these days.

Shopping

New Providence and Grand Bahama offer a huge variety of goods that are noticeably cheaper than in the USA and Canada and in some cases cheaper than items in Europe. There are whole streets, arcades and shopping centres devoted to the tourist market. A huge range of watches, cameras, gems, jewellery, swimwear, designer casuals, T-shirts, gifts, china and crystal are on display. Check the prices of items you wish to buy before you leave home. On the Family Islands the selection will be more restricted. Most shops open at 9.00 or 9.30 and stay open until 17.00 or 17.30. Some close for lunch. Virtually all stores close on Sundays.

Souvenirs

Locally produced goods include polished conch shells, wood carvings and coral jewellery. Several shops exhibit a range of paintings and prints by Bahamian artists. Local industry now produces batik fabrics and clothes, casual wear, countless T-shirt designs, heaps of straw work, Nassau Royale liqueur, sophisticated jewellery designs and countless other items.

Telephone

The international code for the Bahamas is 809.

Time zones

The Bahamas is five hours ahead of GMT.

Tipping

There are a variety of surcharges which may be added to your bill so ensure you budget for them during your stay. In virtually all restaurants and bars a 15% service charge is automatically added to your bill. A hotel tax of 8% is added to the room levy, and $2 to $3 per day for the maid's gratuity may also appear on the bill; possibly even a small charge for 'energy'.

TWELVE

The Bahamas over the centuries

'Beware the white man bearing gifts', would have been an appropriate warning to the peaceful Lucayan Indians who lived in the Bahamas prior to the fateful day when Columbus landed on Guanahani and renamed it San Salvador. The first meeting of the two races from different sides of a vast ocean was friendly enough, gifts were exchanged and attempts were made at communication. Relations were soon soured as Columbus took seven Lucayans by force to serve as pilots.

The Lucayans had inhabited the Bahamas for at least 500 years before Columbus arrived. They were a timid people who had moved north to escape the raiding parties of the warlike Caribs. A few years after Columbus' visit the Spanish returned and carried away the Lucayans to work as slaves in the gold mines of Hispaniola. This act of genocide left the islands unpopulated for over a century.

The Bahamas were of no interest to the gold hungry Spanish. Charles I of England formally claimed the islands in 1629, but it was not until 1648 that a group of 70 settlers came to live there. They were Puritans from Bermuda, who like the early settlers in America had found themselves persecuted for their religious beliefs. The island they chose was named Eleuthera 'Freedom'. As these refugees approached their new home their ship hit a reef and was lost with all their supplies. Left to fend for themselves the new colony almost perished. Though many later returned to Bermuda the sturdiest souls stayed put and endured great hardships.

Soon afterwards the fine natural harbour on New Providence began to be used and a settlement grew up containing a few respectable citizens and a lot of opportunists out in the New World purely to seek their fortunes. It was not long before the 'black flag' of piracy flew on many ships and Nassau became a market for plundered goods. The governors of the Bahamas were eager for a share of the loot and were easily corrupted. The Spanish, who suffered greatly from the cut throats, attacked Nassau and destroyed the town several times.

Finally the English Lords Proprietors, who in theory owned the Bahamas, sent a tough man of action to put things right. This was the new governor Woodes Rogers, who offered a pardon to pirates willing to 'go straight', but drove out the rest. By 1718 his task was complete and he was confirmed as the colony's first Royal Governor. He built fortifications to protect Nassau from the Spanish, proclaimed 'Expulsis Piratis Restituta Commercia' (pirates expelled, commerce restored), and set up the House of Assembly to assist in administering the islands.

The islands remained at peace until 1776 when the 13 colonies declared their independence from Britain. The Bahamas were dragged into a war that they had little wish to fight as they had always maintained close trading links with the mainland. That year the new United States navy raided Nassau seeking gunpowder. The governor lost his nerve and quickly surrendered, but the Americans captured the town only to find that the gunpowder had been secretly shipped away.

In 1782 a huge Spanish invasion fleet came and occupied Nassau until liberated in a daring raid by Colonel Andrew Deveaux, an American who remained loyal to the British crown. When the 13 colonies gained their independence in 1783 many other loyalists sought refuge in the Bahamas. They brought their slaves with them, determined to build large plantations and continue to live in the manner they were accustomed to, but poor soil and pests soon brought an end to their dream. Many migrated elsewhere and in the process their slaves became free. In 1834 any remaining slaves were set free by the Emancipation Act. Thereafter it was a constant struggle for inhabitants of the colony to find ways to make a living. Many lived by the ghoulish profession of wrecking, salvaging the goods from stricken ships. Others tried growing sisal or turned to harvesting sponges.

The only real booms in their economy came when Bahamians took advantage of the suffering of others. During the American Civil War blockade runners took supplies into Confederate ports, making fortunes whilst the conflict lasted. During the US Prohibition period (1919-33) many gangsters frequented the hotels of Nassau and Bimini and found the wealthy Bahamian merchants eager to do business running illicit liquor to the USA.

From 1940 to 1945 the Duke of Windsor served as governor of the islands and tried to improve the economy, but he was unable to prevent a major riot breaking out in 1942 when underpaid black labourers looted the property of infinitely richer white shopkeepers. Troops were able to quell the riot only after several fatalities. A year later the Duke of Windsor had to contend with another controversy when Sir Harry Oakes, one of the richest men in the world, was brutally murdered in the Bahamas (see page 110).

After the Second World War the tourist industry began to develop though only a small group of elite white businessmen saw any profit from it. A white oligarchy known as the 'Bay Street Boys' controlled the House of Assembly and resisted any changes that might better the conditions of black citizens.

In the 1950's a new political group, the Progressive Liberal Party (PLP), began to challenge the Bay Street Boys and through a series of constitutional changes the electorate was widened. In 1967 the PLP won the elections and set the Bahamas along the road to independence, which came in 1973. The change from colonialism to independence, and from white dominance to desegregation, went peacefully and smoothly. The democratic tradition has been maintained and the Bahamas remain in the Commonwealth of Nations.

THIRTEEN

The Bahamas today

The political scene

The Bahamas are one of the most politically stable countries in the world. Sir Lynden Pindling, the current the Prime Minister, came to power in 1967 and is the longest serving elected leader in the western world.

The Progressive Liberal Party (PLP) holds two thirds of the seats in the House of Assembly and the opposition party, the Free National Movement (FNM), holds the remaining third. Politics in the Bahamas is a two horse race, with both parties having a remarkably similar political platform. Both support a free market economy and recognise the importance of tourism and foreign investment in the country's continued prosperity.

Bahamian politics are about leadership and accountability, is the platform from which the opposition continually attack the government. Pindling's long tenure as Prime Minister has not been without its scandals, and the opposition has been much strengthened by disillusioned PLP members. One of the most noticeable features of Bahamian politics is the degree to which attacks are made on individuals rather than the policies.

Sir Lynden Pindling has steered the country through times of greater and greater affluence and remains an enormously popular figure. As leader of the PLP he was one of the key figures in the independence movement. On one occasion he dramatically threw the Speaker's mace out of the window, symbolically giving the emblem of power to the masses. The PLP has worked to maintain a healthy economy and over the years it brought in modern health care and a system of education for all.

The opposition argue that it is time for a change, that the country has been under one person's rule for too long. Members of the FNM attacked Pindling over his failure to act against Carlos Lehder's drug smuggling ring at Norman's Cay (see page 249) and his personal finances. Others argued that many posts went to PLP supporters rather than those most suited for the job, that the PLP were borrowing heavily to finance development and highlighted growing problems in schools.

The heated debates, accusations and rebuttals are all signs of a thriving democracy. Bahamian politics may become very personal but people follow developments keenly. Many participate avidly as well, discussing politics over a game of dominoes or reading with glee the stinging editorials or wickedly satirical cartoons that appear daily in the 'Tribune' newspaper.

The physical environment

The Bahamas comprise of limestone outcrops in a shallow sea cooled daily by south-easterly Trade Winds. The first settlers found the soil thin but the oceans abundant with marine life. Unlike many Caribbean islands, there are no mountains of any height. Mount Alvernia on Cat Island boasts only a 63m (206ft) summit. The islands consist of flat, gently rolling shrub or wooded areas and there are no surface streams or rivers running out to sea, which is one explanation for the breathtaking clarity of the water.

The Bahamas have an abundance of natural cave systems, which have been sculpted over millions of years by water seeping through the limestone. Many caverns contain formations of stalactites and stalagmites and are now the home of various harmless species of bats. Grand Bahama boasts the largest charted underwater cave system in the world at the Lucayan National Park, and Preacher's Cave and the Gregory Town Cave on Eleuthera are other outstanding above-water examples which can easily be visited.

Andros boasts the third largest barrier reef in the world. Beyond it the 'Tongue of the Ocean' (TOTO) plummets down to depths as yet unmeasured. Many islands have their own 'blue holes', which contain salt water and are mostly tidal, being linked to the sea by underground passages. Those on Andros were made famous when Jaques Cousteau dived to investigate them, but most have never been explored; some have been found to go so deep that their extent has not been sounded.

The dollar enterprise

The Bahamas have few natural advantages apart from the wonders of the sun, sea and sand. Throughout their history, attempts to earn a fast buck — pirateering, wrecking, blockade and rum running — have been interspersed with long periods of economic stagnation. Permanent industries have been less successful until the advent of tourism after World War II. Today the tourist industry has the thriving, hustle and bustle attractions of casinos, multi-million dollar resort complexes or small inns and the remote, serene, sun-drenched Family Islands. The annual number of visitors should soon top the 3.5 million.

Tourism accounts for over 80% of GDP. The majority of tourists are Americans, though hundreds of thousands of Canadians and a similar number of Europeans vacation each year in the Bahamas. As a result, a huge army of Bahamians service these requirements, from hotel construction to taxi drivers.

Off-shore banking is the second largest industry with much interest shown throughout the Americas because of the strict secrecy laws governing Bahamian accounts. The government is keen to promote Spanish as the second language in order to expand this operation. Other industries are salt, crawfish (Bahamian lobster), pulpwood and vegetable exports. In recent years the government has borrowed heavily to diversify and expand, and incentives are given for all activities.

Flora and fauna

Every Wednesday the Nassau Guardian newspaper has articles on all aspects of gardening, presenting intriguing insights into the problems of plant cultivation in Bahamian climate. The parks and botanical gardens on both New Providence and Grand Bahama have hosts of exotic plants, both naturalised and native species. (Unfortunately some of the rare species are not always labelled.)

Despite poor soil there are numerous kinds of trees, shrubs, climbers, vines and grasses as well as flora such as humming-bird cactus in the Bahamas. Edible plants are also grown, including bananas, sea grapes, hog plums, bread fruit trees and many more. The majority of plants flower in winter, but in summer the poinsettias are a magnificent sight. The national flower is the yellow elder (a tubular-shaped yellow flower with delicate red stripes on each petal). The lignum vitae or tree of life is the national tree.

There are few native animals because most have been hunted to extinction. The hutia is a unique rat-like rodent, which survives on Atwood Cay. The Bahamian iguana exists on some of the remoter cays such as the 'Bahamian Dragon' on Allan's Cay in the Exumas.

The Bahamian parrot can only be found in the dense forests of southern Abaco, but the Bahamian national bird, the Caribbean flamingo is safely making a comeback in the protective National Trust Park on Inagua.

All these species and more can be seen at the Ardastra Gardens, Nassau.

FOURTEEN

The Bahamian people

The family is an important symbol in Bahamian life and most Bahamian can trace their ancestors back several generations. It is as a family unit that they have had to meet the confusing social pressures that have faced them over the years. In colonial times status was conferred on those who were the most 'British' in their complexion, education and culture, but these overtly racial barriers ended in the years leading to independence. Some pockets of white settlers still cling to outdated prejudices, however most play a full life in the community. The social distinctions of today tend to be far more discreet.

Black Bahamians comprise 85% of the population today, the remainder are whites of a northern European origin, plus small minorities of Chinese, Greeks and Jews. There are virtually no traces of African heritage amongst the black population of today, although some fashions from that continent are in vogue and the Bahamas do have Rastafarian adherents. Most cultural fads now come from the USA.

Meeting the people

One of the pleasures of visiting the Bahamas is the people. Like anywhere else you will come across that unfriendly taxi driver, unhelpful shop assistant or rude waiter, yet most will be courteous, convivial and return the respect shown to them. To help foster real understanding of the culture and country, the Bahamian Ministry of Tourism have established an imaginative programme called 'People to People'.

It is hard to praise the programme highly enough. It is a community wide venture whereby the Ministry of Tourism selects volunteers from all walks of life to host visitors. Care is taken to match visitors and volunteers with similar interests. Encounters are left at the discretion of both parties and it is the responsibility of the volunteers to collect their guests at the agreed time and location. It is a remarkable opportunity to meet Bahamians at their home, social or civic club or at a church service. It is not a dating agency nor do the visitors live with the volunteers.

On the last Friday of each month between January and August there is a Government House Tea Party for members of the programme. The guests usually number about 200 and are greeted by the wife of the Governor General. Pastries and tea are provided, plus a display of art and crafts. Attendance is by invitation only. Ask at the Ministry of Tourism if you wish to go.

Introduced in Nassau in 1975 and extended to Freeport a year later there are now over 1000 hosts in Nassau and about 400 in Freeport. To participate in People to People collect an application form from Bahamas tourist offices or from the Manager, People to People Programme, PO Box N-3701, Nassau, Bahamas or PO Box F-251 Freeport, Grand Bahama. The forms should be returned at least three weeks in advance of your visit. Alternatively, in Nassau you can call in at one of the tourist offices or telephone 326 5371 or in Freeport 352 8044.

Values and beliefs

Religion plays a pivotal role in Bahamian society. No major political speech is uttered without some reference to biblical text. The church offers a sense of belonging and identity to a people who are at their happiest in groups and communities than as individuals. Attendance at the place of worship is a family affair. As elsewhere many do not always see 'the word' applying to their own circumstances. It is common to have children out of wedlock and Bahamian males are under pressure to help to take care of all their children but not all do.

Folklore

On Andros, an island of saltwater creeks and forests, the people talk of red-eyed, three toed, feathered and bearded folk called chickcharnies. Such tales have been used to keep children both enthralled and disciplined. Obeah, the art of witch-craft, is less apparent now but Cat Island is especially reputed as a centre of practise. Its people are sometimes referred to as Obeah people.

Bush medicine

Among the older generations on the Family Islands, especially the more remote communities, the knowledge of bush medicine has not been lost. No scientific study on its benefits or otherwise has ever been undertaken. At one time these would have been the only medicines available. In her book The Outmost Island, Virginia White lists a number of such remedies including the following:

For a cold or flu, loss of appetite and high fever make a tea with the leaves of Gale of Wind (Phyllanthus amarus), add sour lime and salt, then drink. For sunburn or insect bites slice up aloes (Aloe babadensis) and rub the cut edges on the skin. Other cures are for rheumatism or back pain, constipation, menstrual pain, worms in children etc.

Handicrafts

A few traditional crafts are still practised, especially on the Family Islands, such as the art of making goods palm leaves (all sorts of straw hats and other items), painting and wood carving.

Festivals and regattas

Bahamian celebrations come with rhythm and a riot of colour. 'Junkanoo' lasts over the Christmas week and has its roots in Africa. It celebrates the time of year when the slaves got their only real holiday. The word is said to derive from either 'John Canoe', supposedly an African king or 'Gensinconnu', which describes the dressing up in masks that is a vital part of the celebrations. Lavish costumes are made out of bright fabrics or paper and rhythm is supplied by drums, cowbells and conch shells.

Goombay lasts from June to September and derives its name from small goatskin drums. In Nassau, Bay Street is closed off on Wednesday nights and the Royal Bahamian Police Band are guests of honour. The emphasis is less on costume and show and more on partying and dancing. Goombay shows are regularly organised in Freeport and on many of the Family Islands.

Come the spring and summer, the spectacle of sail boats racing returns to the Family Islands. The boats are the traditional Bahamian sloops or schooners, wooden hull and mast with canvas sails. As with most things Bahamians do, it is yet another perfect excuse for a party and everybody is welcome.

Bahamian music

Many of the influences in the contemporary music scene come from the rhythms of Goombay and Junkanoo. A musician who emphasises the African roots in his music is Tony McKay, known as 'Exuma' or the 'Obeah Man'. Many tunes provide sharp and witty insights into everyday life, such as 'Shame and scandal in the family', an old song about the common Bahamian practise of having children both inside and outside the marriage, a story with a twist in the tale. A modern musician with great local standing is KB who mixes a calypso and soca beat with more modern influences from the USA in songs such as 'Only meat', 'She fat', and 'Juicy Suzy'. KB plays regularly at the Family Island Lounge, Soldier Road, Nassau.

Just 'Cos She Fat?

'Gussy Mae' is a term of affection used in the Bahamas to describe a portly woman, a large frame being judged an asset.

A hugely popular song by the vocalist KB sums up Bahamian tastes in 'She Fat', describing in ribald and cheeky style a love affair between the singer and his sweetheart 'Gussy Mae' and a Bahamian male's preference for overweight women. Looks are a big thing here. At a recent 'Mr Universe' competition, women fought and jostled each other over too few seats. A Gussy Mae beauty contest was another tribute to the pulling power of flab. And to Bahamian women bulging biceps are high on the menu; wimps need not apply.

In the Family Islands a local combo is traditionally known as a 'rake'n scrape' band. Using an assortment of instruments they play a selection of calypso and soca songs both traditional and current Bahamian favourites.

FIFTEEN

Nassau and New Providence

The island of New Providence is only 33km (20 miles) long by 11 km (8 miles) wide, much smaller than many others, yet its excellent harbour ensured it would become the nation's capital. Nassau is now a modern city of some 175,000 people, where over half of all Bahamians live. In the capital's hinterland there are several other settlements including Gambier Village, Adelaide, Mount Pleasant and Carmichael, whose citizens were once farmers or fishermen, but are more likely to be commuters working in Nassau's offices, banks or tourist resorts.

The colonial seat of Her Majesty's Governor, here decrees were passed to rule this tiny outpost of the British Empire. Murderous pirates set out to prowl the sea lanes from the same port that later became the rendezvous point for Prohibition-busting gangsters, then a longstanding tax haven that attracted the rich and powerful, then welcomed the Duke and Duchess of Windsor. Famous trendsetters have subsequently been followed by innumerable visitors. All have left their mark on historic Nassau.

The original town had lowly beginnings, starting life in the 1660s with a few ramshackle buildings beside the water's edge, wooden huts thatched with palmetto leaves. Though it was not the first Bahamian island to be settled, it soon became the most successful because of its large sheltered harbour and the seafaring community which settled here soon took up a life of wrecking and attacking passing Spanish ships. The people grew rich through piracy but their lifestyle soon provoked the wrath of the Spaniards, who sent a fleet of galleons whose crews razed the town and took great delight in roasting the governor on a spit.

Undeterred, another group of pioneers erected a new town on the ashes of the old, naming it Nassau after William III who was Prince of Orange Nassau before ascending the British throne. The new inhabitants also took to piracy and made such a nuisance of themselves that in 1703 another fleet was sent to destroy the town, this time both Spanish and French. Nassau was again rebuilt soon

becoming a lawless town where stolen goods were bought and sold and buccaneers came ashore to drink and womanise. The few surviving respectable citizens left or moved inland.

In 1718 Woodes Rogers, the first Royal Governor brought order to the town and built a fort to thwart further Spanish attacks. Nassauvians continued to plunder foreign ships, but now did it legally by attacking only the King's enemies. In 1776, during the American War of Independence, Nassau was captured by the new American navy. Then in 1782 the hated Spanish came, intending to stay, but were driven out by a band of American loyalist refugees from the newly independent United States.

These new arrivals commenced a new phase of building and with increasing numbers of slaves brought to New Providence, Nassau became split by contrasting areas of housing: whites lived on the seafront along Bay Street; blacks were settled 'over-the-hill'. These rigid distinctions blurred as the town grew. In terms of population, Nassau has expanded most noticeably since the end of the Second World War.

Previous page: *Glitzy song and dance shows are a vital part of all the casino operations in the Bahamas. This performance is part of the Bahamas Rhythm Theatre at the Crystal Palace Casino.*
(Photograph courtesy of Carnival's Crystal Palace)

Opposite, top: *The British Colonial Hotel, perhaps the most prominent landmark in downtown Nassau. It has stood there since the 1920's and is known affectionately as the 'BC'.*

Opposite, bottom: *A statue of Christopher Columbus stands before Government House in Nassau. The Governor General's residence stands in its own tropical gardens and hosts the changing of the guard ceremonies and Ministry of Tourism tea parties.*

New Providence

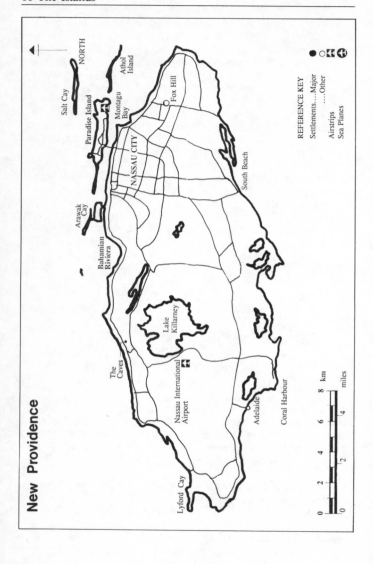

NORTH

Salt Cay

Athol Island

Paradise Island

Montagu Bay

Fox Hill

NASSAU CITY

South Beach

Arawak Cay

Bahamian Riviera

Lake Killarney

The Caves

Nassau International Airport

Adelaide

Coral Harbour

Lyford Cay

REFERENCE KEY

Settlements....Major
         .....Other
Airstrips
Sea Planes

0   2   4   6   8 km
0   2   4 miles

Arrival

By air

A number of international airlines have direct flights to Nassau International Airport.

Europe British Airways fly direct from London four times a week. PanAm, with its extensive network, flies from all over Europe to Miami and New York, with daily connections to Nassau (and Freeport). Other airlines with direct connections are Delta via Atlanta, TWA via New York and US Air via Charlotte and Fort Lauderdale.

North America Nassau International Airport is linked to a host of North American cities including Tampa, Chicago, Boston, Philadelphia, Orlando and Washington DC. Air Canada has direct flights from Toronto and Montreal. PanAm is a regular, reliable carrier connecting many cities with the Bahamas.

Worldwide the Bahamas, being only a short 35 minute run by plane from the gateway of Miami, is open to worldwide destinations. The airlines linking the two cities include Bahamasair, Aero Coach and PanAm.

At the airport the terminal has all the facilities of a major international airport: news stand, liquor and perfume stalls (duty free), bank, post office with a philately section, tourist information desk (which will happily make or confirm hotel reservations) and car hire outlets. The snack bar opposite the domestic flight check-in (all one building) has hamburgers, hot dogs and pastries from $2. The Pre-flight Restaurant (open 7.00-18.00), upstairs above the departure check-in area, has basic food and no pretensions. It serves Bahamian and American dishes (breakfast from $2.50 and $6, from cost $3 to $10).

Paradise Island Airport is the other terminal, serving Paradise Island and Nassau. The resort has its own private airline which flies several times each day to Miami and Fort Lauderdale and once daily to Palm Beach. Chalks Airlines, who fly to Bimini and then Miami, also operate from here. The terminal is a small building with check-in desks, a waiting hall and a small snack bar. Luggage is brought in by trolley and claimed in the main waiting area beside the immigration desk. There are no buses, but a steady stream of taxis waits in the terminal's forecourt; the fare to hotels on Paradise Island costs approximately $5.

By sea

Nassau is a popular port of call for many cruise ships and regularly has several liners in dock at one time, including Fantasy, the largest passenger cruise ship in the world (2,600 passengers). All major cruise line operations in the Caribbean have Nassau on their itineraries.

The Crown Der Mar of Crown Cruise Lines has two-night cruises with such personal touches as a complimentary bottle of champagne and fruit basket in each cabin. It departs on Friday at 17.00 and returns to West Palm Beach on Sunday at 7.00. Cruises cost from $179, with a 10% discount for 90-day advance bookings. The Carnival Cruise Lines operates three ships to Nassau: the Mardi Gras, Carnivale and Fantasy. All have three- and four-day cruises leaving Fort Lauderdale, Port Canaveral and Miami respectively. The four-day cruises all call in at Freeport. Three-day cruises cost on Mardi Gras and Carnivale from $395, departing on Thursdays; on the Fantasy $445 departing Fridays. Four-day cruises start from $525, departing Sundays; and on the Fantasy $545, departing Mondays.

The Star/Ship Oceanic and Atlantic have three- and four-day cruises out of Port Canaveral leaving on Fridays and Mondays, also calling at Salt Cay, a private island. Prices range between $445 to $1,295. Contact Premier Cruise Lines.

At the quayside Nassau Harbour has undergone a major expansion over 1989-90 giving it births for up to 14 ships. A new port administrative office block and control tower was completed at the end of 1990, the entire area resurfaced and the old offices are being demolished. On leaving the harbour you are immediately facing Rawson Square in the heart of Downtown Nassau. On your right is a Ministry of Tourism information building. Welcome to the Bahamas.

Transport

Taxis

There is no bus service from the airport. Taxi fares from Nassau International to Cable Beach are approximately $10; to Downtown Nassau $16; to Paradise Island and $18 (plus $2 for the toll). There is no shortage of taxis on the island and if there is no cab driver waiting outside your hotel one can be rapidly called by reception.

Companies include Meter Cabs (tel. 323 5111), or the Taxi Cab Union (tel. 323 4555).

Car hire
All the major companies have branches on New Providence. Avis have offices at the airport (tel. 327 7121), at the Holiday Inn on Paradise Island (tel. 363 2061), and beside the British Colonial Hotel on West Bay Street (tel. 326 6380). Rates start at $59 daily, $354 weekly, rising to $84 daily, $504 weekly for a luxury model. Comprehensive insurance is $10.95 per day.

Hertz offices are located at the airport (tel. 327 8684) and in the Wyndham Ambassador Hotel (tel. 327 6866). Their cars range from A to D standard at rates from $50 to $70 respectively, insurance is an extra $10 per day.

Budget has branches at the International Airport (tel. 327 7406) and Paradise Island Airport (tel. 363 3095), with vehicles priced at $50 to $70 per day with an optional $9.95 daily insurance charge.

National Car Rental (tel. 327 7231) has agents at the airport, the British Colonial and Crystal Palace. Their daily rates start at $49 economy to $98, luxury or $292 to $588 weekly, respectively. Insurance is $9.50 per day.

It is strongly recommended that all motorists take the insurance scheme offered by all dealers. Minor bumps are common here, the result of left-hand driving with left located steering wheels. A deposit with rental agencies of up to $200 is the norm.

Motorbike and bicycle rental
Contact Ursa Investment Scooter Rental (tel. 326 8329). Alternatively, most hotels and some car rental agencies have a selection of scooters available for $25 to $30 per day or $15 to $20 per half day. Bicycles can be hired daily for approximately $10.

Bus service
The minibus or **Jitney** service operates from the Downtown Bay Street area. For 75 cents you can ride as far as you want along virtually all the bus routes. There are very few 'bus stop' signs around the island so people flag down the Jitney and pay when they reach their destination. To get off simply shout 'bus stop' at the point you require.

Frederick Street just off Bay Street is the main terminal for the Jitney service. Most routes serve the outlying suburbs as many Bahamians use them to get to work (see map for more details).

Routes 14 and 16 run along Shirley Street. These should be taken to get to the Paradise Island Bridge and Potters Cay Dock. Routes

4, 24 and 27 follow Kemp Road; and route 17 turns off down Village Road.

A small number of buses leave from Marlborough Street (routes 5 and 12B), which work the East Street, Blue Hill Road, Robinson Road area.

The third departure point is for buses heading for the Bahamian Riviera (routes 10 and 12A), which are those most frequently used by tourists. These leave from the side of the British Colonial and run along the length of Cable Beach. If you need to go on to Delaporte Point ask the driver nicely and he or she may take you the extra distance.

The Jitneys may return either along West Bay Street (this bus stops near Coral World), or turn along Prospect Road and on to John F Kennedy Drive. Either way the bus will return to the town centre. Most Jitneys stop running between 18.30 and 19.00. After this there are only two scheduled services.

A complimentary bus operated by Crystal Palace runs up and down the hotels on Cable Beach, taking guests to and from the casino from noon until 4.00 the next morning.

Western Transport operates the only timetabled bus service on the island. This runs from the bus station on Frederick Street west past Orange Hill to the Divi Beach Resort. Look out for the blue bus with a bright yellow band along it; fare $1.75. Timetable:

Out of Nassau	Out of Divi
8.00	9.00
10.00	12.00
13.00	14.00
15.00	16.00
17.00	18.00
21.00	20.00
midnight	22.00

On the hour when this bus is not running a complimentary service from Divi Beach Resort to Frederick Street is in operation. Contact Divi (tel. 393 4391), for more details. This is the bus that goes nearest to the airport — the turnoff to the International Airport is at Orange Hill — but it is still 3km (2 miles) walk from here.

On Paradise Island a complimentary bus service is offered by Paradise Island Resort and Casino. This transits between the casino, Club Med, Paradise Paradise and Pirate's Cove Holiday Inn.

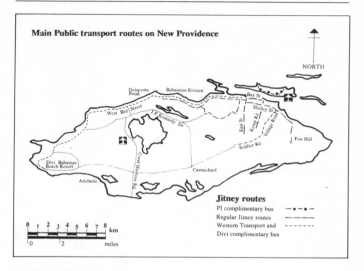

Horse drawn surrey

An excellent way to have a first glimpse of historical Nassau (see under 'The sights' for more details).

Ferry

Services emanate from Prince George Wharf and Union Dock heading for either Coral World or Paradise Island.

Coral world

A two storey water taxi ferry commutes between the cruise ships and the marine world park. The fare is $3 oneway; round trip every two hours.

Paradise Island

Privately operated ferries leave when full from Prince George Wharf. The price of a oneway passage is $2, with the boat captain occasionally throwing in a narrated tour of the harbour. The ferry stops twice at Paradise Island, first at the jetty where passengers for Club Med, Holiday Inn and Paradise Paradise should alight. The boats terminate in the lagoon at the Paradise Resort and Casino, pausing until they are almost full before making the return trip (count on about 20 to 30 minutes between ferries).

The Harbour Cove operate a water-taxi between the hotel and Prince George Wharf. Boats leave the hotel at 10.00, 11.30, 14.15

and 15.30, returning at noon, 14.45, 16.00 and 17.30. The cost is $4 round trips.

Finally, Club Med operate a boat between the resort and Union Dock for use by its guests only, whilst the Pilot House Hotel maintains a similar service to Paradise Island Beach and downtown.

Accommodation

For hotel costs refer to page 5.

Downtown Nassau

High to Top
Greycliff Hotel West Hill Street, adjacent Government House and five minutes walk from Downtown. (PO Box N-10246, tel. 322 2796). A grand old colonial building dating back to the eighteenth century. This hotel continues to have generous accolades heaped upon it (featured in *Lifestyles of the Rich and Famous,* for example), having played host in the past to the Beatles, Sir Winston Churchill, Lord Beaverbrook, Lord Mountbatten, Aristotle Onassis and many others. The house contains 14 sumptuously furnished rooms, each 'personalised' by its furniture and antiques, and excellent value for money. The swimming pool is set in the tropical gardens and the downstairs is given over entirely to the restaurant and lounge. CP; AMEX, V.

High
Best Western British Colonial Beach Resort (PO Box N-7148, tel. USA 800 528 1234). The 3.25ha (8 acres) tropical and beachfront grounds are some of the most historic land in the Bahamas; once a British fort then a pirate's den and more recently, a James Bond movie location.

The present day hotel was built in 1922 and an additional wing was added in the mid-1960s. It dominates the Downtown area and the recently completed $8,000,000 refurbishment programme will ensure that this grand 325 room building continues to attract guests. Various types of rooms are available, ocean or downtown Bay Street views there are and some particularly odd shaped rooms, full of character, in the old wing. Amenities include a private beach, complimentary water sports, tennis courts lit for night play and simply being centrally located. Children under 12 stay free with parents; AMEX, MC, V.

Middle

New Olympia Hotel (West Bay Street PO Box N-984, tel. 322 4971). This 1960s hotel has 50 large air-conditioned bedrooms with twin queen size beds, en-suite bathroom, television, telephone and private balcony. Centrally located, it is just two minutes' stroll from the British Colonial and across the street from the beach. The desire, in the words of its owner-manager, Kate Kiriaze, 'is to try and to give a personal service to all our guests'. Children under 16 stay free with parents; AMEX, MC, V.

Postern Gate (West Hill Street, PO Box FH14547, tel. 326 8028). Amongst the most spacious bedrooms you will find in the Bahamas the rooms here are richly furnished, with huge wardrobes with mirror doors, two queen size beds, en-suite bathroom, air-conditioning and a wooden-shuttered enclosed seating area on the veranda. This is a small hotel (only six rooms), in the colonial style being slowly restored to all its glory. AMEX, MC, V.

Buena Vista Hotel and Restaurant (Delancy Street, PO Box N-564 tel. 322 2811). Famed for its gourmet restaurant (reviewed later) this is another memorable hotel. Spacious rooms, well maintained, clean, richly furnished and steeped in colonial tradition, it is ideally suited for those seeking a quiet, majestic vacation. AMEX, MC, V.

Moderate

Lighthouse Beach Hotel (West Bay Street, PO Box N-915 tel. 322 4474). A modern 1960's building with a rooftop swimming pool taking in the sights and sounds of Nassau. The 92 pleasantly decorated rooms are very popular with North American students on their spring break, being adjacent to the public beach and only five minutes' walk from the British Colonial. AMEX, MC, V.

Ocean Spray Hotel (West Bay Street, PO Box N-3035, tel. 322 8032). Run by Mr and Mrs Brdemeier (he is also the German Consul), with Teutonic efficiency. The rooms are air-conditioned with en-suite bathrooms, comfortable though somewhat old fashioned furnishings. The staff are very friendly and many Europeans stay here. It is located opposite the public beaches, a few minutes' walk from the British Colonial. AMEX, MC, V.

Towne Hotel (George Street, PO Box N-4808, tel. 322 8450). Recently refurbished, with a friendly ambience provided by two talking parrots 'Peewee' and 'Ziggy'. It is located in one of the oldest streets, just up from the British Colonial. The 46 air-conditioned, tastefully furnished rooms are entered off an internal courtyard which has a swimming pool and sundeck with chaise longues. The luncheon buffet and evening specials are great value. MAP $19; AMEX, MC, V.

Parliament Hotel (Parliament Street, PO Box N-7530, tel. 322 2836). Revitalised by new ownership in 1990 this is now an attractive small inn offering a friendly, lively personal service. Its restaurant, the Pick-a-Dilly (reviewed later), is fast becoming one of the premier lunchtime spots, and it is right in the middle of town opposite Rawson Square and the Civic Centre. AMEX, MC, V.

Parthenon Hotel (West Street, PO Box N-4930, tel. 322 2643). Described as 'the most out of the way hotel in Nassau', it is a very convivial, 18 air-conditioned room hotel within its own landscaped garden. The beach or Bay Street lie only three minutes' walk away. AMEX, MC, V.

Budget to moderate
Casa Martha Hotel (PO Box N-4432, tel. 322 5422). A small hotel offering rooms with air-conditioning or ceiling fans. Efficiently run by Geoffrey Collie, the Casa Martha is located on Delancy Street, ten minutes walk from the city centre. The small on property restaurant serves predominantly Bahamian dishes. No credit cards.

Budget
Mignon Guest House (Market Street, PO Box N-7896, tel. 322 4771). Opened in 1969 by Mary and Steve Antonas, it comes very highly recommended by previous customers. It has six comfortable, very clean, air-conditioned rooms in the centre of town. The owners are very helpful and friendly. No credit cards.

Diplomat Inn (Delancy Street West, PO Box N-4, tel. 325 2688), is typical of a number of guest houses, offering basic, reasonably clean facilities, room, shared bathroom, kitchen plus backyard, but no air-conditioning. No credit cards. Pearl.

Pearl Cox's Guest House (Augusta Street, PO Box N-1268, tel. 325 2627), with about the cheapest rates around. Mrs Cox, now aged over 90 is a known and respected person in the community, but no longer takes an active role in looking after her guests. Over the years the place has somewhat declined but remains popular with the budget-conscious traveller. The facilities include sagging bed mattresses, shared bathroom and kitchen plus patio. No air-conditioning. No credit cards.

East Bay Street, Nassau

Middle
Nassau Harbour Club (PO Box N-646, tel. 323 3771). Recently placed under new management it continues to be upgraded. The atmosphere is of an informal, very pleasant, business executive club, situated in a rather elegant building with its 50 air-conditioned large rooms overlooking Nassau Harbour or the club's swimming pool and sun deck. The Ivory Coast restaurant and the Shooters Bar are very popular with the local and expatriot communities. MAP $25; AMEX, MC, V.

 The Orchard Garden Apartment Hotel (Village Road, PO Box N-1514, tel. 393 1297), is a secluded cottage colony congregated around a circular swimming pool amidst 0.8ha (2 acres) of fully enclosed, semi-tropical gardens. Within a residential area of Nassau, the one bedroom housekeeping units are within 450m (500 yards) of Montagu Beach and under five minutes' drive from a large supermarket, several restaurants and a bowling alley. AMEX, MC, V.

New Providence - outside Nassau

Top
Coral World Hotel (Silver Cay, PO Box N-7797, tel. USA 800 221 0203), is an unparalleled secluded retreat hidden away from the crowds flocking to the marine park. Each of the 22 oceanfront villas has its own concealed free-form swimming pool and sun deck. This is your 'world apart'; complete privacy behind your own enclosed terrace. Comfort in contemporary, secure surroundings awaits your pleasure. Inside is a king-size bed, a fold away queen-size sofa-bed, rattan furnishings, tropical wall paintings, a fully equipped kitchen with a microwave and a mini-bar. From the oval bathtub you can sit in seclusion admiring through full length windows the ocean waves breaking against the rocky shoreline. Complimentary continental breakfast is delivered to your private terrace on request, just raise the flag by your mailbox the night before. Probably the most unique feature is the unlimited complimentary access to the marine park at any time of day or night - take a leisurely sunset stroll after all the daytime visitors have left. Car hire and honeymoon packages are available. AMEX, MC, V.

Divi Bahamas Beach Resort and Country Club (South Ocean Village, PO Box N-8191, tel. 326 4391), lies on the opposite side of New Providence from Nassau. It is the complete 'barefoot elegance' getaway. The championship golf course by Joe Lee is rated par 72 by the US PGA. All levels of diving instruction are catered for with up to 30 spectacular scuba diving sites to be visited. There are four plexi-pave tennis courts, two lit for night play, a superb long stretch of white sand beach with complimentary windsurfers, sailing, paddle-boats and snorkeling equipment. This entire complex, including more than 180 air-conditioned luxury guest rooms with private terraces or balconies, two restaurants, swimming pool and bar, can be found amidst the 75ha (1,800 acres), of privately owned woodland and gardens.

The French and colonial style buildings along the beach have raised mahogany four-poster beds and own jacuzzi in each suite. Special dive, golf or honeymoon packages are available. A free bus service operates in tandem with Western Transport to take guests into Nassau or Cable Beach. Alternatively there is a $29 taxi ride back from late night entertainment. MAP $44; AMEX, MC, V.

Moderate

Orange Hill Beach Inn (Orange Hill, West Bay Street, PO Box N-8583, tel. 327 7157), is an informal, distinctive, family run inn nestled on a hillside, surveying the vivid turquoise ocean water below. Before long the family atmosphere and the casual ambiance draws everybody together for a convivial chat in the television lounge/bar or around the swimming pool. The accommodation is either in spacious family apartments with cooking facilities, rooms with two double beds or studio efficiencies, all in blocks set amongst the landscape garden. For those travelling light the hotel laundry is available for use in the afternoon, free of charge. Popular with Europeans, especially the British visitor, your hosts Judy and Danny Lowe extend a warm welcome; come and join them. Approximately 15 minutes from Downtown, seven minutes from the casino on the Bahamian Riviera, by taxi or scheduled bus service. Children under 12 stay free with parents; honeymoon specials; AMEX, MC, V.

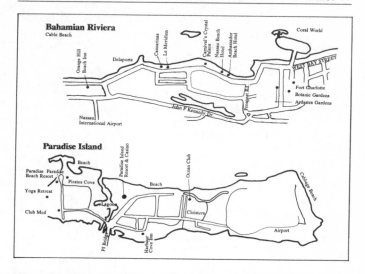

The Bahamian Riviera on Cable Beach

Top

Carnival's Crystal Palace Resort and Casino (1815 Griffin Road, Suite 400 Dania, Florida 33004, tel. USA 800 722 2248). This is the largest entertainment complex in the Bahamas. The fun and games start for 5-12 year olds at Camp Carnival, including finger-painting, hula-hoop contests, obstacle races, sea shell hunts, aerobics, dodge ball and many others. For everyone there are watersports from Sunfish sailing, banana boat rides, parasailing and jet skies to a bi-level pool with a 90m (100ft) waterslide. Near by are 18 tennis courts and a par 72 PGA championship golf course, plus tennis and golf clinics. In the Sport Centre are squash and racquetball courts, and a health spa. For a change of pace there are free gaming lessons, tropical fashion shows and drink-mixing demonstrations, plus a 30,000sq ft casino.

The accommodation is provided in 1,550 rooms of varying categories, including the most expensive suite in the world, 'Galactic Fantasy' at \$25,000 per night. This 'futuristic world' has its own robot, Ursula to greet you at the door and operate the room's sophisticated electronic gadgetry. Other theme suites include Arabian, African, Italian and Imperial French. The Bahamian sunset colour towers are immediately recognisable along the coastline and the design is continued through the remaining bedrooms. Most rooms have a sea facing balcony. Golf and honeymoon packages are available, plus numerous three-, four-, seven-night packages with Carnival Air Lines. MAP $36; gourmet MAP with access to all 19 restaurants $52; children under 18 stay free with parents; AMEX, MC, V.

Trusthouse Forte's Nassau Beach Hotel (tel. 327 7711). This has completed a major refurbishment following the construction of Crystal Palace, and is now back to its former glory. The grey and white building in colonial style combines an old world charm with modern entertainment. Its 411 rooms are rather large, most with a balcony overlooking the pool or oceanfront. The decor is tropical-colonial.

Registered guests are welcomed to the resort membership club, giving them complimentary us of windsurfers, aquabikes, paddle-boats, Sunfish, hobbie cats, scuba lessons and watersport clinics. Tennis clinics and tournaments operate five days a week on six floodlit courts. A children's clubhouse is open daily for 3-12 year olds. The 'Ambassadors' is designed for the teenagers. In the club lounge there are complimentary tea and coffee, daily newspapers, board games and movies. Complimentary tropical cocktails are served on the Ocean View Terrace between 17.30 and 18.30 daily. Enjoy 50% off menu prices with 'Two for One Dining' at all restaurants except Frilsham House. (Children under 18 stay free with parents; AMEX, MC.)

Le Meridien Royal Bahamian (West Bay Street, PO Box N-10422, tel. 327 6400) is for that casual elegant vacation or business meeting location. Grace and grandeur awaits your discovery at this fine pink and white manor house. Inside the tropical grounds is one of the Bahamian Rivieras' more renowned secluded establishments, with a majestic ballroom, excellent conference facilities and private meeting rooms. Ornate decor abounds, typified by the stately courtyard with a stone foundation pool. The 146 guestrooms and 27 villas are comfortably furnished, most with balconies overlooking the ocean or gardens. Complimentary use of the health spa facilities which consist of sauna, steam room, whirlpool, exercise bike and treadmill are provided for guests. There is also a pool room and adjacent bar a few steps away. AMEX, MC, V.

High to top
Wyndham Ambassador Beach Hotel (PO Box N-3026, tel. 327 8231). The wide lobby of the hotel offers a selection of gift shops, a hairstyling salon, car rental and a games room. The two wings containing most of the guestrooms overlook the large swimming

pool, sun terrace and gardens. Rooms come complete with cable television, telephone, air-conditioning and balcony. The Wyndham adjoins a wide section of Cable Beach where a large range of watersports are available. The hotel restaurant, the Pasta Kitchen, serves Italian cuisine; during the day snacks can be obtained from the beachside bar. AMEX, MC, V.

Apartments and villas

Middle to high
Cable Beach Manor (PO Box N-8333, tel. 322 7785), is an informal, relaxed establishment offering the freedom of homelife and the services of an hotel. There are 33 air-conditioned studios, one- or two-bedroom apartments with fully equipped kitchens, plus a television lounge with free video movies and library off a central swimming pool and sun terrace. The beach is just down the lane with the apartments set amidst landscaped surroundings. A supermarket, liquor store, pharmacy and a video store are located around the corner on West Bay Street. Children under eleven stay free; AMEX, MC, V.

Middle
Sun Fun Resorts (PO Box GT2625, tel. 327 8827), is located out past Delaporte on the way to the airport. The casual resort has one bedroom apartments and suites in a collection of two storey buildings around a small swimming pool. Each unit is air-conditioned, comfortably furnished and has satellite television. A kitchenette is in the process of being installed into each room. The staff here are very friendly and the Pisces Restaurant has the cheapest buffet on the island at $6.50. AMEX, MC, V.

Casuarinas of Cable Beach (PO Box N-4016, tel. 327 7921), has both hotel and villa accommodation on either side of the main highway, West Bay Street. The air-conditioned units are pleasantly decorated with views of attractive courtyard terraces shaded by palm and Casuarina trees. There are two swimming pools, a small private beach and a piano lounge with satellite television and two good restaurants. Families are welcomed and there is a reliable babysitting service available. A coin operated laundry is located on the premises. AMEX, MC, V.

Middle
Guanahani Village (PO Box N-7754, tel. 327 7568) consists of large three bedroomed air-conditioned villas for rental or timeshare. Spacious fully furnished self-catering facilities; choice of ocean front or garden villas, the latter being noticeably cheaper. A tennis court and swimming pool are located on the property which backs on to a narrow beach. MC, V.

Paradise Island (PI)

Top
Ocean Club (PO Box N-4777, tel. 363 2501), provides personal service in a secluded colonial hideaway. The 71 luxury rooms have a serene ambience, overlooking the aquamarine waters of the Bahamian seas or the tropical gardens. Enclosed terraces with jacuzzis are the hallmark of the private villas. These are truely historic surroundings, there being a fourteenth century French cloister reassembled stone by stone in the grounds. The surroundings are further enhanced by the white, broad, sandy beach. Rising up the hillside are nine Har-Tru tennis courts which hosts the Bahamas International Open and the Paradise Island Classic, drawing the world's top players. The Paradise Island golf course is only moments away. Dining is at the Courtyard Terrace Restaurant presenting fine continental cuisine. AMEX MC, V.

Paradise Island Resort and Casino (PO Box SS-6333, tel. 363 2000). This is the very core of the island, with 24-hour gambling on over 700 slot machines and a wide array of casino tables open from 10.00 to 04.00. There are 12 gourmet and speciality restaurants, including the acclaimed Cafe Martinique, and a Las Vegas style show.

Over 1100 guests can be housed in the three towers. All rooms have balconies commanding views of the glorious ocean waters. Five two storey villas with 16 units each provide more spacious private accommodation. The Paradise Concierge, a hotel within a hotel, is designed for those wishing extra luxury.

There are over 5km (3 miles) of sandy beaches, 12 tennis courts, an 18 hole championship golf course and 2 swimming pools, a rather cramped health room and a range of watersports.

A free daily 45 minute bus tour of Paradise Island is provided for guests. MAP $28; gourmet MAP $52; children under 17 stay free with parents; AMEX, MC, V.

The Sheraton Grand Hotel (PO Box SS-6307, tel. 363 2011) is situated directly on Cabbage Beach one of the best stretches of powdery fine white sand on the island. The modern 14 storey hotel tower provides each room with a commanding view. Rooms are richly furnished and have well-stocked honesty bars. The VIP floors have their own butler on call. The restaurant prepares excellent cuisine and the staff pride themselves in the professional conference services. During the summer months, Easter and Christmas vacations there is a free children's camp ('Camp Caribbean') for ages 5-13. MAP $36; gourmet MAP $46; AMEX, MC, V.

High to top

Paradise Paradise (PO Box SS-6259, tel. 363 3000) is the mecca for the watersports enthusiasts. This informal resort makes the most of its superb location on the outstanding half-moon shaped Paradise Beach, with its naturally protected bay and wide sandy shoreline. A whole range of watersports and instruction are offered complimentary to guests, including sailing, snorkeling, waterskiing and windsurfing; tennis (day and night), bicycling, volleyball and aerobics.

The 100 rooms, recently refurbished, provide simple, comfortable accommodation stepped back from the private beach. All are air-conditioned with two queen-size beds, en-suite bathroom and satellite television. MAP $29 children under 17 stay free with parents; AMEX, MC, V.

Pirate's Cove Holiday Inn (PO Box SS-6214, tel. 363 2101) is a family orientated resort residing on its own lagoon at Pirate's Cove. The 535 air-conditioned pleasantly decorated rooms in pastel hues look out over the deep blue Atlantic. Facilities include two restaurants and special theme nights, three tennis courts and a fabulous pool which twists and turns around the island bar. The 'natural' jacuzzi sends water cascading down over the surrounding rocks. There is also a children's club ('Captain Kid's Camp') for 4-12 year olds, plus a whole range of activities for 'young at heart adults'. This includes demonstrations on Bahamian food and drink, explanation of the People-to-People programme and an entertaining commentary on bush medicine all by the Social Hostess. Children under 12 stay free with parents; AMEX, MC, V.

High

Harbour Cove Inn (PO Box SS-6249, tel. 363 2561), has excellent views of Nassau from its 242 large, comfortably furnished rooms, some with private balconies. The inn is part of the Loews hotel chain, popular with guests who require a relaxed environment and personal service. It has a large L-shaped swimming pool with and Dip' bar, a sun terrace and a little sandy beach.

beaches are a ten minute walk away. Other facilities are two teneflex tennis courts lit for night play and a health club with massage, steam bath, facials and heat treatments. A guest ferry operates four times a day to Downtown Nassau (except Wednesdays and Sundays). Two shows with buffet dinner are offered each week and the Joker's Wild club performs comedy shows every week. Children under 16 stay free with parents; AMEX, MC, V.

Middle

Club Mediterranee Limited (Bahamas), (PO Box N-7137, tel. 363 2640) is a self-contained 8.5ha (21 acre) village site spanning landscaped tropical grounds from Paradise Beach to Nassau Harbour waters. Sports are its hallmark, with the GO (staff) who try to involve everybody. Activities featured are 20 Har-Tru tennis courts (8 floodlit for night play), plus an intensive tennis clinic with video critique, an 18-hole golf course with clinic a few minutes' drive away (extra charge), water sports, fitness centre, aerobics, calisthenics, volleyball, basketball, ping-pong and others. There is a small charge for materials used in the arts and crafts.

As with all Club Med resorts the price includes accommodation, all meals accompanied by free wine or beer, plus unlimited use of in-house facilities. Breakfast and lunch are buffet-style in the main restaurant overlooking the harbour. The GO's will seat you in groups of eight and eat with you. In the evening, two other restaurants are also available, one serving Italian cuisine, the other international dishes for more intimate dining set in the remnants of the Georgian stately home of the former owner. (These must be booked the day before). The GO put on nightly entertainment followed by a midnight disco around the pool or Harbour Bar. All additional expenditure such as drinks and souvenirs are paid for by beads purchased at the bank.

Accommodation is in basic, sufficiently furnished twin-bedded rooms with en-suite bathroom, grouped in three-storey lodgings with beach or garden views. AI: AMEX, MC, V.

Budget to moderate

Yoga Retreat, (PO Box N-7550, tel. 363 2902). Amidst all the luxury of the neighbouring resorts is the singularly distinctive International Sivananda Yoga Vedanta Centre. Refuge is offered from the stresses and strains of modern life, based on Swami Vishnu Devananda's Five Principles: proper exercise, breathing, relaxation, diet, plus positive thinking and meditation.

The day begins at 6.00 for an hours' meditation, Mantra chanting, an educational chat and long closing prayers. At 8.00 the first Asanas exercises begin. You are taken through breathing techniques and gentle Yoga exercises. The aim is to stretch and invigorate the body. The second daily Asanas exercises commence at 16.00. The day closes with meditation at 20.00. All are required to attend the days events. In between times the day is yours. Vegetarian buffet-style meals, free of eggs, garlic, onions, tea or coffee are served twice daily. Everybody is encouraged to help with the daily tasks. The lodgings are simple and basic. The timber hut cabins either overlook the ocean or grounds. Alternatively you can stay in the dormitory or pitch your own tent. You are requested to bring your own blanket and exercise mat.

The retreat is truely a world apart, a tranquil setting amongst tropical grounds warm and inviting waters off a sun drenched beach. It is hoped that through the Yoga techniques, both physical and mental inner peace can be experienced. The average length of stay is two weeks though the longer the stay the greater the benefit. Upon arrival in Nassau telephone the retreat and their boat will meet you at Mermaid Dock, Downtown. Meals inclusive; AI; AMEX, MC, V.

Apartments and villas

Top
Club Land'Or (PO Box SS-6429, tel. 363 2400) nestles besides the seawater lagoon and canal of Paradise Island resort, in a tropical setting of palm, pine and casuarina trees. The 72 fully equipped and tastefully furnished self-catering units have either a patio or balcony. A short walk away is the casino and Cabbage Beach. The Blue Lagoon Restaurant is conveniently situated on the site. AMEX, MC, V.

    Sunrise Beach Club and Villas (PO Box SS-6519, tel. 363 2234), is a luxurious, stunningly beautiful complex with prices to match. The courtyards, freshwater pools, waterfalls and patios abound with lush tropical plants and flowers. All the apartments are plushly furnished, air-conditioned with satellite television and fully equipped kitchens or kitchenettes. AMEX, MC, V.

Interval ownership

Such complexes on New Providence are:
  Divi Resort and Country Club, PO Box N-8191 (tel. 326 4391).
  Paradise Island Beach Club, PO Box N-1060 (tel. 363 3530).
  Westwind Club, Cable Beach, PO Box N-10481 (tel. 327 7680).

Purchasing a vacation home

For those whose dream is to own house on a tropical island the
Bahamas have built a number of 'planned communities' with
facilities not generally available elsewhere. Two sites are: Port New
Providence (PO Box N-3043, tel. 322 8967), is located passed
Culbert's Point at the eastern tip of New Providence. On the 40ha
(100 acre) site the residents enjoy a private beach, tennis club (with
baths, bar and three clay courts), on the oceanfront, with 24 hour
security. If you wish to bring your 'private yacht' to the Bahamas
there is a canal system so you may anchor it on your doorstep. The
design of your dream house is up to you within certain architectural
principals. Sandyport Marina Village (PO Box N-8585 (tel. 327
8500). The publicity for this exclusive village describes it as a 'little
Venice' of secure turquoise lagoons and waterways fringed by
imposing private homes, each with its own boat mooring space. It
may be viewed from West Bay Street, just before Delaporte.

Places to eat

The guide is sub-divided into various types of cuisine. Inevitably
some restaurants could be classified in two or more categories. At
the end of each section a cross reference is given. Please note, both
Carnival's Crystal Palace and Paradise Island Resorts have gourmet
eating plans (MAP's) which are exceptionally good value if you are
eating out in such style.

Elegant dining
Buena Vista (Delancy Street, tel. 322 2811). Exquisite dining infused
with charming Old World grandeur a few minutes drive from the
British Colonial. Under the care of Mr Stan Bocus this 200-year-old
colonial mansion, in landscaped private grounds, is home to one of
the finest restaurants in the Bahamas. Its graceful ambience
compliments the impeccable cuisine. Presentation and service is
exemplary and it has a loyal and discerning clientele.

The array of delicacies starts amongst the appetizers such as coquille of seafood gratinee (seafood baked in a creamy white wine sauce), to house specialities filet de boeuf Wellington (heart of tenderloin wrapped in puff pastry with pat and mushrooms, gently baked and served in Madeira sauce), to homemade rum raisin ice cream. Set meals cost $30; a la carte from $45; reservations and jacket required; AMEX, MC, V.

Graycliff (West Hill Street, tel. 322 2796). For the wine connoisseur this 250-year-old house is the place to dine — one of the proudest claims is to have in stock wine of any note you care to name (the list is comparable to the Oxford English Dictionary!). The native and French cuisine are equally superb. Mr Enrico Garzarroli has worked his own special magic, from the welcoming complimentary cocktail, to Graycliff's personalised fine china dinner service. The guest book is a veritable who's who. Located within five minutes' walk of the British Colonial. Dinners cost from $50; reservations and jacket required; AMEX, MC, V.

Frilsham House (Cable Beach, tel. 327 7639). Formerly the private house of an English newspaper baron, Lord Edward Mauger Iliffe, it marked the furthest development along Cable Beach when constructed in 1942. Much has changed since the Lord enthralled his guests with fine classic French gourmet cuisine blended with the island's best seafood. However, now reinstated to its former glory, Frilsham House once again delights its guests with excellent gourmet cuisine in a refined, graceful setting. Note the handpainted classical Bahamian cement floor tiles, the mahogany and rattan furniture, whilst seated in your Chippendale chair.

Dinner starts at $40; jacket and tie required; reservations necessary; AMEX, MC, V.

Cafe Martinique (opposite Britannia Towers on Paradise Island, tel. 363 3000). Overlooking the lagoon, this stylish concern hosted one of the scenes from the James Bond movie *Thunderball*. With a white lattice-work ceiling, wide arched windows reminiscent of an elegant Edwardian conservatory and white table linen, the striking black Cafe Martinique fine china dinner service stands out. By candlelight enjoy fine gourmet French cuisine; later round off the evening by ordering Nassau Royale flambe; dinner costs from $60, the Sunday brunch for $29 is rated as one of the best value meals on the island; jackets required; reservations suggested; AMEX, MC, V. Both **Sole Mare** (Carnival Crystal Palace) and **Courtyard Terrace** (the Ocean Club) could be included in this section.

Continental

Sun and * (tel. 393 1205). On Lake View Road off East Shirley Street near Montagu Bay. This restaurant has established a fine reputation amongst island socialites. It is located in a charming old townhouse where you dine amid fountains and beside the pool. The emphasis is on freshness so not all the selections may be available at one time. Specialities include sweetbreads with lobster medallion and slivers of truffle glazed with a supreme sauce or filet with crab mousse and mornay sauce. An evening here will cost from $40 per person; jackets preferred; reservations necessary; closed on Mondays and through August and September; AMEX, MC, V.

The Courtyard Terrace (tel. 363 3000). Exclusive dining on the patio amid the gardens of the Ocean Club, Paradise Island. A dinner quartet provide the background to the continental menu featuring chateaubriand, lobster, calves liver lyonnaise and roast rack of lamb. Open all week for dinner only; a meal here will cost from $50 to $70. Jacket and tie expected; reservations suggested; AMEX, MC, V.

The Riviera (tel. 327 6000), at Crystal Palace places a special emphasis on its seafood preparations though a selection of excellent meat dishes is available under the heading 'landlubbers'. Most of the sauces that accompany the entres have a distinctly continental flavour. Jazz music is played discreetly in the background. Open for dinner every evening; jackets and reservations are expected; AMEX, MC, V.

Bahamian and seafood dishes

Pick-A-Dilly (Parliament Street, tel. 322 2643), in the heart of Downtown is a great lunchtime spot, attracting government ministers, business people and visitors alike. Quality is assured as every dish is inspected before leaving the kitchen. In the evening the tempo changes. Dress is casually elegant as befits the tropics. It is recommended for both cocktails and dessert; do not leave without sampling the daiquiris.

Lunch from $8; dinner costs $15; service charge optional but expected; closed Sundays; AMEX, MC, V.

Travellers Rest (West Bay Street, past the airport road, tel. 327 7633). Eating is either in the sun, shade or indoors. Discover why business people leave Nassau to eat here. Your host is Joan Hanah who has served everybody from the Lord Mayor of London to Mick Jagger. Now it is your turn to sign the visitor's book.

Lunch $7; dinner $12; AMEX.

Calypso Gardens (Bay Street, tel. 328 1512). Elegant dining at tree-top level, commanding a view over Bay Street. The decor is spotless, warm pastel colours, tropical in essence. The house specialities are their sauces which enhance and compliment the dishes. Dinner costs between $35 and $40; AMEX, V.

Poop Deck (Nassau Yacht Haven, East Bay Street, tel. 393 8175). Simple, casual island cooking on the waters edge. Dine on the veranda amidst hanging plants, ceiling fans and bare timber boards. Lunchtime snacks such Abaco nantura sandwich served with french fries and salad costs $6; complete dinner from $23. Open daily 11.00-midnight; AMEX, MC, V.

Grill house cooking

The Rotisserie (Sheraton Grand Hotel, tel. 326 2011). To the accompaniment of a wandering guitarist and the backdrop of an ocean view, tuck into a range of meats from roast beef, fresh game, fowl and fish plus, of course, steaks. Grilled precisely to your instructions, its preparation is visible through the glass screen in front of the kitchen grills. Jackets required, reservations necessary; AMEX, MC, V.

Grill Room (Paradise Island Resort and Casino tel. 326 3000). The dinner bounty comes either charcoal broiled or flambed at your table. The medley of dishes includes duckling l'orange to brochette of chicken with peanut sauce. The service is good, the staff are smartly attired and the bird-of-paradise motif is emblazoned everywhere.

Meals cost from $45; closed Mondays; reservations suggested; also jackets; AMEX, MC, V.

Beef Cellar (Nassau Beach Hotel, tel. 327 7711). T-bone steak is king here, though other dishes are available, including seafood. This small warm restaurant has built-in table top grills. Meals are served with side salads and freshly baked bread — cost $25. Casual attire; AMEX, MC, V.

Le Grille (Carnival's Crystal Palace, tel. 327 6200). Le Grille affords the opportunity for all guests to become a chef. Select your meal from such traditional favourites as broiled double breast of chicken basted with teriyaki sauce ($19.50), to New York blackened steak crushed with herbs and spices, seared in olive oil on a hot iron skillet (10oz -$27.50, 14oz -$33.50). The dish is cooked at your table to your personal taste. The surroundings and service match the style expected of Crystal Palace.

Closed Sunday; full meal costs $35; reservations and jackets required; AMEX, MC, V.

Blackbeard's Forge (British Colonial, tel. 322 3301). The scene has a nautical theme and a hearty set meals are cooked at your table-top gas grill (e.g. boneless twin breast of chicken-$18, to Blackbeard's centre cut sirloin-$27). Soup, green salad, baked Idaho potato and dessert are all part of the same price. Casual attire; reservations required; AMEX, MC, V.

Paradise Grill (Pirate's Cove, tel. 363 2100). Surf and turf (charbroiled filet mignon and broiled lobster tail), $24.95 to Mahi-Mahi (delicate white fish fillet lightly marinated in a ginger-teriyaki sauce and charbroiled to perfection), $16.95 are all here to savour. The emphasis is on charbroiled cooking served with a bit of imagination. Try Goombay chicken; charbroiled chicken breast marinated in garlic, lemon and butter, tossed with fettuccine al fredo, steamed broccoli, artichoke hearts and tomatoes, $14.75. There is something here to suit most palates. AMEX, MC, V.

Seafood and steakhouse

Boat House (tel. 363 3000). Casual dining at the Paradise Island Resort where you take a hand yourself by preparing the main course at your own table over a charcoal grill. Conch chowder is served to start; a salad and rice or baked potato are served with your entre;selection of desserts. A typical meal will cost between $40 and $45. Dinner only, except on Sundays; AMEX, MC, V.

Captain Nemo's (tel. 323 8394), at the end of Deveaux Street Dock beside the Ritz Nightclub. One of the best places to eat for a harbourside view, especially in the evening when fish, attracted by the light, swim close up to the windows.

Generous portions of Bahamian style food for $25 to $30 per person for dinner, topped off by a complimentary glass of Nassau Royale; at lunchtimes a wide range of sandwiches and salads are available. The restaurant contains a pleasant bar where it is often possible to obtain free passes to the Ritz Nightclub. No credit cards.

Ivory Coast (tel. 393 0478), located in the Nassau Harbour Club, an African theme with a Bahamian and Caribbean flavour. The staff dress up in khaki shorts and pith helmets to compliment the tribal masks and animal heads on the walls. Shrimp, lobster, steaks and chicken are on the menu, typically served with peas'n rice and coleslaw. Between $18 and $25 a head; lunch and dinner; AMEX, MC, V.

Bahamian native cooking

Bahamian Kitchen (Trinity Place, off Market Street, Downtown, tel. 325 0702). This is your mother's kitchen Bahamian-style. Good portions (both meals and drinks), presented without fuss. An informal and very friendly place with no music, just the chatter of fellow diners. Breakfast $6; lunch from $10-$20 and dinner $18-$24; Take-away available. Closed Sundays and holidays (with a 'small number of staff and we deserve a rest', says Mera Wallace the owner).

Cellar and Patio Lounge (11 Charlotte Street, Downtown, tel. 322 8877). Daily lunch specials such as curried chicken or steamed conch, both served with peas and rice for $7. Popular with locals at lunchtime and visitors in the evening when the setting moves to the patio gardens. Complete dinners for under $20. Closed Sundays; AMEX, MC, V.

The Shoal (Nassau Street, 'Over-the-Hill', tel. 323 4400). Good value meals from about $9. Frequented by the locals, word of its quality is spreading to the visitor. The taxi fare is about $4 for two passengers from the British Colonial. No credit cards.

French cuisine

Del Prado (West Bay Street, tel. 325 0324). With a master chef schooled in the CIA (Culinary Institute of America), expect something special. Starters include shrimp speared with seafood mousse on a saffron sauce, or lobster bisque with Armagnac followed by a wide range of seafood and meat entres. The high standard of service, soft music and subdued lighting combine to give Del Prado a refined atmosphere. The price of a full meal here is near to $50 though a six course gourmet meal called the 'Sundowner Special' is excellent value at $32.50. Dinner only; jackets expected; reservations suggested; AMEX, MC, V.

Le Cafe de Paris (Le Meriden, tel. 327 6400). The decor and setting are elegant with crystal chandeliers, large windows and blue and white decor. The evening menu includes escalope of veal with bernaise, lobster thermidor and sauted pork medallions with cider sauce. Open all week for breakfast and dinner; The Hamak, offering lunchtime French cuisine is also part of this hotel. Dinner $30-$40 per person; jackets required in the evening; AMEX.

Italian

Sole Mare (Crystal Palace Resort, tel. 327 6200). A gourmet Italian restaurant in a sophisticated setting. Dinner only is served here in subdued lighting with sweeping views over the seafront. A selection of French and Italian wines may be ordered with the meal. Service is exemplary. Selections include scallopine parmigano (veal in a tangy marinara sauce with mozzarella and parmesan), or baked lobster with fresh herbs and garlic. Unusually for the Bahamas several vegetarian dishes are featured in the menu. Closed Mondays; reservations and jackets necessary; $40-$50 per person; AMEX, MC, V.

Pasta Kitchen, at the Wyndham Ambassador (tel. 327 8231). An informal Italian restaurant offering a range of pasta dishes, steaks, seafood and pizzas. Dinner only; about $20 or less; AMEX, MC, V.

Da Vinci (West Bay Street, tel. 322 2748). There is a cosy ambience with glass chandeliers and a piano player. Vitello alia plinio (veal) is the house speciality. The portions are small though taste superb. Dinner only; minimum charge $35; jacket required; reservations suggested; AMEX, MC, V.

Villa D'Este (Paradise Island Resort and Casino, tel. 363 3000). A classical, graceful ambience abounds, enhanced by the Italian singer and guitarists. The featherlight fettuccine Alfredo or the tender veal parmiganna, and the delightful pastries are recommend. Dinner only $60; jacket required; reservations suggested; AMEX, MC, V.

Papagayo (Divi Beach Resort, tel. 362 4391). Situated in the hillside golf club house in tropical, elegant surroundings. In addition to Italian cuisine the selection includes steak and seafood such as lobster Francaise, all served with fresh seasonal vegetables. The assorted pastries are exquisite. Dinner only from $40; jackets required; reservations preferred; AMEX, MC, V.

Chinese delicacies

Oriental Palace (Carnivals Crystal Palace, tel. 327 6200). Excellent food and fine attention to detail are the hallmarks here. Chopsticks, snacks, dips and a pot of green tea served as you order. Expertly prepared appetisers such as Palace dumplings and shrimp fantail are followed by a host of mouthwatering entres, including moo shu pork sauted with eggs, mushroom and bamboo shoots served with Mandarin pancakes and hoisin sauce, Peking duck and kung po chicken with bok choy, mushrooms, water chestnuts, peppers and peanuts. Closed Tuesday; about $40 per person; reservations suggested; AMEX, MC, V.

Coyaba (Paradise Island Resort and Casino, tel. 363 3000). Located just off the casino floor, the decor gives the restaurant an Oriental atmosphere. The selection is Szechuan, Cantonese and Polynesian, including a few dishes which have an intricate and lengthy preparation, such as duck imperial. Closed Mondays; $40-45 per person; AMEX, MC, V.

Oriental Express Restaurant (Bay Street tel. 326 7110) and Madeira Street, Palmdale (tel. 326 6444). Café style, cheap and cheerful; good food and large portions; all the regular favourites such as curry and sweet and sour dishes at $5.25; plus beef with ginger and scallion $6.75,crispy eggplant with garlic sauce $6.50. Open 11.30 to 21.00 Monday to Saturday. No credit cards.

Mai Tai (Waterloo Lodge, East Bay Street, tel. 326 5088). Polynesian, Szechuan and Cantonese dishes; plenty of food and attentive service. To start the evening off taste a 'lover's paradise' or 'a fog cutter' — lethal cocktails from the Orient. Open daily 11.30-15.00 and 17.30-23.00. Meals from $35; AMEX, MC, V.

Mexican experience

Margaritaville (Carnival's Riviera Towers, tel. 327 6200). Tasty, fun food served by attentive staff in Mexican dress. The menu gives you a multitude of choices; huge portions, are huge, each a spicy experience. Try the fried jalapeno cheese $4.95 to start, followed by quesadilla (pronounced k-sa-deea; $14), or fillet of beef chipotte ($25.95). A complete meal starts from $26. Closed Sundays; casual dress; reservations suggested; AMEX, MC, V.

Taco Bell (Woodes Rogers Walk, Downtown, tel. 326 7069). Fastfood chain; about the lowest prices Downtown. The seating area gives good views across the harbour. Open 10.00 to 21.00.

German munchin'

Europe (tel. 322 8032), on West Bay Street, five minutes' walk from the British Colonial. The German food here is well complimented with a variety of international and seafood dishes. Swiss mountain sausage salad, knackwurst, bratwurst, Vienna schnitzel and sauebraten are all part of the fare. Lunch is available daily except Sunday; dinner throughout the week. A meal here will cost between $20 to $30; AMEX, MC, V.

Charley Charleys (tel. 322 2425). A quiet bar and restaurant on Delancy Street with its own loyal following among the expatriot community. It is a take it as you find it establishment, run in a style that Dieter Languillon, the owner, has found appeals to his regular customers. Some visitors make it up here for a schnapps at the bar or to dine on a range of German and international dishes for $20 to $25 per person. Closed Sundays; AMEX, MC, V.

Vegetarian choice

Choosy Foods (Market Street, tel. 326 5232). Healthy eating comes to Nassau — opened in 1987, it offers a new experience in dining where oil and fats do not dominate the taste buds. Presentation is excellent and the dishes, from vegetable moussaka to broccoli-tofu stir fry, taste of fresh ingredients. The apple pie melts in your mouth. Seafood and meat dishes are available. Lunch $10; dinner $15; no credit cards.

Chatters (Market Street, tel. 326 5232). Owned by Choosy Foods proprietor, it opened in the summer of 1990 to provide for a more up-market clientele. The principles are the same with an abundance of fresh fruit to compliment the dishes. Dinner only; $20; no credit cards.

English/Bahamian

The Green Shutters Inn (tel. 325 5702). Lunch and dinner served in the casual surroundings of an English pub. Doughty steak and kidney pie, roast beef and Yorkshire pudding, fish and chips or bangers and mash are conjured up alongside several Bahamian dishes. To wash it all down several English ales are available on draught. Particularly busy around midday when the ring of British expatriot voices around the bar could easily make you believe you are on the other side of the ocean. MC, V.

Italian/Bahamian

Roselawn Cafe (tel. 325 1018). A casual restaurant in an old wood panelled house operated by the owners of the Buena Vista hotel. Open for lunch and dinner its menu includes some interesting Italian dishes and a range of Bahamian favourites. A small band is part of the evening set up and much later videos are shown through to the early hours of the morning, along with a variety of snacks, which are guaranteed to perk up any passing insomniac. AMEX, MC, V.

Feasting on ribs

Paradise Pavilion (Paradise Paradise Beach Resort, tel. 363 2541). Prime rib dishes; barbecues are its specialities; informal atmosphere. Breakfast, lunch and dinner daily; full meal costs from $15; AMEX, MC, V.

Tony Roma's (West Bay Street, past Coral World, tel. 323 6502 and East Bay Street, adjacent Paradise Bridge, tel. 393 0770). Advertised as 'the place for ribs' they come dressed in their secret barbecue sauce, marinated or charbroiled over an open flame. The onion rings are famous. Prices range from $6.95 to $15.95; AMEX, MC, V.

Also see grill house cooking.

Conch, conch and more conch
Mandi's (tel. 322 7260), is in the Palmdale area on Mount Royal Avenue. Its not got the best decor in town (no candlelight dinners), but here you will find conch in all its possible permutation; Mandi's opens for lunch and dinner except on Sundays. Meals from $10 to $20; no credit cards.

Buffet eating
Lunchtime. The ranks of dishes consist of salads, hot buffet and desserts. Eat as much as you can of what you fancy. Salads will include fresh fruit, cheeses, meats, various vegetables and dressings. Hot buffets range from roast beef, lamb, chicken, chilli, curry, ribs and seafood dishes, plus all the trimmings, though not all available on the same day. Ice cream, gateaux, fruit cocktails, flans, pastries and cakes are amongst the dessert choices.

Breakfast. Fresh fruit, juices, cereal, cold ham, cheese, hot dishes such as sausages, bacon, scrambled eggs, together with toast, pastries, tea and coffee.

Hibiscus Cafe (Nassau Beach Hotel, tel. 327 7711). Lunch $10; AMEX, MC.
Seaside Buffet (Carnival Crystal Place, tel. 327 6200). Lunch or breakfast $12.50; AMEX, MC, V.
The Pineapple Place (Nassau Beach Hotel, tel. 327 7711). Breakfast $12; AMEX, MC.
Seagrapes Buffet (Paradise Island and Resort, tel. 363 3000. Lunch $12; AMEX, MC, V.
Pisces (Sun Fun, tel. 327 78827). Cheapest lunch about $6.50; AMEX, MC, V.
Bayside Restaurant (British Colonial, tel. 322 7479). Lunch $11.50; AMEX, MC, V.
Flamingo Cafe and Terrace (Wyndham Ambassador, tel. 327 8231. Lunch $11; AMEX, MC, V.

Cafe eating
These are places where all three meals are available at any time of the day. All are located on or near Bay Street in the centre of town. The emphasis is on food to assuage the appetite rather than cuisine to delight the palate.

Palm Restaurant (tel. 323 7444). Perhaps the cafe with the widest range of dishes in the Bahamas. Soups, huge helpings of salads, 25 different types of sandwich, pasta, burgers, seafoods and over a dozen meat dishes. For dessert there is a multitude of ice creams and cakes to choose from, with wines, beers and liqueurs available with any meal. A full meal here will cost from $15; snacks considerably less. AMEX, MC, V.

    Co-Co's Cafe (tel. 323 8778). Offers similar prices to other snack bars though the portions are poor value for money. Equally getting the waitresses' attention may involve the frantic waving.

Fast foods
Tired of all this fine cuisine and native dishes? The multi-national chains and local outlets are here to ensure the minimum of culture shock.

Pizzeria
Downtown	Dolce Vita (Charlotte Street near the harbour).
	Sony's Sports Bar (West Bay Street).
Bahamian Riviera	Swanks (Cable Beach Shopping Centre).
	Beachcomber Grill and Pizzeria (Nassau Beach Hotel).
Paradise Island	Swanks (Paradise Island Shopping Centre).
Suburbs of Naussa	Pizza Hut (Mackey Street. Swanks (Village Road).

Burgers
Downtown	Burger King (Prince George Shopping Arcade).
	McDonalds (British Colonial Arcade).

Fried Chicken
Downtown	Kentucky Fried Chicken (Charlotte Street and West Bay Street).
Bahamian Riviera	Kentucky Fried Chicken (Cable Beach).
Suburbs	Kentucky Fried Chicken (East Bay Shopping Centre).
	Chicken Unlimited (Mackey Street and Nassau Street).

Deli

Downtown	Dina's Delita (Bay Street).
	Dunkin Donuts (Bay Street).
	Seaside (Colony Place off Bay Street).
	Subway Sandwiches and Salads (Bay Street).
Cable Beach	The Deli (Crystal Palace).
	TCBY (Cable Beach Shopping Centre).

Basics

Banks

As the Bahamas has grown into a major offshore and investment centre, there is no shortage of banks. Opening hours are from 09.30 to 15.00 Monday to Thursday and 09.30 to 17.00 on Fridays. With over 300 licensed banks in the Bahamas this is only a small selection of them (all located in Downtown): Bank of Nova Scotia (tel. 322 1071), Barclays (tel. 322 4921), Chase Manhattan (tel. 323 6811), Lloyds (tel. 322 8711), Royal Bank of Canada (tel. 326 5650) and the TDB American Express Bank (tel. 326 0337).

Churches

Most Nassauvians are deeply religious and go to church at least once a week. There is a proliferation of different Christian denominations on New Providence island. The main ones are:

Denomination	Church	Address and telephone number	Time of main service
Anglican	Christ Church Cathedral	George Street (tel. 24186)	Sunday 11.15 am
Baptist	Zion Baptist Church	East and Shirley Streets (tel. 53556)	Sunday 11 am
Christian Science	First Church of Church Scientists	Collins Avenue and First Terrace (tel. 58029)	Sunday 11 am
Greek Orthodox	Annunciation	West Street (tel. 24382)	Sunday 10.30 am
Islamic	Jamaat-Us-Islam	House No 13 (tel. 50413)	Friday 1 pm

Denomination	Church	Address and telephone number	Time of main service
Methodist	Trinity Methodist Church	Frederick Street (tel. 52552)	Sunday 11 am
Lutheran	Lutheran Church of Naussa	J F Kennedy Drive (tel. 34107)	Sunday 11 am
Presbyterian	St Andrews Kirk	Duke and Frederick Streets (tel. 24085)	Sunday 11 am
Roman Catholic	St Francis Xaviers Cathedral	West Hill Street (tel. 28528)	Sunday 11 am

Credit cards

Agents for the major credit cards for reporting in lost or stolen cards:

American Express — Playtours Travel Agency, Shirley Street (tel. 322 2931).

Master Card — Bank of New Providence, Charlotte Street (tel. 322 8134).

Visa Barclays Bank, Bay Street (tel. 322 4921).

Opposite, top: *Just a friend dropping in. The great white shark, busting through the wall at UNEXSO's Brass Helmet Restaurant is only one of the Society's many attractions.*

Opposite, bottom: *The pool at the Princess Country Club, Freeport is perhaps the best in the Bahamas. Its well designed shutes and waterfalls provide hours of amusement to the hotels younger guests.*

Following page, top: *A picture postcard sunset over the Abaconian community of Hope Town.*

Following page, bottom: *The Glass Windows Bridge on North Eleuthera shows clearly the striking differences between the choppy Atlantic swells and the Pacific waters of the Bahamian Bank.*

Communications

The Main Post Office, East Hill Street (a tall concrete building overlooking the city — tel. 322 3344); several branches at the Bahamian Riviera (tel. 327 7642), and one out at the airport (tel. 327 6500). Opening hours are 08.30 — 17.30 Monday through Friday and 08.30 — 12.30 on Saturday.

Most hotels will place overseas phone calls if a credit card imprint or a sufficient deposit is left at the front desk. If this service is not available use the Telecommunications Building on East Bay Street, which is open 24 hours a day, seven days a week. You must first pay for the call, then wait for your name to be called. Typical rates are: $4.50 for three minutes to Miami; $8.25 for three minutes to San Francisco; $15 for three minutes to Britain on weekdays or $12 on Saturdays and Sundays. Calls to other Bahamian Islands count as overseas calls. Refunds are available for unused time provided a minimum of three minutes time has elapsed.

Emergency services

Police: 919 for immediate assistance; or 322 4444. If you wish to report an incident the main police station is on East Street in Downtown Nassau. Alternatively there is a small tourist police office on West Bay Street.

Fire Department: 919.

BASRA: 322 3877.

Library

This is an impressive octagonal building that used to be the town gaol (see 'sights' section). It has a reference section with specialist materials on the Bahamas, including bird watching, flora and fauna, etc. There is a selection of newspapers, usually the previous day's edition, including the Wall Street Journal, New York Times, USA Today, International Herald Tribune and Financial Times. Visitors may join the library to borrow books for a $20 deposit plus $5 per book, for periods of a fortnight (money refunded when books returned).

Medical

Ambulance (tel. 322 2221); prescriptions — City Pharmacy on Bay Street, (tel. 322 2061), or Britannia Drug Store on Paradise Island (tel. 363 3000). The main hospital — government run Princess Margaret Hospital (tel. 322 2861) — is on Shirley Street, with 450 beds and a wide range of specialist departments. There are several dentists and opticians with offices Downtown.

Newspapers
There are two dailies on New Providence: the Nassau Guardian in the morning and the Tribune in mid-afternoon Nassau Guardian is a soft—spoken newspaper while the Tribune tends to be a vitriolic critic of the government. A number of US papers are available in good newsagents especially the International Herald Tribune, Miami Herald and Wall Street Journal.

Tourist information
There is a small tourist information desk at the airport, who will gladly contact a hotel for you if you have not already arranged one. For cruise ship passengers there is an office at Rawson Square (tel. 328 7810), which has a large selection of maps and brochures. During most of the year Bahamashost personnel can be found on Bay Street and in the Downtown area. Feel free to ask for any information you require.

The Ministry of Tourism is beside the Strawmarket on Bay Street. For public relations call 322 7500. The Ministry of Tourism operates several tours (see Excursions).

Nightlife

Theatres
New Providence has one cinema showing the latest releases for $5 or $6 (tel. 393 2884), located near the intersection of Shirley Street and Mackay Street. An afternoon and evening show is offered.

The Dundas Centre (Mackay Street) puts on a variety of plays and musicals throughout the year. Ring 393 3728 for details.

Shows
For comedy the **Harbour Cove Inn** (tel. 328 0499), hosts the 'Jokers Wild' Club on Wednesdays to Sundays, featuring a selection of Bahamian and touring stand up comedians followed by a 'snapshot' of one of the more established local bands. On Tuesday the Harbour Cove Inn offers a buffet with native show, featuring a calypso and steel band, fire eating and dancers.

The 'Experience the Bahamas' show at Crystal Palace Resort and Casino offers an excellent introduction to the islands for all the family. The show costs $6 lasts 30 minutes and starts on the hour from 10.00 — 21.00. Seven days a week (for reservations call 327 6200 ext. 6861). The presentation cost a million dollars to make and is presented on five screens, filling a 130 degree angle of the wall.

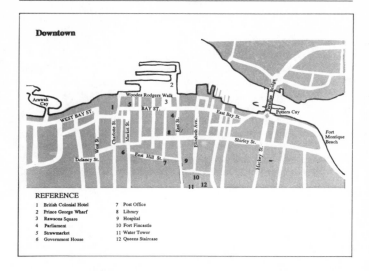

Downtown

REFERENCE

1 British Colonial Hotel
2 Prince George Wharf
3 Rawsons Square
4 Parliament
5 Strawmarket
6 Government House
7 Post Office
8 Library
9 Hospital
10 Fort Fincastle
11 Water Tower
12 Queens Staircase

Scenes cover Family Islands such as Abaco, Eleuthera, Exuma, Harbour Island and Grand Bahama as well as New Providence. It flashes through the history of the islands: Columbus, pirates, rum smugglers, the abolition of slavery and independence as well as the Junkanoo, singing church choirs, the Strawmarket and a host of other familiar Bahamian images.

Calypso Gardens on Bay Street present a 55 minute show celebrating of Bahamian culture and song, telling the story of the islands from the Arawaks and Columbus through slavery to modern day Junkanoo, with a series of lighthearted music and dance routines. The show is well produced and good entertainment value: Mon. 13.15 and 20.00; Tue 13.15, 20.00 and 22.00; Wed. 13.15, 15.00 and 20.00; Fri. 13.15 and 20.00; Sat. 13.15, 20.00 and 22.00; no shows Thur. or Sun. The show with a drink and gratuity costs $15, in the evening this can be combined with dinner for $25. For reservations call 322 1550.

The Drumbeat Club (West Bay Street opposite the New Olympia Hotel; tel. 322 4233), run by a local celebrity, 'Peanuts' Taylor, offers a comprehensive native show including a limbo artist, fire dancers and comedians. The music comes from 'Peanuts' Taylor in person on the drums, the calypso band 'High Voltage' and Portia Butterfield performances start at 20.00 or 20.30 nightly except Sundays; second sitting at 22.00 or 22.30. The show costs $10 or $30 with dinner. A beachfront bar is on the premises beside the concert hall.

Casinos

Crystal Palace Casino on Cable Beach and the **Paradise Island Casino** offer gambling virtually round the clock. In theory you have to be 18 to enter a casino. More formal attire is preferred in the evenings.

Crystal Palace's glittering casino (tel. 327 6200) is open round the clock, though the tables start at 10.00. The vast 30,000sq ft casino floor is festooned with rows of slot machines and tables for blackjack, baccarat, big six, craps and roulette. It is adjoined by several restaurants and overlooked by a balcony bar. The minimum stake at the tables is $5. Gambling lessons offered are around midday. Special deals are also on offer such as the Slot Club, which apparently 'lets you win from the very start'.

The Palace Theatre's Las Vegas-style show features lavishly costumed dance routines, cabaret singers, an hilarious juggler-comedian and a master of illusion who merrily saws members of the cast in half and makes big game cats appear and disappear to the total bewilderment of the audience. Reservations can be made at the booking office on the casino floor or by ringing 327 6200. The show is performed twice nightly except on Mondays and costs $25 including two complimentary cocktails. For $35 a three course dinner is served offering entres such as chicken calvados — (chicken filled with apples and walnuts in a rum raisin sauce) or grouper served with almonds and dill, followed by a range of enticing desserts.

Paradise Island Casino (tel. 326 3000) offers 30,000sq ft filled with over 700 slot machines plus blackjack, roulette, wheels of fortune and baccarat. The minimum stake is $2. Slot machine tournaments and free gaming lessons are held during the day. Beside the casino is the Sports Bar which, true to its theme, offers televised sporting events.

Cabaret Theatre boasts the most extravagant show in the Bahamas (at a cost of over $3 million). It comes complete with laser special effects and an impressive cast, including an illusionist working with a lion, tiger and black panther, a stand-up comedian, and ambitious dance routines by acrobats and an ice skater. This culminates in the finale when 50 white doves are released into the theatre. The show costs $25; or $38 with dinner. Le Cabaret is performed at different times through the week except Sundays. For details of times and reservations call 326 3000.

Nightclubs

Club Waterloo (tel. 393 1108), set back in the grounds of a converted mansion, is widely recognised amongst residents and expatriates as the number one nightspot. Its doors open before midday but most people turn up around 23.00. The club caters to all tastes with a live band Tuesday to Saturday on the large dance floor and chart hits played on the smaller dance floor. Outside on the patio there is a bar and seats for those who prefer to chat, mingle or just people-watch. Occasionally special parties are held around the swimming pool. The establishment's dress code is anything goes except scruffy. Burgers, conch fritters, fries and such snacks are on sale inside. Drink prices are reasonable, especially on Wednesdays when it is happy hour until midnight. There is a $15 cover charge at the door, but free tickets are widely available — ask around (at the time of writing they were available with purchases at Dina's Delita or Supermacs, both on Bay Street opposite the British Colonial; alternatively, try Shooters Bar down the road. On Thursdays the club offers free entry to women. Club Waterloo closes at between 03.00 and 04.00. If you only try one nightclub in Nassau come here.

Ritz Nightclub (tel. 323 8394 and enquire via Captain Nemos) on Deveaux Street features live bands and calypso and soca music. The crowds are mainly locals with a smattering of tourists, who come for some of the best Bahamian music. Entry costs $15 (however complimentary passes can often be obtained from Captain Nemos restaurant, or you may find an enterprising local selling tickets for less on nearby Bay Street). Drinks are bought with tokens and range from $2 to $4.50 apiece. It's definitely come as you are here and the club keeps going until around 03.00.

Family Island Bar and Lounge (tel. 325 6235) is a lively and friendly Bahamian bar and restaurant featuring live music until the early hours, except on Mondays and Tuesdays. When he is not off on world tours this is the home of Bahamian singer KB, a household name in Nassau. Located on Soldier Road the Family Island Bar is a fair way from Bay Street. The crowd is exclusively local. Entry is $7 including the first drink, prices are very reasonable.

Fanta-Z (tel. 327 6200), recently opened at Crystal Palace attracts a mainly tourist crowd. The music is generally a selection of chart hits with some calypso and soca; impressive lighting and sound system. Smart dress is expected; cover charge $10.

The Palace (tel. 325 7733), Downtown just off Bay Street, attracts a young crowd. It offers live music and a disco, and the only talent show in town. This is filmed on Bahamian television so if you want to become a local celebrity or just want to watch other people trying to be, this is the place to head for.

Le Peon (tel. 326 2011) at the Sheraton's a large discotheque that attracts mainly visitors. Seating is either round the edge or right in the middle. The music is chart hits and calypso. Open from Wednesday until Sunday; entrance charge of $10 includes two free drinks. Smart dress preferred.

Club Pastiche (tel. 326 3000). A bar and disco area beside the Paradise Island casino stays open until 04.00. (The bar opens at 20.00 and the disco starts up around 22.30). It is a better place for a drink than a dance as the floorspace is a little limited. Entry is free Monday through Thursday; on other evenings admission is $12, including two free drinks. Dress is casual.

Pirates Cove Holiday Inn (tel. 363 2101 ext. 23) offers two special events. On Thursdays the Island Luau and Native Show from 18.30 — 21.00 features limbo dancers, fire eaters and Bahamian Music and an endless supply of food. The charge is $24.95 for adults and $11.95 for children under 12. On Sundays there is the Calypso Music and Comedy Show, also from 18.30 — 21.00. The food is bountiful and costs $18.95 for adults or $8.95 for children under 12. The acts are aimed to entertain all members of the family.

Bars

Palm Patio Bar (tel. 322 3301). Downstairs at the British Colonial, and one of the film locations for *Never Say Never Again*. Furnished with small circles of chairs or barstools overlooking the beach and garden area.

Deep End (tel. 328 3301). West Bay Street, five minutes' walk from the British Colonial. Frequented by a young lively crowd of tourists and expatriates. A popular place — it contains the best jukebox in the Bahamas. Seating outside on the sidewalk or in the rather small interior. Bar snacks from $3 to $5 and coffee are available throughout the day. Open all week from 11.00 until late, with a happy hour from 17.00 — 19.00. One of the cheapest bars in Nassau. The best time in the week to go is on Tuesday nights from 21.00 until 22.00 when all beers go for $1 (just before 21.00 the bar is subdued, then five minutes later the whole place is jammed solid).

Smiley's Place (tel. 352 1997), right on the beach, ten minutes walk from the British Colonial along West Bay Street; open only until the early evenings. It is very popular with locals as it serves the cheapest beer in town and a variety of inexpensive local food. The bar gets particularly crowded at weekends when Bahamians come down to the beach.

Sonny's Pizzeria and Sports Bar (tel. 322 4971), West Bay Street. Reasonably priced drinks and good value freshly baked pizzas (large with extra toppings costs $12 to $14). There are two television screens showing the evenings sports matches and tournaments, or videos of any major game during the day. Sonny's attracts a particular crowd and if there is a sports event you missed whilst you were out on the beach, this is the place to head for.

The Billa Bong Pub (tel. 326 7774), on Cumberland Street, two minutes' walk up the hill from the British Colonial Hotel. A cosy bar with low ceiling and pub decor. Vague Australian theme and loud music, with terrace seating for those with sensitive eardrums. Microwaved bar snacks are available.

Shooters (tel. 393 0478), downstairs in the Nassau Harbour Club overlooking the quayside. Currently in vogue with Nassau expatriates and frequently used as a watering hole on the way to Club Waterloo, the bar hosts popular rock, pop or calypso bands on Fridays and Saturdays. During the week there are selections on the Wurlitzer jukebox to choose from. Shooters is open until 02.00; reasonable bar prices. (Free passes to Waterloo are frequently available here, so if you want some, tip the hard-working staff generously and who knows?)

Delaporte Bar (tel. 327 7377), out at Delaporte Point past the end of Cable Beach. Not at all the place for a romantic night out, but if you fancy trying a raucous local men's bar this could fit the bill. A range of drinks and snacks are sold at reasonable prices.

Coconuts or 'Le Shack' (tel. 352 2148), on West Bay Street out of town, before reaching Paradise Island Bridge. A bar and tables under the stars; Gets busy around 20.30 with a largely Bahamian and expatriot clientele. As well as drinks a wide range of local food is served. An easygoing atmosphere prevails here with the soca and calypso music complimenting the hum of conversation.

The Roselawn (tel. 325 1018), mentioned under restaurant reviews, is a gathering place for the very late night crowd. It fills up after the nightclubs close, around 03.00, with a mixed crowd of locals and tourists. The Roselawn is a favoured haunt of the croupiers who come here to unwind after the tables at the casino finally fall silent.

The Sights

Paradise Island

Lying 500 metres out of Nassau Harbour it was known for centuries by the less romantic name of Hog Island. Little happened here — a few pigs were left to graze and the occasional recluse made a home here. During the Second World War a Swedish millionaire Dr Axel Werner Gren bought much of the land and began to develop it. The lagoon was hollowed out by Nassau labourers, who earned a mere $1 a week for their efforts, and properties were constructed.

In 1961 Hog Island was sold to Huntingdon Hartford of the F and P family. He immediately set to work pursuading the government to change the island's name to 'Paradise' and then sinking millions of dollars into construction and landscaping. The Mary Carter Paint Company later bought out Hartford. By subsequently obtaining a casino license, the island turned into one of the world's main tourist destinations.

The toll on the bridge linking Nassau with 'PI' is $2 for cars, 25 cents for pedestrians. Other visitors may cross on the regular ferry service from Prince George Wharf for $2. On the western end of the island is the lighthouse constructed in 1816 which, as a tribute to its builders, managed to survive a devastating hurricane in 1866. It can only be visited by walking along Paradise Beach.

Paradise Lagoon can be entered by the ferry from Nassau or driven to by road. Beside it is perched the Cafe Martinique, once Werner Gren's boathouse. Nearby at the Paradise Island resort, a pair of dolphins perform daily (call 363 3000 for show times). The footpath beside the lagoon leads round to Cabbage Beach, perhaps the most popular sweep of sand in the Bahamas.

To the east on Paradise Island Drive is the Ocean Club, once Huntingdon Hartford's private retreat, now an exclusive hotel. Here stretching across the width of the island from Cabbage Beach to Nassau Harbour, are the Versailles Gardens and French Cloister. The landscaped gardens are an imitation of Louis XIV's grounds at Versailles. The tropical shrubbery is complimented by an assortment of statues from Mephistopheles to Dr Livingston to F. D. Roosevelt.

Across Paradise Island Drive is the Cloister, a favourite spot for wedding photographs. Here are a collection of arches and columns painstakingly reconstructed from the stones of a fourteenth century monastery brought over by Huntingdon Hartford.

Historic buildings of Nassau

Bay Street is the usual starting point for tours of Downtown. This road originally faced the seafront. At its centre, facing Rawson Square, is a statue of Queen Victoria, the buildings on three sides of which were once the pillars of colonial administration: the **Post Office, Court Room, Colonial Secretary's Office, Treasury** and **House of Assembly.** They were built in the early 1800s when Nassau was receiving an influx of refugees from the newly independent USA.

Facing Queen Victoria across Rawson Square is a Bahamian of another era, Sir Milo Butler, the country's first locally born governor. Overlooking Rawson Square is the present House of Assembly of the independent Bahamian government. Along Parliament Street is the Supreme Court.

Bay Street was and still is the centre of commercial activity, and was the main powerhouse of the 'Bay Street Boys', a stubborn group of white merchants who tried their hardest to thwart independence. Near the junction of Bay and Market Streets is a reminder of the darker side of the island's past: the present Bahamas Electricity Corporation building was formerly Vendue House, the island's slave market from 1769 to 1833.

Other historical buildings of Nassau lie further inland from Bay Street and include:

Nassau Public Library (Parliament Street opposite Shirley Street), a three storey octagonal building, was formerly the island's gaol. The library also houses a small collection of historial artefacts including documents, stamps and shells. Open weekdays and Saturday mornings.

The Bahamas Historical Society Museum (junction of Shirley Street and Elizabeth Avenue) opens twice a week, Tuesdays from 10.00 until 16.00 and Wednesday from 10.00 to 14.00. On display are prints, paintings, photographs, maps and a collection of artefacts from different periods of the nation's history: Arawak pottery and jewellery, plantation tools and artefacts and a display of sponges, the staple industry of the late nineteenth century.

Fort Montagu, built in 1741, is the oldest surviving defensive work on the island. Built at the waters edge, its guns cover the eastern entrance to the harbour and Montagu Bay. The fort has seen plenty of action in its time having been fought over by the Americans, Spanish and British. The powder room and its cannon may still be seen. Open daily; entrance is free.

Fort Fincastle was built in 1793 with slave labour when it was decided extra protection was needed for the eastern harbour entrance because Fort Montagu had fallen to all previous attacks.

It was built on the ridge overlooking Nassau of an unusual design, being shaped like a paddle-steamer. It is perpetually open, and reached by the Queens Staircase, built so that the garrison could speedily reach the cannon. The staircase was later named in honour of Queen Victoria with each of the 66 steps marking one year of her reign. Children should be kept in hand as there are no safety rails on the ramparts.

Fort Charlotte was the most ambitious military work in the Bahamas. It took nine years and over £32,000 to build, an incredible sum at that time. It earned the nickname 'Dunmore's Folly' after the governor who built it, but ensured that no one ever attacked Nassau again. Open every day except Sundays, its walls, cannons and dungeons have recently been restored by the Bahamas National Trust.

Government House on Mount Fitzwilliam has been the residence of the Governor General since 1803. Neo-classical in style the interior was extensively renovated by the Duchess of Windsor during her husband's tenure as governor from 1940 to 1945. Regrettably, it is closed to the public, but the grounds are open for special occasions, including on the last Friday of every month a tea party organised by the Ministry of Tourism as part of their 'People-to-People' programme (for a reservation call 326 5371 or 322 7500). Another piece of colonial pageantry is the Changing of the Guard

---

The Duke and Duchess of Windsor

In 1940 the Duke and Duchess of Windsor came reluctantly to the Bahamas. It was a decision imposed on them by the wartime government rather than an appointment of their own choosing. Prior to the Duke's new posting, the couple had been living in Portugal. Here the British Government discovered a Nazi plot to kidnap the Windsors. Horrified at the possibility of a member of the royal family falling into German hands, British agents brought them safely to England.

Why were the Duke and Duchess whisked away to the Bahamas? Was it really only for their safety? Before the outbreak of war they had drawn much criticism for a tour of Hitler's Germany. The Duchess had many fascist friends and acquaintances and the Duke was an outspoken critic of Britain's policy of war with Hitler. He would have preferred to have seen a negotiated peace. While the royal family suffered with other Londoners, the hardships of Luftwaffe bombing, the Duke of Windsor was making speeches in the USA against the War. This was the kind of action that infuriated many members of the British Government. Was it any wonder that the Windsors remained here until virtually the end of the war?

ceremony at 10.00 every other Saturday: spectators are welcome. A 4m (12ft) high statue of Christopher Columbus guards the steps leading to the governor's residence.

Gregory Arch beside Government House spans Market Street, which was extended to allow the old slave settlement, 'Over-the-Hill', to have access to Nassau.

The **Water Tower** beside Fort Fincastle stands 38m (126ft) tall and is the highest point on New Providence. For 50 cents the visitor can take the elevator to the observation platform on top. Take your camera for the sweeping views of Nassau; closed Sundays.

Potters Cay is located two kilometres (one mile) out of town by Paradise Island Bridge and holds a bustling market where many Bahamians go to buy their vegetables and seafood. Agricultural produce from the Family Islands and the day's catch are brought here. Shop around to find the best prices and haggle before you make your purchases.

Historic churches of Nassau

Christ Church Cathedral on George Street in Downtown was built in 1837 on the site of an older church, it houses some beautiful stained glass windows. Since 1861 this has been the seat of the Anglican Bishop.

St Andrews Presbyterian Church beside Shirley Street, Downtown, was constructed in 1810 with additions in 1864.

St Francis Roman Catholic Church, West Street was the island's first Catholic church, dating back to 1885. The Priory, however, is much older and was built in 1787 as the governor's residence, then known as Dunmore House.

St Matthews Church on Shirley Street is the oldest surviving church on the island, dating back to 1800. It is a mixture of the neo-gothic and neo-classical. Near by is the only Jewish cemetery in the Bahamas.

Gardens and retreats

The Botanical Gardens are situated off West Bay Street near Port Charlotte. They were founded and developed by the Nassau Garden Club in 1937, as the Coronation Gardens, to commemorate King George V's enthronement then transferred to the government in 1954. Of the 7.2ha (18 acres), 3.6ha (9 acres) are open to the public

(08.00-16.30 Monday — Friday and 9.00-16.00 Saturday — Sunday; admission $1 adults, 50 cents children). It is a lovely setting with numerous mature trees, but sadly the lush tropical grounds have been somewhat neglected. Hardly anything is labelled and the paths and steps are in a state of disrepair.

Victoria Gardens, opposite Nassau Public Library, is in the grounds of Royal Victoria Hotel, the oldest establishment on the island and is now closed and delapidated. (It is a possible location for a new parliament building.) The once famous and attractive grounds full of exotic plants are now rundown. Admission is free.

Ardastra Gardens (tel. 323 5806). One of the more attractive sites on New Providence, it has at its centre a parading flock of pink flamingoes. The gardens (with the more exotic plants labelled) were begun in 1938 and are still privately financed. Amongst the 1.6ha (4 acres) of tropical plants are some of the rarest Bahamian creatures, some of which are not found anywhere else in the world. Reptiles such as the Acklins iguanas, brown headed tamarins (monkeys) and hutias (a native rat-like animal) can be found. The Bahamian parrot and duck, living in the same aviary, are a lovely sight. The Caribbean flamingoes are the national bird. Since 1964 a flock of these exotic creatures performs three times daily for the public, who are also informed of the need for conservation. Open 10.00-17.30 Monday — Saturday; admission $3.

The Retreat (tel. 323 1317). The headquarters of the Bahamas National Trust is set in a 4.5ha (11 acre) garden which includes one of the most complete collections of palms in the world. Open weekdays 09.00-17.00; tours available on Tuesday, Wednesday or Thursday for $2. A small collection of books and gifts are for sale in the reception.

Coral World Marine Park and Underwater Observatory (tel. 328 1036). The secrets of ocean marine life are revealed and explained at this fascinating, well planned and maintained aquatic attraction. Experience the thrill of the shark tank, handle star fish, conch and other creatures of the ocean. Visit the reef tank which houses the largest man-made reef in the world and view scores of coral, sea fans and a multitude of tropical fish. This is no ordinary aquarium.

The objective is as much about conservation and education as it is about giving the public a spectacular insight into the undersea world. Coral World has pioneered the 'open-system' of aquarium management, developed to meet their desire to exhibit marine life in their native environment. Seawater is perpetually recirculated from the ocean in each tank, not chemicals. It is the only way many 'exhibits' can be kept alive.

The 6.5ha (16 acre) sea park is recognisable by the 'space station-like' observation tower. As well as the shark and reef tanks there are the Marine Gardens Aquarium, showing the tidings of life on the reef, including such wonders as sea horses and baby sea turtles; and the stingray pool and turtle pool, where the endangered green turtle actually breed. Everything is layed out in beautiful tropical grounds. At various times throughout the day the creatures are fed, always an added bonus - divers surrounded by a flurry of fish make a popular photo opportunity (a schedule of times is provided upon entry).

If you are here for lunch the Clipper Restaurant, built overlooking the ocean is open from 10.30 to 17.30 with snacks from $3 and meals from $7. There is the typical choice of souvenirs available plus a Pearl Bar. You select your own oysters containing pearls right there on the spot. Bring your swimwear if you want to explore the snorkel trail off-shore. Finally, step down 6m (20ft) below the water surface and observe natures sea world from behind glass-plated windows or take in the panoramic view of the surroundings from the top of the observation tower.

Open 09.00 to 18.00 daily; admission $14 for adults, $7 for children.

Sea Gardens Still within the waters of Nassau Harbour, but away from the main shipping lanes, are the fascinating undersea-gardens. Because there are no rivers in the Bahamas, very little silt gets washed down into the ocean and the waters retain their astonishing clarity. Thus the magic of nature's reef and multi-hued shoals of fish are plainly visible from glass bottomed boats. A number of such vessels are moored along Woodes Roger Wharf from Rawson Square. Enquire with the captains for times of sailing; price usually $7.

Sights of New Providence

To see the rest of the island it is necessary to hire a car or moped, join a bus tour or negotiate a fee with a taxi driver. Leaving Nassau by West Bay Street you will soon pass through the Bahamian Riviera, previously known as Cable Beach after the first cable link to Florida made in 1892. The area was noted for its race track before this was built over. One of its more famous residents was Sir Harry Oakes, who was murdered in his manor here. The Wyndham Ambassador Hotel now stands in the place where this infamous deed took place.

Who killed Sir Harry Oakes?

One of the most infamous and grisly murders of the twentieth century was committed on Cable Beach on the night of 7-8 July 1943. The victim, Sir Harry Oakes, was one of the richest men in the world, having made his fortune through gold prospecting in Canada. He had subsequently married and moved to New Providence where he lived the life of a wealthy philanthropist.

Sir Harry was killed in a most gruesome manner. He had first been hit about the head, then covered in petrol and set alight. Rumours of hidden gold and ritual murder flew around the island; the news was flashed overseas. From the start the governor, the Duke of Windsor, played an ambiguous role in the subsequent investigation. He brought over two detectives from Miami who were later shown to have acted in an incompetent or even corrupt manner.

Two days later Alfred de Marigny, Oakes' son-in-law, was arrested and charged with the murder. In a tense trial, closely watched by the world's press, the defence lawyers managed to cast grave doubts on the reliability of the prosecutor's witnesses. The jury reached a verdict of not guilty, Marigny was deported and no one was ever again charged with the murder. Several speculative books have been written on the controversy, but the weight of evidence now suggests that the deed was done by a leading Nassau businessman.

Outside the Bahamian Riviera is a modern development project at Delaporte Point and a luxurious housing project called Sandyport. Several kilometres further on is **Gambier Village** which was settled by freed slaves in 1807. This overlooks Love Beach, a popular swimming place.

Out at the extreme western end of the island is **Lyford Cay** frequented by perhaps the greatest concentration of the affluent in the world. This 4,000 acre piece of real estate now contains over 200 villas and mansions set in their own landscaped gardens. Luxurious yachts moor along canals and multi-millionaires dine at the exclusive Lyford Cay Club. The residents are protected from the outside world by a high wall and security guards, entrance is strictly by invitation only.

On rounding Clifton Point you will pass the **Commonwealth Brewery** where the local brew 'Kalik', as well as 'Heineken' and 'Vitamalt', are made. Further along the southern coast is **Adelaide,** a village originally established by freed slaves. This settlement is nearly surrounded by water. It was recently the centre of a Bahamas National Trust project where a channel was dug to long-stagnant marshes. This now allows the tide to flow into these estuaries to preserve their natural habitat.

A few kilometres east is the site of **Coral Harbour** an ambitious residential project that went bust. It is now used as a base by the Bahamas Defence Force, whose fast patrol boats have the mammoth task of catching the drug smugglers who operate in these waters. The **Bacardi Rum Distillery** is located down a turn off on Carmichael Road, which joins Blue Hill Road and leads back to Bay Street.

'Over-the-Hill' and Eastern New Providence

The term 'Over-the-Hill' is used to refer to the twin settlements of **Bain Town** and **Grant's Town** which sprawl for some distance down the ridge from Nassau but are not considered part of the city proper. Grant's Town was originally designated as a slave settlement in the 1820s and over time became a suburb of Nassau. Some of the poorest housing in the Bahamas exists here.

These areas consist of brightly painted wooden houses which are gradually being replaced by more substantial stone structures. The area is dotted with the occasional bar or store and, of course, a large number of churches. Many of todays leading figures, including the Prime Minister himself, come from here.

Heading out of Nassau along East Bay Street are many fine colonial style buildings. One is the **Hermitage,** built in the eighteenth century by Lord Dunmore, now the official home of the Roman Catholic Bishop of Nassau. Further along is an old ruin romantically if somewhat dubiously named **Blackbeard's Tower.** Along Bernard Road is the **St Augustine Monastery** and **College** designed by Father Jerome, the 'Hermit of Cat Island', which was finished in 1947. During the day it is possible to call at the monastery for tours. Near by are the old settlements of **Fox Hill** and **Sandilands Village.** Fox Hill holds a colourful fair in August and is named after Samuel Fox who bought land here when he his freedom from slavery. The Sandilands village is on the site of an old estate which was broken up into smaller plots.

Excursions and tours

Many local tour operators offer day and evening-excursions either to one of the uninhibited offshore cays or to a scenic reef area. Most trips include items such as snorkeling equipment and often a complimentary drink and meal. Night trips can vary from an intimate dinner for two to a boozy night on a party boat.

The Wild Harp, a 17m (56ft) schooner offers day-cruises departing Nassau at 10.00 and the Harbour Cove Inn on Paradise Island at 10.15. For $35 you sail to a neighbouring islet for snorkeling, swimming and sunbathing, followed by a picnic lunch. The 'sunset dinner cruise' off the coast of New Providence is offered for an evening's entertainment costing $40. For information on either excursion call 393 6085.

The Exuma Island one day trips offer excursions on board a 9m (30 ft) scarab. This races through the shallow water from Nassau to the Cays in the Exuma chain in about an hour. The remainder of the day is spent visiting iguanas, snorkeling and picnicing. The boat accommodates eight people. For prices and information call 322 3724.

Nautilus, a 30m (97ft) glass-bottomed submarine, made originally as a set for a James Bond movie, offers trips out to nearby reefs and the wreck of the Mahoney. Despite being billed as a submarine the Nautilus does not actually submerge. For bookings call 325 2871; departure from New Mermaid Marina beside Captain Nemo's Restaurant on Deveaux Street, he submarine leaving at 09.30, 11.30, 13.30 and 15.30; the cruise lasts nearly two hours and costs $20; a dinner cruise boarding at 18.00 is offered for $25.

For cruises to Rose Island complete with lunch and snorkeling equipment call 393 0820. The Wind Dance or Liberty Call leaves the British Colonial dock at 09.45 and the Harbour Cove Inn on Paradise Island at 10.15, arriving back in the harbour at about 16.00. Complimentary transport to the boarding point only is included. The charge is $45.

Sea Island Adventure offer a similar arrangement with lunch, snorkeling equipment, volleyball and free drinks. Call 325 3910 for more information.

The MV Calypso and MV Calypso II take large groups on day excursions to Blue Lagoon Island. The boats have three decks for sunbathing, partying and dining, with a fully stocked bar on board. The fun continues on the island which offers modern amenities rather than the desert island touch, including two bars, a gift shop and a range of watersports. The island used to be called Salt Cay and walkers can explore the oldest customs house in the Bahamas, built in the 1830s, which still stands here. The day cruise costs $40 including a lunch and complimentary wine and fruit punch. In the evenings the Calypso I and II offer dinner cruises for $35: the ships stay out at sea for three hours then return. All cruises depart from Hurricane Hole Marina on Paradise Island. For reservations call 363 3577.

The Lucayan Queen's booze cruise departs Woodes Rogers Wharf once a day at 13.15. Free return transportation to the Bahamian Riviera and Paradise Island is available. The $28 ticket includes all drinks and snacks. The trip lasts four hours and includes snorkeling (for the sober). To find out more call 393 3772.

The El Galleon is a reconstructed eighteenth-century Spanish galleon which offers day-trips to Discovery Island, departing from the dock at Victor's Department Store at 10.30 and returning about 16.00. The $35 includes lunch, as much punch as you desire, a disco and snorkeling. Dinner-cruises run from 19.30 to 22.30 for the same charge. Upon the ships return to harbour in the evenings the disco and partying continues. The El Galleon does not run every day of the week. For details of the schedule and reservations call 328 7772.

Majestic Tours (tel. 322 2606) can make reservations with a number of the above excursions. They also offer ones of their own, such as the 'Robinson Crusoe' which has all the hallmarks of other cruises including a desert island, buffet lunch and unlimited wine for $35. A similar cruise by catamaran for $13, excluding food and drink, is another variant.

Majestic Tours also have a variety of guided minibus excursions around the island. These last from two to four hours and cost from $16 to $27 per person.

Treasure Island Cruises offer a $35 trip to this small cay with the usual trimmings. An interesting touch is the chance for a couple to spend the night on Treasure Island at Kings Kastle, a two-room hideaway. Your sojourn comes complete with a valet-cook to ensure you enjoy being marooned here overnight. For more details call 326 2606.

A 'booze cruise' for landlubbers could well be a trip to the Bacardi Distillery (tel. 362 1412). The company has a Visitor's Bar where a variety of rums and liqueurs can be sampled. Drinks are complimentary, but no transport is provided. Open 10.00 to 16.00 Monday through Friday.

Horse drawn surreys. Horses like 'Tina', 'Venus' or 'Ritchie' provide tours at a leisurely trot around Downtown Nassau. The drivers have all taken courses laid on by the Ministry of Tourism and so are well informed on Nassau's historic buildings and gardens. Feel free to ask as many questions as you want. The carriages will comfortably seat four people at a charge of $5 each. Surrey drivers usually rest their horses for an hour in the mid-afternoon.

Guided walking tour. The Ministry of Tourism provide free tours of Nassau which depart from the Rawson Square tourist office, starting at 10.00 and 15.00. The tour highlights old buildings and Nassau's history. Telephone 326 9772 for more details.

Most of the tours and excursions can be arranged through hotel desks in the larger establishments. Many hotels have activities desks where a wide range of up-to-date brochures are on display.

An excursion with a difference
Hartley's Undersea Walk (tel. 393 8234). One of the true wonders and attractions of the Bahamas are the warm and inviting waters. This singularly distinctive excursion combines diving, snorkeling and aquarium gazing into one spectacular operation.

You are invited to stroll along the ocean bed on a guided tour of the sea's flora and fauna, surrounded by shoals of mult-coloured fish. If you are lucky, and most groups are, you will be introduced to 'Harry' the grouper and 'Dorothy' the angel fish. The beautiful and varied types of coral, sea-fans, etc. can be seen as nature truely intended. All this is achieved in perfect safety and breathing natural air.

The system was devised over 30 years ago by the father of your host Chris Hartley. It relies on the same principle as placing a cup upside down in water. The air is trapped inside. In this case it is a brass helmet with three glass vision panels. Air is fed in under pressure, but have no fears, even if (as in some Hollywood dramas) the air host is cut, there is enough oxygen to comfortably last the 20 minutes that you are on the ocean floor. Swimming is not even a requirement just the ability to walk.

The whole adventure lasts about three and a half hours; spent on the Pied Piper, an 18m (57ft) yacht which leaves Nassau Yacht Haven on East Bay Street twice a day. On the journey to the reefs, Chris Hartley gives a humorous, educational chat on the operation, the wonders of the ocean life and what there is to be seen. Each group of up to six people is escorted personally by Chris while the remaining adventurers sunbathe and relax on board. It costs $35 per person, with a maximum of 24 people. If you desire an underwater photograph of yourself it will cost $5. Sodas are available on board at 50 cents based on an honesty system. Book well in advance as this is a small, personalised operation. Do not forget to bring your swimwear and your glasses (if applicable). Everybody from 5 to 85 years old is welcome to join in this fabulous experience - come along.

Annual events

January
Junkanoo, actually starting on 26 December, has its finale on New Years Day. So it's a time of music, parties, dance and celebration.

The International Windsurfing Regatta is organised from the Nassau Beach Hotel though the entrants compete along the length of Cable Beach for cash prizes.

The opening of the Supreme Court Assizes is an historical ceremony dating back to colonial times, held on the second Wednesday in January, then the first Wednesdays in April, July and October. It marks the beginning of the Quarterly Courts sitting. It is held in Parliament Square.

February
Southern Ocean Racing Conference. The Nassau Yacht Club sponsors the last two races of the international yacht racing series: the Miami to Nassau Race and the Nassau Cup Race, featuring some of the most accomplished yachters in the world. The final legs are held around the shores of New Providence.

April
April to October is cricket season; matches are played over the weekends at the Haynes Oval, West Bay Street.

May
The Annual British Health Run; entry fee $5. All are welcome to compete.

June to August
Goombay Summer Festival is held in Downtown Nassau every Wednesday from 18.00 to 21.00. From late afternoon Bay Street is closed off and stalls selling food and drink are set up. By 18.00 there is music, dancing, drinking and partying with thousands of people out on the streets. Several local groups take part but the most prestigious is the Royal Bahamian Police Band.

August

Fox Hill Day is a fête held on the second Tuesday in August to celebrate the abolition of slavery. The festival includes stalls of craftwork, food and drink. Fox Hill is one of the oldest settlements on New Providence which supposedly found out about the ending of slavery a week later than everyone else because of poor communications. Here Emancipation Day is celebrated with true style in a carnival atmosphere of music and song.

December

Bahamas Blue Water Run. A yearly half marathon organised by the Bahamas Striders Road Running Club, all are welcome to enter.

Bahamas Grand Prix. A powerboat race with an international Formula One field; held around Nassau Harbour for big money prizes.

In addition to the above events a number of sporting events are organised each year, especially golfing tournaments. Visiting sports clubs make frequent tours playing their counterparts on New Providence.

Beaches

Paradise Island

On Paradise Island most of the beaches are owned or adjoined by the main resorts. The two most popular beaches are the Paradise Beach which runs along the front of Club Med, Paradise Paradise and the Yoga Retreat; and Cabbage Beach, which extends from the Paradise Island Resort and Casino to the Sheraton and eastwards. The Holiday Inn has its own small beach at Pirate's Cove while Ocean Club has access to Cabbage Beach. To find a quieter stretch of sand it is necessary to go to the eastern end of the island. Unfortunately a pleasant slumber in the sun out here is often disturbed by jets landing at PI's airport.

New Providence

In Downtown Nassau there is a private beach at the British Colonial Hotel which spreads into Western Esplanade and runs beside West Bay Street to the bridge for Coral World. This beach is served by Smiley's Restaurant and Bar, offering a range of local cuisine and drinks at very cheap prices. To the east of Nassau is Montagu Beach, a longtime favourite of the locals who gather on Sundays to watch a calypso band and party. A bar opens up on the weekends serving snacks and drinks.

Moving westwards there is Gardener's Bay, a favourite of Bahamian families out for the day. Roadside stalls often set up on Saturdays and Sundays, selling a variety of snacks. Cable Beach foots the hotel development of the Bahamian Riviera; it is wide and clean, if a little crowded at times.

Beaches elsewhere on New Providence tend to be quieter but offer fewer facilities. At Cave Beach, a narrow strip of sand, there is a roadside stall open lunchtimes. A kilometre down the road there is a more substantial beach at Orange Hill, merging into Love Beach opposite Gambier Village. The southern coastline is much rockier and the only beach of note there is at Adelaide Village, another popular place for Bahamians out on a weekend break. You will need your own transport to get out here.

A full range of watersports is available at Cable Beach and on Paradise Island. Most hotels provide chaise lounges free of charge for their guests and on the Bahamian Riviera there are a couple of volleyball nets. Hawkers patrol the beach hoping to unload a portion of their endless supply of T-shirts and coral jewellery on you.

Sports

Bowling alley
Located on Village Road; a modern 20 lane facility with a public bar. Open daily from noon, it gets busy from 18.00.

Bridge
There are several possibilities for those looking for a rubber or two. To organise an event before travelling to the Bahamas contact the Bahamas Bridge Association (the National Contract Bridge Organisation), secretary who will help to stage special meetings (tel. 324 1488). The Paradise Bridge Club welcomes visitors to meetings which are usually held at the Buena Vista on Delancy Street, Nassau (call 324 6565 for more information).

Fishing
Most boat rentals are either by the day or half day. Bare boat and deep sea fishing boats are the two types most commonly available. A bare boat with sail will cost about $200 per day, whilst a deep sea fishing boat will cost between $130 to $250 per half day or $300 to $490 per day. For bare boats contact East Bay Marine (tel. 322 3754) or Ocean Reef Charters (tel. 393 3950); for larger vessels,

Nassau Yacht Haven (tel. 322 8173), Nassau Harbour Club (tel. 325 5393), Pick Me Charters (tel. 326 6261) or Hurricane Hole Marina on Paradise Island (tel. 326 3601).

Golf

There are four 18 hole courses on the island. The one at Lyford Cay is strictly for members and their guests. The other three are accessible to members and visitors alike. All courses are rated at par 72.

Cable Beach Hotel Golf Club (tel. 327 6000), charges $18 for 18 holes and $10 for 9 holes. Electric carts are compulsory before 14.00 and cost for $25 for 18 holes, $13 for 9. The clubhouse contains a bar which serves snacks, a pro shop and locker room.

Divi Beach Resort and Country Club (tel. 362 4391), offers a recently restored 18 hole championship Joe Lee course. The clubhouse contains a pro shop, restaurant and bar. Fees for 18 holes are $25 for guests or $35 for non-guests; electric carts cost $25.

Paradise Island Golf Club (tel. 326 3926) is a PGA rated course designed by Dick Wilson. The clubhouse contains a pro shop, restaurant and bar. The fees vary per season: in winter 18 holes cost $25, 9 holes cost $15; in summer $20 and $10, respectively. Electric carts are available for $25 for 18 holes and $12.50 for 9.

All three resorts offer special rates for visitors interested in golfing holidays. Contact the hotels directly for details of rates.

Health clubs

There are a number of privately owned clubs in the suburbs of Nassau, but the larger resorts maintain their own. Of these the best is undoubtedly **Crystal Palace's** (tel. 327 6200), which is located in the basement of Riviera Towers. Guests are charged $16, non-residents $20. The club contains a sauna, hot tub, aerobics room with regular classes and an excellent multi-gym with fixed and free weights. Instructors are available to teach the use of various machines or to work out programmes specific to your needs.

Le Meridien Royal Bahamian (tel. 327 6400) has recently renovated its health club and now provides a hot tub, sauna, steam room, massage and fixed weight multi-gym. It also offers a bath treatment using a natural mud from the Neydharting Valley in Austria: for a mere $25 you can be immersed in a hot dark mud-bath who's substances will 'penetrate through the skin into the circulatory system and reach all parts of the body with their healing power'. Whatever the blurb says it is certainly a refreshing experience, but remember not to shower for 24 hours or you could loose all those healing properties.

Paradise Island Resort (tel. 363 2000) has a small health club with a limited number of machines, sauna and massage.

Horse riding
Happy Trails offer one hour trail rides for $30, accompanied by an experienced guide. English or Western saddles are available with 2-10 being the usual group size. For learners a series of four 30 minute courses at $25 a piece are available. Children under 8 or persons weighing over 200lbs cannot be catered for. The fee includes transportation to and from the stables. Happy Trails are good value to beginner but capable riders may find the trails limited. To obtain more information or make a booking call 362 1820.

The **Harbourside Riding Stable** (tel. 363 3733) offers daily rides in the golf course and Cabbage Beach area of Paradise Island. English or Western saddles are provided and each ride lasts approximately one hour and costs $25. Beginners classes are available.

Jogging
Paradise Island Resort and Casino produce a brochure 'Run Through Paradise' which details a 3km (2 mile) walk and an 8.5km (5 mile) run. The routes follow the main roads around the island and can be easily joined from any of the major hotels. Divi Beach Resort also offers a joggers' track which runs beside portions of the golf course.

The Nassau Hash House Harriers Running Club. During the days of prohibition in the USA, Nassau was famous for its rum smuggling. In an act of religious remembrance men, women and children from all walks of life forget not the heroes of earlier years. Every Monday evening this group of so called athletes (commonly known as ex-pats) run around the island shouting 'on-on, falsie', blowing a horn and eyeing the ground for flour. Eventually after about an hour they reach the 'on-in' for a 'down down'. It is all just a way to break the ice and socialise and visitors are more than welcome to join. Contact Richard Brown (w)322 5630, (h)327 7939 or Jonathan Lloyd-Jones (w)322 4643, (h)324 1113.

Parasailing
The exhilarating sensation of being whisked through the air by powerboat is excellent fun but not for the faint-hearted. Rides begin on an off-shore raft where the harness is strapped on, then off you go, soaring high above the beachfront, waving to the tiny figures on the sand, being buffeted in the breeze.

Operators working from the Bahamian Riviera and Paradise

Island offer parasailing. A ride lasts from 5 — 7 minutes, though you can pay for extra. Contact R and R Watersports outside the Wyndham Ambassador Beach Hotel and Crystal Palace Resort complex or telephone 327 8231 (Wyndham), or 327 6200 (Crystal Palace). R and R's current rates are $30 for 5 — 7 minutes or $50 for 7 — 12 minutes. Similar rates are available at the Nassau Beach Hotel (tel. 327 7711). The Paradise Island Resort (tel. 363 2000) and the Sheraton (tel. 363 2011) offer similar rates.

On days of excessive wind parasailing trips will be cancelled.

Racquetball

Courts are available at the Crystal Palace Sports Centre, across the road from the resort (tel. 327 7070). Three courts are available at $5 per hour; rackets are $3 per hour each and balls at $5.25 per can.

Scuba

The Vulcan bomber used during the filming of James Bond movie *Thunderball* lies off the west coast of New Providence. Near by is a 34m (110ft) freighter which was confiscated after drugs were found on her, and sunk, later to find fame in *Never Say Never Again*. Parts of *Splash* were filmed around Goulding Cay and the Porpoise Pen Reefs were a location using during the making of *Flipper*.

There are other excellent dive sites that, needless to say, have not been used by Hollywood. Other wrecks include the Alcona, another ex-drug-running vessel which was sunk specially as a dive site and or the LCT, a rusting landing craft. There are many dives of great natural beauty to reefs teaming with marine life or wall dives along the edge of the Tongue of the Ocean.

All the sites are open to the different dive operations, but each one tends to specialise in a specific area.

Sun Divers Limited (tel. 325 8927) operate from the grounds of the British Colonial Hotel in Downtown Nassau. Beginners are offered a pool training session and a dive for $40. Boat trips take snorkelers and shallow dive groups out at 09.00 and 13.00. A half day's snorkeling with gear costs $20, the shallow dive costs $30. A half day deep diving down to 27 metres (90 ft) costs $50, including two tanks and leaves at 13.00. Night dives cost $50. Underwater cameras are available for renting.

Bahama Divers (tel. 393 5644) are based at the Pilot House Hotel. They provide free transportation to and from your hotel, with two trips out each day. A 'learn to dive' package costs $50, including one dive, while for experienced divers one tank costs $35, two $50. A dive shop is available on the premises.

Peter Hughes Dive South Ocean (tel. 326 4391) is part of the Divi Beach Resort. It offers certification or an introductory dive for novices. A one tank dive costs $35. Favourite dives include some of the Bond movie wrecks and 'Runaway', a reef area that attracts many huge stingray.

Nassau Undersea Adventures (tel. 326 4171) operate out of Lyford Cay near many of the locations made famous by filming, including most of the Bond sites and some excellent reefs and sea walls. Certification is offered for $350, and an introductory course for $65. One tank dives cost $35, two-tanks $35. Snorkelers are also welcome.

Dive, Dive, Dive of Coral Harbour (tel. 362 1143) offer a range of wall, reef, night and wreck dives. Round trip transportation is included in the price: $50 for two dives, $650 for open water certification, $250 for advanced diver certification or $25 for snorkeling. A shark dive is offered for advanced divers at $75 where sharks gather to be fed and can appear from all directions around the diving group. Check that safety standards are to your satisfaction before signing up for any diving.

Squash
Available at three locations. Three courts at the Crystal Palace Sports Centre (tel. 327 7070): courts cost $5 per hour; racket hire costs $3 per hour; balls $2.50 per box.

At Nassau Squash and Racket Club on Independence Drive (tel. 323 1854), the three courts cost $7 per hour a piece.

The Village Club also has three air-conditioned rooms for hire from 08.00 to 23.30 for $6 per hour; racket rental $1.50 and balls at $2.50 per box. There is also a sauna and swimming pool on the premises.

Tennis
The **Nassau Squash and Racket Club** (tel. 323 1854) have three Har-Tru courts open all week costing $6 per hour. They are located on Independence Drive.

Court rental at hotels varies between $5 and $10 per hour. Some allow guests to use the courts free of charge, most allow non-guests access, though they are usually charged a higher rate. Equipment for rental and lessons may also be available.

Hotels offering tennis facilities include the following:
Downtown: British Colonial (tel. 322 3301); 3 hard courts, guests use complimentary, night play available.

Bahamian Riviera: Crystal Palace Resort (tel. 327 7070); 5 clay, 5 asphalt, guests free until 16.00, night play available.

Nassau Beach Hotel (tel. 327 7711), 6 flexi-pave courts, guests free, night play available.

Meridian Royal Bahamian (tel. 327 6400), 2 flexi-pave courts, guests free, night play available.

Wyndham Ambassador Beach Hotel (tel. 327 8231), 8 asphalt courts, guests only, half lit for night play.

Paradise Island, Club Med (tel. 363 2640). 20 Har-Tru courts, guests only, some night play.

Holiday Inn (tel. 363 2101), 4 asphalt courts, guests free, night play available.

Harbour Cove Hotel (tel. 363 2561) 2 asphalt courts, guests free, night play available.

Ocean Club (tel. 363 2501), 9 Har-Tru courts, guests only, four lit for night play.

Paradise Island Resort (tel. 363 3000), 12 asphalt courts, guests free, lit for night play.

Waterskiing

Paradise Paradise is recommended as the best place to stay for enthusiasts of this sport, as one skiing session a day comes complimentary with the price of the room. Elsewhere you will have to pay for it at a rate of approximately $25 for 15 minutes or $50 for half an hour. The Paradise Island Resort offers rides and lessons (tel. 363 3000).

On New Providence contact the Wyndham Ambassador (tel. 327 8231), the Nassau beach Hotel (tel. 327 7711) or Crystal Palace (tel. 327 6200).

Watersports

There are a growing number of beachside operators who will rent out jetskis at a rate varying from $25 to $40 for 15 to 30 minutes. Vigorous bargaining may get you a discount. Other boats such as catamarans, paddleboats, banana boats and Sunfish are available at the beachfront outfits that operate parasailing, waterskiing and windsurfing.

Resorts such as Club Med, Paradise Paradise, the Wyndham Ambassador Beach Hotel and Divi Beach Resort offer complimentary use of their different sailboats as part of the hotel package. This will mean considerable savings on equipment hire for all watersports enthusiasts. Generally only those things powered by an engine will have to be paid for at these resorts.

For the non-swimmer who wishes to witness the abundant variety of marine life first hand the Undersea Walk is highly recommended (See Excursion section for details).

Windsurfing
Equipment rental varies from $10-$15 for the first hour and $6-$10 for subsequent hours. Lessons cost between $20 and $30 per hour. For keen windsurfers Paradise Paradise, Club Med, Divi Beach Resort and the Wyndham Ambassador Beach hotel are recommended as the use of this equipment is free with both Paradise Paradise and Club Med also include free instruction. The Nassau Beach Hotel (tel. 327 7711), Crystal Palace Resort (tel. 327 6200), and the Paradise Island Resort (tel. 363 2000) have equipment for hire.

Shopping and souvenirs

Visitors to Nassau from North America should find many luxury items on sale from 10% to 40% cheaper than they would back home. Shoppers from Europe will have to be more careful. They are less likely to find such bargains as many of the goods are EEC imports, with extra duty charges imposed on them.

For US and Canadian citizens bargains include watches, European and Japanese cameras, European perfumes, clothes, ceramics, crystal and Colombian emeralds. Shops are open from 09.00 until 17.00 except on Sundays. The Strawmarket hardly ever closes. Shops are happy to close the sale with money, travellers' cheques or credit cards, but in the Strawmarket it is cash only.

Virtually all the main shops are in the centre of Nassau, on Bay Street itself or in an adjoining arcade or road. Some stores have branches in the larger hotels but for the best choice (and the chance to compare prices), there is no better place than Downtown.

On Bay Street
Bernards of Bay Street and 5th Terrace, Centreville is a specialist china and crystal shop featuring ranges by Wedgewood, Coalport, Royal Copenhagen, Royal Crown Derby, Royal Worcester and Royal Doulton in crockery, or figurines by Nao. Crystal brand names include Baccarat, Lalique, Daum, Schott Zwiesel and Kosta Boda.

Body Shop, past Rawson Square heading out of the centre, sells a variety of skin care, beauty products and toiletries imported from England. All the products sold here are cruelty free.

City Pharmacy Limited, opposite the Strawmarket, sells medicines, toys, gifts, perfumes and aftershaves.

Colombian Emeralds, are available uncut and unpolished, or mounted. The emerald jewellery is crafted in Freeport. In addition a selection of plain silver and gold jewellery is on display.

Discount Warehouse. An excellent place to price up items as the store offers a money-back guarantee if you purchase identical items in town for less than it costs you here. Low-priced goods include china, rugs, charms, earrings, special jewellery made from conch shell and coral, as well as a large range of watches.

D'Orsys, on Bay Street, specialises in scents, perfume and skincare products from around the world.

Francis Peek offer an interesting collection of antiques and china, including Vista Alegre individually painted items.

Girls from Brazil sells a wide range of swimwear and casuals, including the latest fashions imported from Europe. A selection of belts and jewellery is also stocked.

Gold Limited, opposite the Strawmarket, sells a range of jewellery, including some 14-kt gold charms made in the Bahamas.

Island Shops stocks the best range of books and periodicals on the Bahamas, as well as gifts, perfumes, cameras, men's and women's casuals, swimwear and jewellery.

John Bull is a longstanding fixture on Bay Street with a wide range of departments. It has one of the best selections of cameras (Nikon, Vivitar, Hasselblad, Ricoh, Minolta, Olympus and Pentax) and watches (it is the only authorised Rolex outlet), and also stocks Concord, Corum, Omega, Pulsar, Longine and Seiko. Other departments carry a wide range of perfumes and accessories. The jewellery section includes a range of pearls by Adeana Creations, a Bahamian Company.

Little Switzerland is to be found at three locations on or near Bay Street and features a large choice of gold jewellery and cut or uncut emeralds. Other ranges include watches (Ebel, Gucci, Rado, Seiko and Tag-Heuer), china (Aynsley, Royal Doulton, Lladro and Wedgwood) and crystals (Cristal de Sevres, Waterford, Swarovski and Cristal d'Arques).

Madamoiselle, on Bay Street, Paradise Island and at Cable Beach offer a wide range of casuals for all the family, including Bahamian Batiks from 'Androsia'. A selection of accessories, gifts and jewellery are also available.

Mr Photo, beside the Strawmarket, develops films in one hour and will even turn a photograph into a postcard upon request. It is the only place in town that will develop slides as well as prints.

Nassau Shop is a long established and large department store. It boasts the largest jewellery collection with watches by names such as Piaget, Concord, Baume and Mercier, Movado, Orient, Nivada and Swatch. In addition men's and women's clothing, scents and a huge range of souvenirs may be found within its walls.

Pipe of Peace, on Bay Street and at the Paradise Shopping Centre, sells a large range of tobacco related items, cameras and hi-fi equipment.

Treasure Box, across from the Strawmarket, stocks a range of original crushed coral jewellery including pins, bracelets, rings, earrings and necklaces, each item retailing at less than $30.

The Strawmarket on Bay Street

A place to visit even if you do not intend to buy anything. Amongst its narrow passageways, balconies and wide courtyard are a myriad of stalls brimming with souvenirs. The enterprising Strawmarket women compete vigorously for the passing tourist's attention. Nowadays you will even see the occasional Bahamian male setting up shop here. Bargaining is part of the etiquette and certainly adds to the fun. Amongst the many items on sale are woven bags, wall hangings, mats, dolls and hats. Carved beads reminiscent of Africa sit beside a selection of prints and drawings by Bahamian artists. Many knic-knacks are made from marine products including polished conch shells, coral necklaces, sharks teeth bracelets and sea fans. Racks of T-shirts with a multitude of logos are on display along with batiks, prints, skirts and beach towels. Due to the boom in tourism a lot of the straw work items are now imported from Taiwan and the Far East so if you do want a genuine Bahamian article choose very carefully. The Strawmarket is a hive of activity until early in the evening and opens every day, every week of the year.

International Bazaar off Bay Street

Candy Bar sells gifts for those with a sweet tooth.

Patricks Camera Specialists displays a wide range of cameras; it also offers a camera repair service.

Off Bay Street

The Brass and Leather Shop is in two premises on Charlotte Street. Designer products by Land Luggage, Fendi, Bottega Veneta, HCL, Desmo and Mali Parmi wil be found, together with a good choice of English brassware.

Coin of the Realm on Charlotte Street has a huge catalogue of gold coins from around the world. Most coins can be mounted in 14 kt or 18 kt gold or a sterling silver chain. Also featured are uncut diamonds, European gemstone jewellery and gold watches made from either coins or ingots.

Galaxy, on Patton and Rosetta Streets, are importers of a wide range of men's and women's shoes as well as jewellery, belts, handbags and designer pantyhose. Brand names include Bruno Magli, Bally, Anne Klein, Hugo Bosca, Yves Saint Laurent, Charles Jourdan and Liz Claiborne.

St Michaels, on George Street and in several of the larger hotels, offers a range of clothes, accessories and gifts imported from the very British Marks and Spencers department stores.

The Scottish Shop on Charlotte Street offers a variety of collectors items and gifts, including tartans, heraldic wall plaques, Scottish jewellery, Perthshire paperweights, Border fine arts, kilts, Edinburgh crystal, figurines, pottery and books. An interesting if a little incongruous collection.

Undercover Agents on Frederick and Shirley Streets stocks a range of European lingerie.

Prince George Plaza off Bay Street

Gucci stocks the Gucci designer line: leather goods, accessories, men's and women's sportswear and watches.

Le Bon holds a select range of European menswear. Brand names include Hugo Boss, Lubiam, Tommy Hilfiger, Giorgio Armani, Victor Hugo, Perry Ellis and Alexander Julian.

MGM sells a range of handbags, luggage, clothing, watches and fragrance by the Germany company MCM.

Marlborough Street area

Marlborough Antiques, opposite the British Colonial Hotel, contains a selection of 'olde worlde' maps or prints of birds, flowers and a variety of Bahamian themes. A variety of gifts evoking a colonial English style can be found here.

Optique Shoppe, in the British Colonial shopping arcade, features sunglasses and designer wear by such brands as Ray-Ban, Cazal, Serengeti, Suncloud Rose, Vuarnet and Silhouette.

Tasha Collection, on Marlborough Street, is a glamorous boutique selling Asian ethnic accessories and Austrian crystal evening clutches. Other items include leather, lapis and suede belts with matching bags, Chanel accessories, scarves of silk, chiffon or wool and hair accessories.

Around Nassau

British Home Stores, in the Independence Drive area, selling a range of clothes and accessories imported from the UK.

Jubal Sounds, on Madeira Street of Mackay Street, sells a range of Christian souvenirs including gospel music tapes.

The Androsia Batik Factory Shop, located 'Over-the-Hill', (tel. 368 2020 for details on how to get there) has batik fabric or casual wear which is displayed in many boutiques along Bay Street. But here a blouse will cost $4 to $8 or a shirt $6 to $20, whereas Downtown the 'tourist price' will be at least twice as much.

The Philatelic Bureau of the Main Post Office at the top of Parliament Street has a large catalogue of stamps and is a must for any avid collector. There are many beautifully designed sets which come complete with their own mounts and make pleasant small gifts. A small philatelic bureau has now opened down on Rawson Square.

Preserving the Bahamas' heritage

It was a familiar story to many other countries worldwide: indigenous species in danger of extinction, areas of natural beauty threatened and historic buildings decaying beyond repair or being bulldozed to make way for office blocks. All these factors led to the formation of the Bahamas National Trust, an organisation which despite limited resources has made huge strides in protecting sites of value.

The Trust employs two fulltime staff at its headquarters in Nassau. Its most important projects to date include the huge flamingo reserve on Inagua, the Exuma Cays Land and Sea Park, the restoration of Fort Charlotte and the Lucayan National Park near Freeport. Many of the projects are run entirely by volunteers.

Partly a charity, sometimes a pressure group and often the nation's conscience, the Bahamas National Trust's work has been widely recognised. Its patrons include the Duke of Edinburgh who visited the Inagua National Park in 1989. Fresh emphasis is now being placed on educational material and school visits to inspire the coming generations with the trust's work. For information or membership call 393 1317.

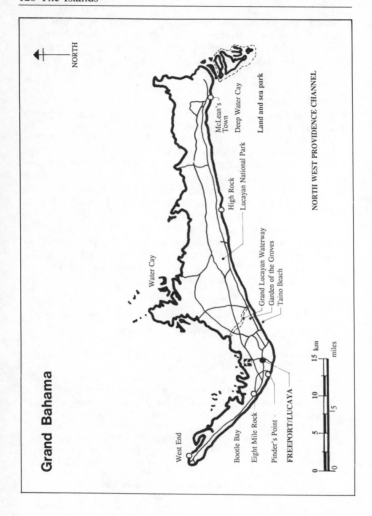

Grand Bahama

NORTH

West End

Bootle Bay

Eight Mile Rock

Pinder's Point

FREEPORT/LUCAYA

Water Cay

Grand Lucayan Waterway
Garden of the Groves
Taino Beach

High Rock
Lucayan National Park

McLean's Town
Deep Water Cay

Land and sea park

NORTH WEST PROVIDENCE CHANNEL

0   5   10   15 km
         miles
0   5

SIXTEEN

Freeport - Grand Bahama

Grand Bahama is one of the largest Bahamian islands. Despite its abundant pine forests it was neglected until comparatively recently. The island is 120km (75 miles) long west to east but only 6km (4 miles) across. Today it is the second most popular island and it owes its unprecedented growth to one man, Wallace Groves. Without his vision and finance the island would have remained a backwater.

The Siboney were the first people to live here but they moved on as the Lucayans arrived. Lucayans cave dwellings have been excavated and can now be visited and Lucayan artefacts are on display in the Garden of the Groves.

The indefatigable Ponce de Leon was the first European to record landing here. He found only one Lucayan, an elderly woman. The rest had probably been carried off as slaves or were hiding to avoid such a fate. Ponce de Leon searched the island for the elusive 'fountain of youth' before sailing on to Florida. He was granted control of the island but was killed before he could return.

Wreckers and farmers were the first settlers in modern times: the Straits of Florida were only 80 miles wide at this point and Grand Bahama is surrounded by many dangerous reefs. It was a good place to start a salvaging business, and in the eighteenth century it had been a favourite hunting ground of pirates.

The main settlement was established at West End which only boomed twice, on both occasions by cashing in on misfortunes occurring in the USA. During the American Civil War it was an excellent site for the blockade runners heading for Confederate ports. During US Abolition it became a haven for gangsters and smugglers. The alcohol just could not be shipped out fast enough and West End grew rich.

The people of Grand Bahama took advantage of these opportunities, but these were not the necessary foundations for secure economic growth. With the growth of US demand for lobster West End became a centre for crawfishing, and in 1946 the island's lumber began to be exploited. An American entrepreneur, Wallace Groves, took over the operation, and gradually became more involved in other business affairs on Grand Bahama, seeing its great potential: a location only a few minutes by plane from Florida or a few hours by ship, lying in another country and not subject to the taxes and duties of industry on the mainland.

Groves negotiated with the colonial government to obtain the freedom and powers he wanted to develop his concept — Freeport. The terms of the agreement were extremely generous: no customs, excise or stamp duties for 99 years, no income or property taxes for 30 years, a grant of 50,000 acres of land and the ability to bring in any expatriate staff required without work visas or immigration procedures. As Chair of the Grand Bahama Port Authority, Groves immediately set to work.

A deep water harbour was constructed by a shipping company and slowly but surely enterprises began to establish themselves. The real expansion did not come until a casino license was granted in 1963, obtained by dubious means, much wheeling and dealing and unspecified amounts of money changing hands in 'consultancy fees'. When the Lucayan Beach Casino and Hotel opened it brought about a tourist boom, and the resultant publicity attracted many others to Freeport.

In the late 1960s there was a growing concern that the licensees in Freeport were discriminating against black Bahamians as foreigners continued to be flown in to do much of the skilled work. The Progressive Liberal Party tried to improve prospects for Bahamians, but most business concerns proved intransigent on the matter. In 1970 the government finally imposed a settlement forcing the Freeport area to accept Bahamian immigration laws.

Some businesses departed or closed down and growth slowed, though more Bahamians were now able to seek employment here. The town still bears all the hallmarks of Groves's influence. Its wide streets, avenues, roundabouts and drive-ins have far more in common with the USA than with Nassau. The layout favours the motorist and the commuter, the pedestrian will be lucky to find a sidewalk let alone a crossing place. Here you will find 'American suburbia' rather than homely village communities. Even so Bahamians have adapted themselves well to these changes and have made the island's economy the second strongest in the country.

Arrival

By air

Freeport is a busy international airport. PanAm (3 times a day, every day), Eastern and Bahamasair connect to Miami. Aero Coach link Freeport to West Palm Beach and Fort Lauderdale. Air Canada fly direct from Montreal. Delta, Eastern, TWA, Piedmont and Com Air have flights in from several other US cities. Bahamasair connect Freeport with Nassau (3 flights a day). Taino Air Services fly out of Freeport to the Family Island (tel. 352 8885): to Marsh Harbour, Abaco for $49 and Bimini for $39, both one-way. The flights to both destinations leave daily except for Tuesdays and Thursdays.

At the airport

A small but busy terminal; baggage can be quickly picked up; customs are cursory. Immediately outside is the taxi rank where numerous drivers will hustle for your fare. There is no public bus service so unless your hotel has a courtesy service you will have to take a taxi. (The Princess Casino/International Bazaar is about 5 km (3 miles) away, which should cost around $5; the Port Lucaya area is about double the distance and twice the fare). Across from the taxi working zone is a row of hire car offices: Avis, Hertz, National and several local firms.

Inside the terminal are a variety of shops, (liquor store, two boutiques, record and tape stall, newsagents — bookshop, restaurant and snack bar) and a telecommunications booth (open for international calls from 08.00 to 18.00 on weekdays and 09.00 to 17.00 on weekends).

By Sea

Crown Cruise Lines offer one day cruises to Freeport on board the Viking Princess, departing Monday, Tuesday, Thursday or Saturday. The Saturday cruise costs $89, the others $79 each. The Viking Princess leaves Palm Beach at 09.30 and returns at midnight.

The Discovery I leaves from Port Everglades, Fort Lauderdale four times a week: Monday, Tuesday and Sunday cruises cost $89, leaving at 08.00 and returning at 23.00; Friday cruises costs $69 and leave at 07.30 returning at 20.30.

Sea Escape have cruises to Freeport out of Miami and Fort Lauderdale, leaving at 08.30 and returning at either 22.00 or 23.00; $79 on Thursdays or $89 on all other days.

Alternatively, with Carnival Cruise Lines Freeport can be visited as part of a larger cruise including Nassau. The Mardi Gras four-day cruise leaves Fort Lauderdale on Sunday with Freeport as the first stop. The Carnivale has a similar programme from Port Canaveral while the Fantasy operates from Miami, leaving on Mondays. Prices for three day cruises start at $295, four-day cruises at $425. This does not include airfare and varies considerably with season. Confirm all sailing times with the relevant company.

In contrast the humble old mailboat leaves Nassau on Wednesday at 16.00, calling at Freeport, Eight Mile Rock and West End. It leaves for Nassau at 19.00 on Friday. The one way fare is $35.

At the quayside

Freeport Harbour is approximately 5km (3 miles) from the International Bazaar area of Downtown — $6 by taxi. Port Lucaya is further, the fare being about $10. Taxis assemble before cruise arrivals and are the only means of transport to town except for the occasional complimentary hotel bus.

Transport

Taxi

There are taxi ranks outside all the major hotels and your reception can call one very quickly. All taxis should be metered, if not enquire about the approximate fare before you get in. The fare for one or two people is the same with an extra $2 per person thereafter. All taxi drivers have participated in the Bahamahost programme so they should know quite a bit about the places to see and things to do around town. Taxis have a monopoly in most areas as there are few bus routes.

Car rental

An average sized car will cost approximately $50 per day or $300 to $330 per week. Insurance is an extra $10 per day. There are car hire firms at the International Airport, the International Bazaar, the Atlantic Hotel, Holiday Inn, Princess Country Club and the Xanadu Hotel.

Bicycle and moped rental

Daily hire can be obtained from the front of the Port Lucaya Marketplace adjacent to the Police Station on Seahorse Road. Bicycles rent for $10 a day, mopeds for $25 for one or $38 with two riders, plus a $2 insurance charge, crash helmet and a $10 deposit.

Bus

The local minibuses are called **Jitneys.** The ones that operate in the Downtown/Port Lucaya area charge 75 cents per person per journey. Jitneys have no set timetable, but leave when full. Do not worry if you have just missed one there will be another along soon.

The most popular route begins at the West Mall Shopping Centre in Downtown Freeport, runs past the International Bazaar and on to Port Lucaya. The last bus on this route leaves at about 19.30. The stopping off point at Port Lucaya is outside the Holiday Inn. The buses are forbidden by the powerful taxi union to go all the way down to the Lucayan Beach Resort.

Other bus routes start and terminate at the West Mall Shopping Centre. One goes out to the eastern portion of the island, another goes hourly to West End. A regular Jitney route goes from the West Mall to and from Eight Mile Rock.

Ferry

There is a complimentary boat service running from 08.00 to midnight across the harbour from the Lucayan Marina Hotel to the Casino and Port Lucaya Marketplace.

Accommodation

For hotel costs refer to page 5

Freeport

High to top

Xanadu Beach and Marina Resort (PO Box F-2438, tel. 352 6782). 186 rooms ranging from an exquisite suite where Howard Hughes the billionaire recluse once resided, to comfortable guestrooms complete with balcony, satellite television and bathroom. In the Xanadu tower there is a laundry service, restaurant and bar. Outside recreations include swimming pool, tennis courts, marina and a concession on the nearby beach which offers the complete range of watersports. The resort now offers a form of club membership.

During the day a complimentary bus service runs to the Princess Casino every half hour. (A taxi to the Princess Casino cost about $5.) At other times the resort is rather isolated, though you cannot get lost as the bright pink 13-storey tower can be seen for miles around. AMEX, MC, V.

Top

Princes Resort and Casino (805 Third Avenue, New York, New York 10022, tel. 352 6721). This is actually two resorts, the Princess Country Club and the Princess Tower with 965 rooms in total. Guests at both centres have access to the two 18-hole championship golf courses, the 10km jogging trail, 12 tennis courts, 2 swimming pools, 2 hot tubs, a fitness centre and sauna. The complimentary bus service to the beach runs every 30 minutes.

The 565 room Country Club is a fun place for kids, with its pool complete with cascading waterfalls and slides and games-room. There is also a babysitting service during the evenings. There are six restaurants and a number of bars and lounges. Rooms have air-conditioning, telephone and television. The resort also offers a wide range of conference facilities.

The Princess Towers is beside the Moorish-domed casino entrance hall and is designed in a complimentary style. Inside are four restaurants, two bars, the Sultan's Tent disco and a variety of boutiques and giftshops. The rooms in the tower are pleasantly furnished with television, telephone and bathroom. The higher floors offer excellent panoramic views of Freeport. Some levels have been converted to timeshare apartments. AMEX, MC,V.

Middle

Caravel Apartment and Beach Resort (PO Box F3038, tel. 352 4896). A resort specialising in self-catering units on Caravel Beach, the units contain two bedrooms, two bathrooms, air-conditioning, kitchen and television. Amenities include coin operated launderette and the Windsurfer restaurant. MC, V.

Moderate to middle

Freeport Inn (PO Box F200 tel. 352 6648). 140 spacious rooms, each with air-conditioning and many with self-catering facilities, are arranged around the swimming pool with courtesy transportation past the International Bazaar to the beach. AMEX, MC, V.

Moderate

Windward Palms Hotel (PO Box F2549, tel. 352 8821). 100 rooms arranged round a freshwater swimming pool across from the International Bazaar. The large number of surcharges (such as 'energy') makes this hotel more expensive than it would first appear. AMEX, MC, V.

Port Lucaya

High to top

Lucayan Beach Resort and Casino (1610 SE 10th Terrace, Fort Lauderdale, Florida 33316, tel. 373 7777). The first casino to open in the Bahamas, it has now been extensively refurbished. Rooms come with satellite television, air-conditioning and balcony. There are several restaurants, tennis, a golf course, gift shops, cabaret and a beach where a large range of waters sports are on offer. The Casino has beginners classes during the morning and early evening and provides a leaflet for first time gamblers. AMEX, MC, V.

Middle to high

Holiday Inn (PO Box F200, tel. 373 1333). This resort aims at the family market and puts on a variety of activities for children throughout the week; under 12s stay free. The hotel is designed in a crescent shape around the large swimming pool. Five room types vary from economy to ocean front.

With 500 rooms, this is the largest hotel in Port Lucaya. There are tennis courts, three restaurants, a poolside bar which offers regular live entertainment and the Panache nightclub. A wide range of water sports are on offer on the beach. AMEX, MC, V.

Atlantic Beach Hotel (PO Box F531, tel. 373 1444). The Atlantic Beach rises up like a block of London council flats but do not be put off by its external appearance. Inside the rooms and suites are furnished with television, telephone, bathroom and air-conditioning. It is located beside the Casino and across from the Port Lucaya Shopping Centre.

The hotel appeals especially to sporty types. It offers regular complimentary transportation to the Lucaya Golf and Country Club, generally considered the best on the island. A large range of water sports are on offer at the adjacent Lucaya Beach. Amenities include a swimming pool, jacuzzi, two restaurants, bar and meeting rooms. AMEX, MC, V.

Middle

Channel House (PO Box F1337, tel. 373 5405). A membership club centrally located in Port Lucaya, but some of the studios and apartments are available to non-members throughout the year. Each unit is fully equipped for self-catering. In the grounds are two tennis courts, a swimming pool and a bar selling drinks and snacks. AMEX, MC, V.

Moderate

Silver Sands Hotel (PO Box F2385, tel. 373 5700). The 144 studio apartments and 20 one bedroom suites come complete with kitchenette, dining area, air-conditioning and balcony. The Silver Sands is two minutes' walk from the beach and about 15 minutes' walk to Port Lucaya. Alternatively the Jitneys regularly pass by the hotel entrance during the daytime.

The La Phoenix Restaurant is above the reception area. In the grounds are two swimming pools and tennis, paddleball and shuffleboard courts. Water sports are available at the Lucayan Beach. AMEX, MC, V.

Coral Beach Hotel (PO Box F2468, tel. 373 2468). Most of this development consists of private condominiums with only 11 rooms available for rent. All rooms come complete with air-conditioning and television, some also have balcony and refrigerator. The building has ramp or level access.

There is a large pool on the terrace beside the beach. The beach bar offers a variety of meals and snacks throughout the day, with Juliat Lins Chinese Restaurant offering food in the evenings. Facilities for children include babysitters, a games room and playground. AMEX.

New Victoria Inn (PO Box F1261, tel. 373 3040). A circular building centred around the swimming pool. Amenities include a restaurant, bar and complimentary transport to Port Lucaya. The 40 rooms are tastefully decorated, coming complete with telephone, colour television and air-conditioning. Special family rates and dive packages available here. EP; AP; AMEX, MC, V.

Lucayan Marina Hotel (1610 SE 10th Terrace, Fort Lauderdale, Florida 33316, tel. USA 305 463 7844). The 142 rooms offer cheap, reasonably furnished accommodation in the centre of Port Lucaya. Complimentary ferry trips link the resort to its sister complex and casino. Facilities include a 150 slip marina, bar, swimming pool, laundry service and restaurant, plus full use of the amenities at the Lucayan Beach Resort available to guests. AMEX, MC, V.

Redwood Inn (PO Box F1417, tel. 373 7881). A variety of comfortably furnished studios and penthouses. The rooms come complete with air-conditioning and there is a small pool and terrace area. Centrally located near the shopping centre. No credit cards.

Other Accommodation

Deep Water Cay Club (PO Box 1145, Palm Beach, Florida 33480, tel. USA 305 684 3958). A small resort catering especially for bone fishing enthusiasts, located right at the eastern end of the island with its own airstrip. The accommodation consists of 11 air-conditioned cottages with a restaurant serving Bahamian food and a bar. There are a variety of custom-built boats for hire. For details of rates contact the Deep Water Cay at the above address. AP; AMEX, MC, V.

High to top
Jack Tar Village (tel. 346 6211). This resort closed down in 1990 and a phased relaunching under new management is planned through 1991. At present it seems that all the old amenities will be on offer: the previous package included all meals, drinks and full use of the amenities. The rooms are air-conditioned with double or twin beds and a telephone. Some have verandas, patios or televisions and there are some suites available. On site facilities include a 27-hole golf course, 16 tennis courts, shuffleboard, volleyball, table tennis, multi-gym and aerobics classes. Instruction is available in most sports and activities. At the beach the range of activities includes sailing, snorkeling, water skiing and pedal-boats. UNEXSO operate a small scuba operation here (see under 'Sports' below). AI; AMEX.

In addition to on-site activities the Village organises a variety of tours to Freeport, the museums, gardens and casinos; and cruises and fishing trips. There are shows in the evenings, the piano lounges to relax in, and the discos later on at night. For the latest developments at Jack Tar Village contact the Bahamas Board of Tourism or your travel agent.

Moderate
Harbour Hotel (PO Box F2670, tel. 346 6432) has nine brightly decorated, comfortably furnished air-conditioned rooms with satellite television. Above the restaurant and bar there is one two-bedroom apartment with spacious lounge and kitchen. Rooms on the oceanfront have private balconies. The restaurant serves typical Bahamian fare, lunch from $8, dinners from $20. No credit cards.

Vacation Resorts

Places offering vacation resort holidays are:
Mayfield Beach and Tennis Club, PO Box F458 (tel. 352 9776).
Ocean Reef Resort and Yacht Club, PO Box F898 (tel. 373 4661).
Princess Vacation Club, PO Box F207 (tel. 352 6721).
Taino Beach Resort and Club (tel. 373 4682).
Xanadu Beach and Marina Resort (tel. 352 6792).

Places to eat

Dining out
It is always best to make a reservation, especially during the winter
season. Some establishments expect men to wear jackets and none
will serve those in swimwear or bare feet. A glossy brochure entitled
'What-to do Freeport Lucaya' contains many suggestions for eating
out and is available at Tourist Information Booths and most large
hotels.

In addition to the cafes and restaurants outlined below there are
many fast food outlets including Burger King, McDonalds,
Kentucky Fried Chicken and Pizza Hut. Frozen yogurt and ice
cream parlours can be found in the International Bazaar and
Lucaya. For Bahamian snacks there are a number of small family-
run cafes in the Port Lucaya Marketplace.

Elegant dining
The Crown Room (tel. 352 6721) is part of the Princess Casino
complex. Lavishly furnished with pink marble, mirrors and
chandeliers it serves until late into the night except on Mondays. The
menu features a large selection of international dishes, including
lobster casino, veal piccata, pepper steak Madagascar and rack of
lamb. A three course meal here costs between $40 to $50 per person,
including gratuity; reservations necessary; jackets expected; AMEX,
MC, V.

Continental
Luciano's (tel. 373 9100). A true pleasure of fine French and
continental dining at the waters edge in Port Lucaya. For something
different why not try salade de carbes au pamplemousse (a
refreshing combination of juicy crab meat and fresh grapefruit
segments in a brandy sauce; $12). Fish and shellfish are the hallmark
of the menu, but there are other popular dishes such as steak
Diane($22.50). For desserts, try crepes Suzette for two, (sweet

French pancakes flamed in Curacao and Grand Mariner). If you haven't had a 'Bahamian coffee' you are in for a lovely surprise (ingredients: Nassau Royale, Tia Maria, coffee, topped with cream chantilly). Dinner only; complete dinner under $50; reservations necessary; jackets required; AMEX, MC, V.

Ruby Swiss Restaurant (West Sunrise Highway, tel. 352 8507), adjacent to the Princess Tower Hotel. Native and house specialities with a flamboyant style. Lobster Armorique (sauted minced lobster flamed with Cognac topped with tomato sauce and Tio Pepe, served with rice) prepared at the table, $23.75. The Bahamian or Swiss coffee, prepared at your table, is a flamboyant display of exquisite pyrotechnics. Prices range from $30 to $40 per person; AMEX, MC, V.

Les Oursins (tel. 373 7777). The premier restaurant at the Lucayan Beach Resort with a blend of French and Continental dishes complimented by a wide range of wines and excellent surroundings. Terrine of sea urchins, grilled frogs legs 'Malaysian style' and mussels St Jacques in saffron cream are examples of the fare. Price of a typical gourmet meal is about $50; AMEX, MC, V.

Bahamian and seafood dishes

Fatman's Nephew (tel. 373 8520) situated across the square from Luciano's in Port Lucaya keeps alive the tradition of excellent cooking that runs in the family. The plaque inside says it all: Two men who had a positive effect on me as a child and later as a man were my two uncles, Joseph 'Fatman' Munroe and David 'Fatman' Simmons. They were both huge men in size and talent. Both possessing the natural ability to do wonders with food. They are both now deceased, but they left me something ... a legacy. This is my tribute. Stanley L Simmons Jr'. Freshness is the concern here — no standard fish menu just 'catch of the day' boards. Meals start from $14; AMEX, MC, V.

Brass Helmet (tel. 373 2032). Open throughout the day all week, the restaurant sits above the dive shop and is decorated with a realistic mock up of great white shark bursting through the wall. A large video screen shows a selection of the days dives while you eat; a wide choice from light salad snacks, sandwiches and burgers through to three course meals. Prices are reasonable with the gratuity discretionary; AMEX, MC, V. (As an interesting sideline the Brass Helmet adds a small surcharge to tuna dishes to fund organisations trying to halt the harmful practices of the tuna fishing industry that lead to dolphin deaths.)

The Stoned Crab (tel. 373 1442). A popular Bahamian hangout at Taino Beach built right on the seafront. As you might have guessed crab dishes are de rigueur, but big game fish are also available — it just depends on the day's catch. Homemade bread and salads go well with the meals, which cost $30 to $40, including the gratuity. Dinner only; AMEX, MC, V.

Hemingways (tel. 373 8888). The restaurant of the Lucayan Marina Hotel overlooking the marina and Lucaya's harbour. Serves breakfast, lunch and dinner. The menu includes a variety of Bahamian and American classics. Breakfast averages $3-$6; a three-course meal costs approximately $20, including the gratuity; AMEX, MC, V.

Morgan's Bluff (Princess Towers, tel. 352 9661). A selection of seafood such as salmon steak, mahi mahi, cracked conch and a variety of lobster dishes. A meal here costs about $30; AMEX, MC, V.

Grill house cooking

Baron's Hall (The Pub on the Mall, tel. 352 5109). Stands on the roundabout opposite the International Bazaar. Ever wished to participate in a medieval banquet? Now is your chance. The hall, with its lances, tapestries and heraldic banners suspended from solid timber beams over a stone flag floor is incredibly authentic. All items have been imported from Britain, down to the tables and chairs. The food, whether it is meat, fish, fowl or steak, is grill house cooking at its best. Complete meals from $24 upwards. For that banquet, just make a reservation once you have got your party organised. AMEX, MC, V.

Guanahanis (tel. 352 6721). Part of the Princess Country Club serving dinner only. Serves a variety of barbecued, grilled and sautéd dishes such as shrimps, lobster and spare ribs. Between $25 and $35 per person; AMEX, MC, V.

Seafood and steakhouse

Charthouse Restaurant (East Sunrise Highway, tel. 373 3900), for seafood kebab, excellent salads and stuffed mushrooms. A very pleasant, friendly dining environment with views of the pine forests. Nice touches are the menus on wooden tablets and the sea charts of the Bahamas laid into the tabletops. For dessert try the homemade pies, truly delicious. Courtesy bus service; AMEX, V.

Rib Room (Princess Country Club, tel. 352 6721). A selection of meat and fish dishes served in an English inn setting. The menu includes crpes of crab meat, baked clams casino, grouper armadine and a choice of standard international meat dishes. A meal here costs $30 to $45 per person, including gratuity; reservations and jackets required; AMEX, MC, V.

Buccaneer Club (tel. 348 3794). A long-established Grand Bahamian restaurant at Eight Mile Rock which offers complimentary transport. Set in its own gardens, patrons may choose the patio or dining room, where a variety of seafood and meats are prepared in a Bahamian or Continental manner. A meal for one will set you back about $30; no credit cards.

Lucayan Lobster and Steak House, opposite Port Lucaya (tel. 373 5101), serves not surprisingly, lobster and steaks. 'Early bird' specials (16.30-18.30) from $18 for three courses. At other times dinner from $25, or entres of boiled half chicken ($11.95), medallions of beef ($19.95) or ocean reef lobster tails ($18.75); AMEX, MC, V.

Bahamian native cooking

Pier I (tel. 352 6674). A large wooden lodge beside Freeport Harbour. Upstairs is a bar which serves drinks and snacks and is decorated with ships tackle, nets, mounted fish and other nautical items. The restaurant serves a variety of Bahamian dishes where prices range from $20 to $30; AMEX, MC, V.

Admiral Nelson Bar and Restaurant (International Bazaar, tel. 352 2673). Open for breakfast - boiled fish with Johnny cake and grits, $8; lunch of fried red snapper with peas n' rice and potato salad at $6; and dinner with complimentary glass of wine, from $13. This can vary from Bahamian seafood to hamburgers. Happy hour, Friday 17.00-19.00. The large room that serves as bar and restaurant will comfortably hold a 100 people. No credit cards.

The Phoenix (Silver Sands Hotel, tel. 373 5700), serves Bahamian and international fare above the hotel reception. The entrance to this pleasantly decorated, elegant dining room is up an expansive flight of external timber stairs. Sit in high back wicker chairs for a traditional island feast. Dinner from $18; AMEX, MC, V.

French cuisine

Escoffier Room (tel. 352 6782), a memorable selection of dishes served with a polished elegance amongst the intricate furnishings of Xanadu's premier restaurant. Dining is by candlelight accompanied by live entertainment. Open for dinner only, with a full meal costing around $40; jackets required; AMEX, MC, V.

Italian
Silvano's (The Pub on the Mall, tel. 352 5111). Your host and owner is Silvano Brutti, a member of Le Grand Cordon D'Or (a membership of the top 600 chefs in the world). This is authentic Italian cuisine with dishes to tempt the palate, such as linguine al pesto (linguine with fresh basil, garlic, pine nuts, parmesan cheese and olive oil, $9.95), or vitello alla Milanese (breaded veal scallop sauted in butter, $17.50). The menu is in Italian with English translations. Complete dinners from under $30; AMEX, MC, V.

La Trattoria (tel. 352 9661). Laid out like a Mediterranean cafe in the Princess Towers complex. 'Early bird' meals, before 18.30. For $15 to $30, including gratuity, you can dine on a variety of pizza or pasta dishes and a selection of meat and seafood entres. Most pasta dishes are available as entres or appetisers; AMEX, MC, V.

Marcelles (The Mall, tel. 352 5085), serves Italian dishes from pizza to pasta. The surroundings include a bar with TV. Prices range from $10-20. Closed Sunday lunch; MC, V.

Oriental delicacies
Mai-Tai (Emerald Golf Course, tel. 352 7277) proffers a selection of Polynesian, Cantonese, Szechuan and American dishes in appropriate surroundings. Can you avoid not trying a sizzling Ga Bar (pronounced 'gay bar'), or a Pu Pu platter? They may sound amusing to the ear but they are excellent for the palate. Prices from $20; closed Mondays; AMEX, MC, V.

Japanese Steak House (tel. 352 9521 International Bazaar or tel. 373 8499 Port Lucayan Marketplace). The setting is a mock-Japanese timber house with subdued lighting and red decor; service is by kimono-clad Bahamian waitresses. A selection of sushi dishes cost $14.95, though there are plenty of other choices on the menu. For budget eating there is an 'early bird' menu with a set meal for $9.98, including such dishes as pork or chicken terijaki and tempura fish fillet; a 15% gratuity is added to these prices; AMEX, MC, V.

China Palace (tel. 352 7661). If you want to escape from a typical menu of grouper and conch try this establishment at the entrance to the International Bazaar. Very good Chinese food at reasonable prices. Closed Mondays; AMEX, MC, V.

China Temple, Hong Street (tel. 352 5610). A couple of doors down from the Palace, managed by the same owner, it offers cheap dishes in basic cafe-style dining from $5.50. Take away service available; closed Tuesday; AMEX, MC, V.

Juliat Lins Chinese Restaurant, Coral Beach Hotel (tel. 373 8061). An informal cafe serving Mandarin and Szechuan cuisine. The luncheon prices are approximately $7; dinner, including

Mongolian beef or General Chen's chicken, between $12 and $20, including gratuity. Take away service is available; no credit cards.

China Cafe. A small snack bar in the heart of Port Lucaya selling a range of Chinese dishes for $6 to $10, can be eaten inside on the veranda or taken away.

English
Prince of Wales Lounge (The Pub on the Mall, tel. 352 2700). The third of the excellent establishments run by Silvano Brutti. Stop by for a lunch of sizzled brown English sausages with vegetables and choice of mashed or French fried potatoes ($4.25); or alternatively, 'The Prince's Favourite' — cheddar creamed with Bass ale and toasted to perfection for Welsh Rarebit ($4.25). With English imported draft beer on tap and a large selection of bottled beers, it is a popular drinking place for both locals and visitors. AMEX, MC, V.

Pusser's Co (tel. 373 8450) is situated underneath Fatman's Nephew. The chef has prepared good old English pastry recipes such as steak and ale or fisherman's pie. Complete meals from under $18. Before leaving try one of Pusser's infamous drinks, (e.g. The Painkiller': Pusser's Rum, coconut, pineapple and orange over rocks; not blended, no dilution, $2 to $6). AMEX, MC, V.

German/Bahamian
Bavarian Beer Garden/Hurricane Lounge/Zanzibar Snack Shop (tel. 352 5050). A set of restaurants and bars selling bratwurst and knockwurst with sauerkraut as its German dish and a variety of Bahamian and international snacks, including some of the cheapest lobster dishes you will find anywhere in the Bahamas. The Bavarian Beer Garden is decorated with a mural of a German town scene and sells a variety of Continental beers. A light meal here costs from $5 to $10, including gratuity. The African theme Zanzibar Snack Shop and Hurricane Lounge share the same menus. All three are open seven days a week; located in the International Bazaar.

French/Bahamian
Cafe Michel (French Quarter, International Bazaar, tel. 352 2191). Dinner specials $10.95: New York Strip 10oz steak, homemade garlic butter, served with salad, baked potato, bread and butter. Good value, but not very French. Other dishes priced from $3 to $8; AMEX, MC, V.

English/Bahamian
Sir Winston Churchill (International Bazaar, tel. 352 8866). The nearest thing in the Bahamas to a London East End gin palace. Four locations: pub, restaurant, the 'cave' or the patio, serve a range from fish and chips, barbecue chicken and pizzas to native dishes. Open 11.30-02.00, it has various special nights during the week, including ladies night 09.00-23.00 Mondays with free champagne for women. AMEX, V.

Buffet/American
Arawak Dining Room (tel. 373 1066), Port of Lucayan Golf and Country Club, which can be reached by complimentary bus, running hourly from the Atlantic Hotel. Decorated with rattan fittings and furniture in pastel green hues, set against a backdrop of sweeping views over the landscaped fairways. A pianist entertains accompanies patrons in the evenings. Food is served on crockery decorated with a bust of Columbus. Lunch is buffet style complete dinner will cost between $40 to $50; reservations and jackets required; AMEX, MC, V.

Cafe eating
The Pancake House (tel. 373 3200), located on East Sunrise Street midway between Port Lucaya and the International Bazaar, an ideal stop for lunch. A few Bahamian dishes and sandwiches are also on offer. The pancakes vary from $3.60 to $5.40 depending on the sauces and extras; a full meal costs about $10, including the gratuity; no credit cards.

The Lemon Peel (tel. 352 9661), and **The Patio** (tel. 352 6721), located in the Princess Tower and Princess Country Club offer identical breakfast, lunch and dinner menus. The food consists of a variety of salads, sandwiches, burgers and Bahamian dishes. American breakfast costs up to $10; lunch and dinner combinations vary from $10 to $25; AMEX, MC, V.

Garden Patio (tel. 373 1333), sited at the Holiday Inn. American cuisine in a casual setting and relaxed atmosphere. Breakfast range from $3 to $8; lunch and dinner choices vary between $15 and $25, including gratuity. The restaurant is open every day of the week. Special theme nights are also organised: Tuesday is the Caribbean Luau with a buffet and 'native' show for $23. Thursday brings a wide range of Italian dishes for $17; Friday is the Bahamian Luau, which is another buffet with live band and revue. AMEX, MC, V.

Hibiscus Brassiere (tel. 373 7777). Part of the Lucayan Beach Resort. Serves throughout the day. American or Continental breakfast costs up to $12. The afternoon and evening menu presents a cosmopolitan selection of dishes varying from light snacks to hearty meals. Each day there is a set meal of Bahamian dishes for $14 to $22 including gratuity. There is an especially wide selection of desserts to indulge those with a sweet tooth. AMEX, MC, V.

Abbey's Bakery. Port Lucaya's pastry shop which sells sweet cakes, fresh bread, pies and pastries.

Basics

Banks
Banking hours are 09.30-15.00 Monday-Thursday; 09.30-17.00 Friday. Many international banks have branches here, including The Royal Bank of Canada at the Port Lucaya Marketplace and Barclays and the Canadian Imperial Bank, Downtown.

Churches
There are a large number of denominations all in Downtown Port Lucaya.

Denomination	Church	Address and telephone number	Time of main service
Anglican	Christ the King Anglican Church	Pioneers Way Tel. 352 5255	Sunday 10 am
Baptist	St Johns Native Baptish Church	Coral Road Tel. 352 2276	Sunday 11 am
Christian Science	Christian Science Society	East Sunrise Highway Tel. 373 1082	Sunday 11 am
Hebrew	Luis de Torres Synagogue	East Sunrise Highway Tel. 373 2008	
Methodist	St Pauls Methodist Church	East Sunrise Highway Tel. 373 5752	Sunday 11 am
Lutheran	Our Saviour Lutheran Church	East Sunrise Highway Tel. 373 3500	Sunday 11 am
Presbyterian	Lucaya Presbyterian Church	West Beach Road Tel. 373 2568	Sunday 11 am
Roman Catholic	Mary Star of the Sea Church	East Sunrise Highway Tel. 373 3300	Sunday 10 am

Communications
The phone system is privately operated by the Grand Bahama
Telephone Company. International calls can be made from the
Telecommunications Building in the Downtown shopping centre or
from most hotels. Most hotels post mail and sell stamps and
postcards. The Main Post Office is in the Downtown area opposite
the fruit market.

Library
The Sir Charles Heywood Library is on East Mall Drive opposite
the Downtown area (tel. 352 7048). Opening hours are Monday,
Wednesday and Friday 10.00-17.00; Saturday 10.00-noon. Selection
of international newspapers; well stocked.

Medical
The Rand Memorial Hospital, East Atlantic Drive, Freeport (tel.
352 6735); is a modern government hospital whose staff are well
equipped to deal with any emergencies.

For prescriptions there is LMR Prescription Drugsin Downtown
at the LMR mini-mall, 08.30-18.00 Monday-Saturday (tel. 352
7327).

For an ambulance call 352 6735 or 352 2639.

Newspapers
The local daily is the Freeport News which comes out every
afternoon except Sundays. Nassau papers: The Tribune and The
Nassau Guardian as well as some US dailies are usually available.

Tourist information
The Bahamas Board of Tourism's headquarters is at the Library on
East Mall Street (tel. 352 8356). Other offices are at the
International Bazaar, West Sunrise Highway (tel. 352 8044),
Freeport International Airport and the Harbour Cruise-ship Port.
To participate in the People-to-People programme contact the main
office.

Casinoland for beginners

With four casinos and a gamesroom in every cruise ship there is plenty of opportunity for the newcomer to dabble at the tables. You have to be over 18 and suitably dressed (no swimwear or barefeet). On offer are:

Blackjack (also called 21 or pontoon), usually begins with $5 minimum bets. The aim is to get as close to 21 as possible, you win if you beat the dealer. After the cards have been dealt the dealer keeps one card face down and does not reveal it until all players have finished. It is best to assume that this card is a face card. Craps is a dice game where players bet on the outcome of the roll. There are many different combinations of betting allowed.

Roulette also offers many different betting permutations. Payoffs start at 35 to 1 for the correct number and decrease to 1 to 1 for correctly predicting red or black, odd or even, high or low.

The **Big 6 Wheel** (wheel of fortune), is the easiest game to play. You simply place your bet on a note of currency. The higher its monetary value the less probability there is of it winning. Baccarat is a game for highrollers where the object is to achieve a score as close to 9 with a minimum of cards.

Naturally in all games the odds are stacked in favour of the house.

All the casinos offer gaming lessons and you can learn a lot from watching experienced players at the tables.

Fortune does not favour the brave but rather the cool and calculating.

Nightlife

Freeport Movie Theatre, East Mall Drive (tel. 352 7478), shows a variety of recent releases. Two screens, showings 14.00 and 20.00.

Yellow Bird Show Club, Castaways Resort, which offers a Caribbean show of limbo, steel drums, fine eating and story-telling.

Performances by **Freeport Players Guild** are held about four times a year at the Regency Theatre. For information on the dates and type of production tel. 352 5165. **The Bahama Players** (tel. 373 2299) put on more cultural shows including works by Bahamian, West Indian and US playwrights, also at the Regency Theatre. Tours by professionals are arranged by the Freeport Friends of the Arts from November to May; for details call 373 1528.

Casinos

Lucayan Beach Casino. Lavish, Las Vegas style revues are performed daily (except Sundays) at the Showcase Theatre, 20.30 and 22.30. The acts are changed regularly and are frequently booked solid. A seat with two drinks and gratuity costs $19.95.

The 20,000 sq ft Casino Room is decorated in a mock Edwardian style. It features over 550 slot machines, blackjack tables with stakes beginning at $5, craps, roulette, big six and baccarat. The Casino Cabaret Bar offers an elongated happy hour from 11.00 to 19.00 for 99 cents a drinks. Beginners gaming lessons are held every day in the mornings and early evenings. The Lucayan Beach Resorts restaurants are only a minutes' stroll away from the casino floor.

Princess Casino. An opulent Moorish palace featuring the Princess Casino Royale Theatre which competes with the Lucayan Showcase to present the brightest and brashest revues in town. Showings are at 20.30 and 22.45 (except on Mondays); tickets available at the booking office in the casino. Expect to pay about $20 per person, which includes two drinks.

On the floor are blackjack tables starting at $5, craps, roulette, money wheels, video games and 450 slot machines. Around the casino are the Crown Room Coffee Shop and the King's Court Bar which is an excellent vantage point to watch the bustle and activity around the tables. Adjacent to the casino floor is the Crown Room, a high class gourmet restaurant.

Nightclubs

The Club Estee (tel. 373 2777) at Port Lucaya is the newest late night-location. The club insists on smart dress (no shorts, T-shirts or jeans) yet charges a reasonable entrance fee. The interior is spacious and pleasantly furnished with a central bar. One side is given over to seating and conversation, the other to the dance floor. Club Estee has a pleasant easygoing atmosphere with state of the art sound system and lighting. The entrance fee includes a complimentary drink. Open 21.00-02.00 in the week, later at weekends. The music is a variety of top 40 hits, calypso and soca. Ladies are admitted free on Wednesday nights and receive a complimentary glass of champagne.

Panache Nightclub (tel. 373 1333), Holiday Inn, hosts some of Freeport's most popular local bands. The cover charge of $12 includes the first two drinks, thereafter bar prices are quite expensive. Open 21.00-03.00.

The Sultan's Tent (tel. 352 6682), Princess Tower, is open 21.00-03.00; entrance fee $10, includes two drinks. The interior is decorated in Moorish style. The music selection consists of the latest chart hits and a selection of soca and calypso from live Bahamian groups.

(Studio 69, Midshipman Road used to be an extremely popular disco, but was forced to close down in 1989. It may re-open in the future.)

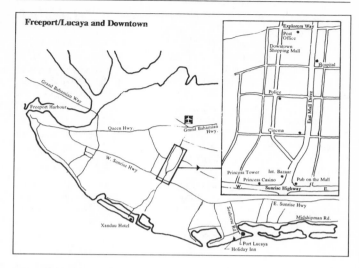

Freeport/Lucaya and Downtown

The Sights

Freeport

Garden of the Groves, a 4.8ha (12 acre) landscaped, botanical garden dedicated to the memory of Wallace and Georgette Groves. Waterfalls, ponds, cacti, hibiscus plants and hanging gardens plus curious plants such as the sausage tree, are to be found in this beautiful and well-nurtured setting. The flowerbeds, shrubbery and pathways are properly maintained but unfortunately not all the plants are labelled. Open every day 09.00-17.00; admission free.

Grand Bahama Museum (tel. 373 5668), Garden of the Groves. A fascinating but small museum with, models, plaques and photographs depicting the history of Freeport and Grand Bahama, the marine life, geological structure of the island, Lucayan burials and early settlements. There is even a slide show. Admission $2 adults, children $1; open 10.00-16.00 daily, except Wednesday.

Rand Nature Centre (tel. 352 5438) is a preserve for the natural Bahamian habitat and an opportunity to enjoy the Bahamian wildlife while learning about their environment. Founded by Mr and Mrs Rand and now dedicated to their memory, you are treated to an hours' guided walk through this 600m (½-mile), nature trail and bird sanctuary ending up at the flamingo pond. No children under eight are admitted; walks at 10.30, 14.00am, and 15.00 Monday —

Saturday, and 14.00and 15.00 Sundays; admission $2. (The taxi fare is $7 from International Bazaar.)

The National Trust hold talks at the Rand Nature Centre every first and third Wednesday at 19.30. Guests are most welcome.

Hydroflora Garden (tel. 352 6052) is an amazing natural demonstration of what plants can be grown in the Bahamas from bare rock. Absolutely no soil has been used, merely limestone rock crushed to form gravel beds releasing various nutrients and fed hydroponically (with a solution of mineral enriched water) every 15 days. Fruit trees, many kinds of vegetables and flowers are grown. Admission is $2; while guided tours by Professor S. Roger Victor an additional $2 (worth the extra for the insight given).

Bottle Museum, Ye Old Pirate Bottle House, Port Lucaya, contains various exhibits diagrammatically illustrating the history of bottle making over the centuries and the reasons behind their different shapes. The museum is a treasure trove of fine antique bottles, some dating back to 1650 and has taken Jim Brice 30 years to collect. A 15 minute video explains clearly all the developments and brings the museum alive. Entrance fee $3 for adults, $2 for children; closed Sundays.

There are two intriguing excursions around working 'factories' which can make a pleasant diversion:

The Colombian Emeralds International factory tour, International Bazaar. The tour explains the techniques of 'Lost Wax Investment Casting', the traditional and most extensively used manufacturing process. You can view work in progress through a glass screen and a six-minute video gives more detailed explanations of the process. The company is in fact the foremost emerald jewellers and their sea-treasure range (inspired by the Bahamian seas), is unique.

The Perfume Factory, rear of the International Bazaar. The free tour lasts about seven minutes, taking a behind-the-scenes look at perfume production. Your tour guides will explain how up to 150 oils are used to make the 6 fragrances used in the 16 different products. The four production staff manufacture 15,000 perfume filled bottles a week. There is even the opportunity (for $20) to make your own personalised fragrance from a choice of up to three oils in the Mixology Laboratory, including a certificate and its own name. The tour ends with a free sample gift and six tips on making the most of your perfume purchases.

Out east

On the road eastwards from Freeport is the Grand Lucayan Waterway, a canal which cuts the island in two. Further along are the remains of Old Free Town — the villagers were forcibly removed when the Port Authority purchased their land. Near here are two blue holes: Mermaids Lair and Owl Hole.

The Lucayan National Park is approximately 25km (15 miles) from Downtown. Here the Bahamas National Trust are the proud custodians of the longest known underwater cave system in the world. This consists of over 11,000m (36,000ft), of charted passageways with entrances at several places. Dives can be arranged through UNEXSO, though the park also offers plenty to see above ground.

There are two accessible caves to the north of the road. Ben's Cave is a large chamber with a staircase leading into it, containing many stalagmites and stalactites, most lying underwater. During summer it is a resting area for harmless brown fruit bats.

The burial cave mound was a site of former Lucayan Indian habitation. In a nearby underground chamber several skeletons were discovered arranged in a ceremonial pattern and Indian pottery has been found in the vicinity — all now on display at the Garden of the Groves Museum.

South of the road are a series of wooden boardwalks (built by Operation Raleigh in 1985) across the mangrove swamp. The mangrove swamp area serves as a hatchery for numerous species of fish which can be seen clearly in the shallow water. The paths lead on to the charming Gold Rock Beach and picnic area.

Out west

West End, now somewhat delapidated, is the oldest settlement on the island with a selection of colonial era buildings. The Jack Tar Village is also part of Grand Bahama history. This was originally constructed by Billy Butlin who hoped to attract US visitors to his English style holiday camp. Unfortunately the project ran out of money and the hotel was forced to close down. Despite this Butlin's original idea inspired other entrepreneurs to take over the property and see the project through to fruition.

Excursions

Reef Tours, Port Lucaya Marketplace, operate what they claim to be the worlds' largest glass-bottomed boat. They offer 90 minute trips out to sea, leaving at 10.30, 12.30 and 14.30 every day. This includes a tour of the reef and the chance to watch a dive feeding the fish: $12 for adults, $7 for children.

Alternatively there are a pair of sailing and snorkeling trips leaving daily: a 4-hour trip leaving at midday, including picnic lunch on a beach for $25 per adult, $15 per child; or a 1-hour trip, $15 per adult, $10 per child. These leave three times a day at 11.00, 13.00 and 15.00.

Viva Cruises (tel. 352 7871) offer two snorkeling trips, leaving at 10.00 and 12.30, both lasting two hours: adults only, $15, including drinks, snacks and include free transportation to the departure point.

Both Viva and Reef Tours offer the ever popular 'booze-cruises', where after paying a lump sum all drinks are free. The Viva cruise departs at 17.30 or 20.00 and lasts two hours for $22. Reef Tours leave at 18.00 returning at 20.00 for $20. Both cruises include a disco and snacks. Reef Tours also offer a cruise at 20.00 for $10, with drinks two for the price of one.

Executive Tours (tel. 352 8858) offer cruises on board the El Galleon I, a mock-up of an old pirate's vessel. The day cruise lasts from 10.00 to 16.00, taking passengers out to an islet for lunch, snorkeling (with complimentary equipment), swimming and sunbathing. Children are free; enquire with Executive Tours for current adult fare. The dinner cruise leaves at 19.30 and returns at 22.30: adults $35, children $10, drinks extra.

The dolphin experience

There are many places in the world where dolphins are kept penned up in aquariums to perform to the public. However at the Undersea Explorers Society (UNEXSO), Port Lucaya Market place, a group of five bottlenose dolphins have been trained in a human-dolphin familiarisation process. They are regularly set free into the harbour but they have always chosen to return to their enclosure. This free release programme is the first of its type in the world.

Members of the public are invited to participate in this programme, either by swimming with the dolphins or just observing them closely. During the seminar there is a general talk about dolphin behaviour while their underwater communication is relayed through earphones. There are many opportunities to ask questions and interact with the dolphins by feeding or stroking them. At the end of the session the swimmers get into the enclosure or the harbour depending on preference.

The swim is certainly a vivid experience. The dolphins move with startling dexterity and grace. Participants get the opportunity to feed, be 'rescued' and towed back to shore, or to be leapt over by the dolphins. Seminar alone $10; swim $50.

Annual events

January
New Year's Day is the final day of Junkanoo. In the late afternoon the traditional parade moves through the town - bright, exotic costumes, plenty of music and lots of partying. Later in the month is the Grand Bahama Vintage Grand Prix (tel. 352 8357 for more details): a collection of old cars which have assembled here since 1986 for several races around the town. Many sideshows are also organised.

February
The Grand Bahama 5000 Road Race (formerly known as the Princes 10k Road Race) attracts an international field of runners (tel. 352 5658 for details).

June to August
Goombay Summer Festival, yet another time of partying, dancing, colourful organised events and elaborate shows.

October
On the 12th, Discovery Day, a conch-cracking contest is held in McLean's Town, out east. A real Bahamian tradition though foreigners can participate, but be warned you will be up against stiff competition as islanders can 'jewk' (open) about 20 in five minutes.

November
Conchman Triathlon, all are welcome to participate in this swimming, running and cycling event.

December
At the end of the month it is back to the Junkanoo festival again, this begins on Christmas day and continues non-stop into January.

A variety of specialist sports tournaments are organised regularly throughout the year. There are several golfing events held over the year and frequent rugby and sports club tours. For more information call the Bahamas Sports Hotline on 800-32 SPORT in the USA or contact the Grand Bahama Island Promotion Board (tel. 352 7845).

Beaches

The most popular beach area is at Port Lucaya adjoined by the Holiday Inn, Atlantic Hotel and the Lucayan Casino; a selection of water sports on offer. Almost as busy is the Xanadu beach, which has a complimentary bus service to and from the Princess Towers Hotel and a watersport concession.

Taino Beach is a favourite amongst Bahamians while the Coral Beach and Silver Sands hotels overlook the Silver Point Beach. East of Freeport are Fortune Beach and Barbary Beach. There are a selection of secluded beaches on the drive to West End, culminating in a nice stretch of sand along the front of Jack Tar Village.

The most magnificent beach on Grand Bahama is fortunately in the hands of the Bahamas National Trust. Gold Rock Beach lies in the grounds of the Lucayan National Park (see Sights above). It is a short walk from the car park to the beach (both free). The waters offshore are clear and shallow for some distance; the sand is a fine white powder; picnic benches and tables provided.

Sports

Fishing

Grand Bahama is highly regarded for bone fish, snapper, grouper, yellow-tail, grunts and king fish, and further out marlin and wahoo. Boats start at $40 for small motor boats to $300 a half day for deep sea fishing. Contact any of the following: Lucayan Harbour Marina (tel. 373 1639), Running Man Marina (tel. 352 6834), Xanadu Beach Marina (tel. 352 6782), Jack Tar Village Marina (tel. 346 6211) or Reef Tours (tel. 373 5880).

Golf

Grand Bahama, with six courses is the island for the golf enthusiast. Many golf courses make the use of golf carts compulsory.

Bahamas Princess Golf Courses (tel. 352 6721) offer two 18-hole championship courses rated at par 72. The 'Ruby' and 'Emerald' courses each has its own clubhouse, restaurant and pro shop. The Princess Resort offers special packages for golf enthusiasts. Costs: $10 for either 9 or 18 holes; use of golf carts $26 for 18 holes or $14 for 9.

Bahamas Reef Golf and Country Club (tel. 373 1055), par 72, adjacent to the Seahorse Road and Royal Palm Way, a few minutes' walk from Port Lucaya. Rates vary with season: winter $18 for 18 holes, $10 for 9 holes; summer, $14 for 18 holes, $8 for 9 holes. Electric carts are mandatory before 13.00 and cost between $20-$24 for 18 holes or $14 to $12 for 9 holes according to season. The clubhouse contains a restaurant, bar, pro shop and swimming pool.

Fortune Hill Golf and Country Club (tel. 373 4500). A small course (par 36 for men, 37 for women); $12 for 18 holes, $7 for 9 all year round; electric cart $20 for 18 holes or $11 for 9. The clubhouse has a bar, pro shop and restaurant (closed on Wednesdays during the summer).

Lucayan Golf and Country Club (tel. 373 1066), is owned by the Atlantic Hotel which provides complimentary transportation to and from the clubhouse for its par 72 course. Guests play for $22 all day or $15 for 9, the fee including the compulsory golf cart. Non-guests pay $18 for 18 holes (cart $24) and $12 for 9 holes (cart $14). The clubhouse contains a cocktail lounge and pro shop; its restaurant is regarded as the finest on the island.

Jack Tar Village, West End (tel. 346 6211), 72 par. Use of the course is free to guests though they have to pay for golf carts at $18 for 18 holes or $10 for 9. Non-guests pay $18 for 18 holes, $10 for 9-holes in addition to the cart hire. The course has three nine hole courses arranged around each other and a nearby pro shop.

Health club

The Princess Country Club (tel. 352 6721 ext. 4606) has the Fitness Centre: a well equipped multi-gym with fixed and free weights; massage service, facials and a sauna can be booked by guests or non-guests. Open seven days a week, Monday-Friday 09.00-19.00 and weekends 09.00-17.00.

Horse riding

Pinetree Stables (tel. 373 3600) has English or western-style riding, but you must make an appointment prior to arrival. The cost is $25 per person for 90 minutes. Lessons are available for adults and children. Experienced guides accompany all groups.

Parasailing

Available at Xanadu and Lucayan Beaches. An amazing experience as you soar up above the ocean and then land without getting your feet wet: $20-$25 for a 5-8 minute flight.

Scuba

UNEXSO, the Undersea Explorers Society, are the most prestigious dive operation in the Bahamas offering a huge range of programmes and facilities. Established in 1965, the company has since gone on to achieve a worldwide reputation as a top class dive resort, located in the Port Lucaya Shopping Centre.

A 'learn to dive' programme is offered for $79: three hours of instruction, first in a swimming pool, then in a 6m (18ft) training tank. By the end of this easy to follow course trainees get a certificate and join one of the shallow reef dives going out next morning. Other courses on offer include certification, instructor training, cave-diving and underwater photography.

UNEXSO offer four dives daily, including night dives and blue holes. The dolphin dive is new and unique 'there is nowhere else in the world where scuba divers can interact with dolphins in the wild on a scheduled basis', is one of the Society's proudest boasts. A fish feeding dive that usually features an appearance by curious reef sharks, or a wreck dive to a 75m steel freighter are other favourites. Recently exact replicas of a 4m hammerhead and a 2m mako shark have been tethered to the seabed 15m down. These prove to be a favourite photography place.

On shore at UNEXSO's base are the Brass Helmet restaurant and bar, a large dive and souvenir shop, a wide range of photographic apparatus for rent and facilities to process film or copy videotapes so people can have a permanent souvenir of their dives. Several dive and hotel packages are available. For more information tel. 373 1244 or write to UNEXSO, PO Box F2433, Lucaya, Grand Bahama.

There are small diving operations at Jack Tar Village which is a sub-branch of the main UNEXSO operation at Lucaya and out at the Deep Water Cay Club at Deep Water Cay.

Squash
Grand Bahama Tennis and Squash Club (tel. 373 4567), open 09.30-midnight; around $5 per game with rackets and balls available for rent. Ring in advance to reserve your court.

Tennis
Guests at the Lucayan Beach Hotel, Silver Sands, Xanadu and the Jack Tar Village have free use of their resort's courts. At Princess Tower and Country Club and the Holiday Inn, guests have to pay a similar amount to non-guests. The going rate for non-residents is $5-$6 per hour. Night play tends to be double daytime rates.

Waterskiing
Available on the beach at the Holiday Inn and Port Lucaya at $10 for three miles and at the Jack Tar Village where rental is $10 for eight minutes.

Windsurfing
Windsurfing equipment is available at a variety of hotels who offer some watersport facilities but the place to go is undoubtedly the Atlantic Beach Hotel (tel. 373 1444). Here a complete set of lessons are offered from beginner to freestyle. Certification and a variety of boards are available; rental rates vary considerably but start at $10 per hour with significant savings on longer periods.

Shopping

Freeport/Lucaya boast two shopping areas where visitors can make about 10% to 40% savings on USA and Canadian prices. If you know what you want to buy, check the prices before you leave home. There is a large range of stores to choose from. Jewellery, cameras, watches, porcelain and clothes with European labels are good buys. Opening hours vary though generally shops open between 09.00 and 10.00 and close between 17.00 and 18.00 Mondays to Saturdays. Virtually all close on Sundays. Stores accept a wide range of credit cards and most accept travellers cheques, though some will charge a commission.

Shopping in Freeport splits easily into two sections, those stores found at the International Bazaar and those in Port Lucaya Marketplace.

International Bazaar

Bahama Coins and Stamps Catalogues of international and Bahamian issues as well as samples of coin jewellery.

Bombay Bazaar Jade, coral and tigerseye jewellery with a distinctive Indian style and a range of clothes.

Colombian Emeralds International The giftshop and factory are located here (see 'Sights' above). The gems are imported straight from the Chivor and Muzo mines in Colombia and made into intricate jewellery here in the Bahamas.

Fendi Boutique Exclusive range of Fendi leather goods: handbags, suitcases, belts and accessories. T-shirts, swimsuits and sportswear are also sold.

Flamingo Casuals European swimwear and some distinctive hand painted T-shirts.

Garden Gallery Canvases from Bahamian artists including R. Brent Malone and several local painters. There are a selection of frames to choose from or canvases can be mailed home in protective tubes.

Island Galleria Bone china, giftware, brand name watches and art. China selection includes Wedgewood, Royal Doulton, Aynsley, Royal Crown Derby and Coalport; also Waterford Crystal and stoneware from Royal Brierley.

Little Switzerland Wide range of luxury goods including watches by Raymond Weil, Tag Heuer and Gucci; china products by Aynsley, Royal Doulton, Lladro and Wedgewood or crystals by Cristal de Sevres, Waterford and Atlantis.

Midnight Sun China and crystal, stocking a range of brand names including Lalique, Baccarat, Daum, Hoya, Swaraski, Stratton, Schott-Zuiesel, Hummel and Royal Worcester.

Oasis Jewellery, French perfumes and aftershaves and leather goods.

Old Curiosity Shop Artwork, antiques and jewellery. More interesting to collectors are the range of clocks and catalogue of old coins.

Pipes of Peace. Watches, cigars, pipes, pipe tobacco and lighters.

Sea Treasures (Spanish section). Rings, necklaces and jewellery crafted by Bahamian jewellers. Many have a nautical theme about them such as a doubloon pendant, a 'pieces of eight' necklace, pink or black corals; also a collection of antique coins.

The London Pacesetter Boutique Sportswear, beach and swimwear (by Body Glove and others) and a variety of other items such as bags and beach towels.

The Unusual Centre (South American section). Jewellery and eelskin (!) products.

The Strawmarket

Located between the International Bazaar and the Winston Churchill pub. A selection of Bahamian souvenirs including carvings coral jewellery, straw-work and a huge quantity of cheap T-shirts. Prices are flexible and dependent on your bargaining power.

Port Lucaya marketplace

Laid out in a mock colonial style with an equal emphasis on shopping and dining. The English touch is set off by the occasional well-sited British telephone box which even has UK charge rates inside. Pavements are spacious with ramps for disabled access. Steel or calypso bands perform in the central plaza in the evenings giving the place a pleasant night-time ambience, easily enjoyed from the surrounding bars and restaurants.

Colombian Emeralds International Jewellery made at the factory in the International Bazaar. The emeralds are significantly cheaper than elsewhere.

Esperanza Imports A main stockist of Panama Jack fashions plus sport, resort and casual wear, suntan products and beach towels.

Gucci Gucci leather goods, including wallets, watches, luggage, handbags and shoes.

Lucaya Knits Ladies knitwear, including a large selection of private label designs imported from around the world.

Pusser's Company Store Gift items and knick-Knacks with the Pusser's British Navy Rum logo: T-shirts, sweatshirts, china and carvings.

Straw Craft A good shop to browse in; interesting selection of craftwork, paintings and carvings with a red, gold and green theme. The T-shirts here feature unique designs and the leatherwork is all handmade.

The Candy Keg Candy and chocolates, including European sweets, cotton candies, dietary cookies; many special gift items are also on display.

Sharks: would you like to know them close up?

There are few creatures that are more persistently portrayed as villains than the shark. No sooner has the movie's hero or heroine fallen into the water than there one or more of these bloodthirsty creatures closing in for the kill. In two quite separate places in the Bahamas, there are people who will challenge these misconceptions.

On Long Island the resort of Stella Maris offers a shark dive (see Long Island chapter) where divers get to view and photograph sharks at very close quarters. Divers perch safely on a reef whilst the sharks feed off baited lines around them. On Bimini the Earthwatch group are conducting research into shark behaviour (see Bimini chapter), which involves a good deal of participation by members of the public.

The real shark is an efficient scavenger who is attracted to the blood and the haphazard movement of wounded fish. They are deep water creatures who normally shun contact with people. Greater understanding of shark behaviour may one day allow us to co-exist safely with these unnerving fish which somehow hold a strange fascination to us all.

Opposite, top: *Fernardes Bay, Cat Island is a place of outstanding beauty and tranquillity. Its anchorage is a favourite of passing yachters.*

Opposite, bottom: *Ruinous buildings like this one on Inagua are a familiar sight on most Family Islands and many young people have to go to Nassau and Freeport to find work.*

Following page: *The astute vendors of Nassau's strawmarket are some of the world's keenest entrepreneurs. The bustling market hardly ever closes and is one of Nassau's most popular attractions.*

SEVENTEEN

Why the Family Islands?

An idyllic existence and some of the most breathtaking scenery in the world are undoubted lures of the Family Islands. Emeralds set in translucent waters, far from rush and bustle. Many people come for the rustic simplicity and the natural beauty, to experience the pleasure of a vacation amongst small, warmhearted communities. This is how Nassau used to be 50 years ago before modern development.

Family Islanders live close to their environment. On many a night a father will take his small child out crab-hunting in a time-honoured fashion. 'Shhhhh! you can hear the crabs walking' is the Ministry of Tourism slogan often used to promote these locations and it is indeed the hope of many a Bahamian to detect the telltale scuttling of these crustaceans — the chance to bring something tasty home for the kitchen pot.

Travel on a mailboat

On the plane you are packed like sardines and rushed to your destination, on the mailboat the day proceeds at a more measured pace - A modern day comparison between the hare and the tortoise. The deck and cabins are open to all so make yourself at home. Hours can be spent reading under the shade or sun bathing in the fresh breeze.

Mailboat travel is cheap but more time consuming. It provides a vital link between the Family Islands and the capital. Typically machine parts, electrical goods and luxuries leave Nassau while farm produce comprises the bulk of the return cargo. Ambitious plans are afoot to modernise the service with a drive-on, drive-off system, regular timetables and better dockside facilities.

For the visitor the mailboat provides a more intimate and personal mode of transport. A chance to meet the other passengers, chat and catch a glimpse of their lives. There are several hours to while away, plenty of chance for coffee or a beer. As the boat moves dreamily on, time slows perceptibly.

We found the five most beautiful beaches in the Bahamas were in these out islands: Treasure Cay Beach, Abaco; Fernandez Bay, Cat Island; Pink Sands, Harbour Island, Eleuthera; Bonefish Bay, San Salvador; and Cape Santa Maria, Long Island.

The choice of accommodation is as bountiful as you could expect anywhere, from exclusive clubs (who routinely cater to the preferences of members of the royal family) to homely guesthouses. Likewise the cuisine encompasses all ranges of quality. The Family Islands are being increasingly opened up to cruise liners with ports of call at Abaco, Bimini and Eleuthera but you will not find glitzy brash casinos here. The appeal is the atmosphere of seclusion, charm and tranquillity.

EIGHTEEN

Abacos

The people of Abacos comprise a thriving community of new entrepreneurs working alongside staple industries of boat-building, farms and fishing. Looking as much to the USA as to Nassau, Abacos has long been a favourite sailing ground for trippers out of Florida. The crystal clear waters of the Abaco Sea, the offshore cays with their zealous loyalist heritage, plus the commercial centre of Marsh Harbour, have much to offer the visitor. Here many people first encounter island life in the Bahamas.

Beginning at Walkers Cay, 180km (110 miles) from West Palm Beach, the Abacos swoop down 170km (107 miles) south-east to Hole in the Wall, approximately 100km (60 miles) off Nassau. The majority of the 9,000-plus population lives on Great Abaco with its great pine forest, flat terrain and settlements at Cooper's Town and Marsh Harbour (the capital). It is perhaps the waters and cays where the visitor will find the essence of Abaco's character and modern day attractions.

The early settlers

Uninhabited for many years, Abacos awaited the arrival of loyalist fugitives seeking the protection of the British crown. The first to begin a new life were a community of mainly black loyalists, who left New York on the ships Nautilus and William in 1783. They set up at Carleton (named after Sir Guy Carleton, the British commander-in-chief for New York) near today's Treasure Cay resort. More were to follow: plantation owners, their slaves from Florida, and later settlers from Harbour Island. Prospects were, however, not good. Many left, while others tried to make a living on the outer cays, combining fishing with subsistence farming.

Their descendants prospered at various times from boat building, wrecking, pineapples, sisal production or, more reliably, sponge collecting and, in today's world, crawfishing. Yet no matter how hard they worked, they always seem to be entering the market place

Abacos

NORTH

Walker's Cay

Strangers Cay

Great Sale Cay

Pensacola Cay

LITTLE ABACO

Cooper's Town

Green Turtle Cay

Ferry

Treasure Cay

Treasure Island
Great Guana Cay

MARSH HARBOUR

Man O War

Ferries

Moore's Island

Elbow Cay

Pelican Cays

Gorda Cay

Cherokee

Sandy Point

GREAT ABACO

0   10   20   30 km
0   10   miles

Hole in the wall
Lighthouse

at its peak, only to have their hopes dashed with its fall. This in many ways was the product of their isolation. Today it is this relative isolation which attracts the visitor.

Abaco's self-reliance led to moves to break away from Nassau when the Bahamas were granted independence from Britain in 1973. There were plans for an armed insurrection backed by an American financier who sought to create a tax free utopia. Enthusiasm for this risky venture faded with increasing reconciliation between Abaconians and the new government.

Arrival

By air

The most important requirement is to use the correct international airport.

Bahamasair fly twice daily to Marsh Harbour, then on to Treasure Cay before returning to Nassau (tel. 322 4727). Return fare $128.

Aero Coach (toll free USA 800 327 0010) is a frequent carrier with fourteen daily flights to both airports from Fort Lauderdale, Miami and West Palm Beach.

Other airlines are US Air, Delta and American Eagle. Taino Air Services fly daily (except Tuesday and Thursday) from Freeport.

Walkers Cay (toll free USA 800 327 3714) flies out of Fort Lauderdale (journey time 45 minutes).

By sea

Two mailboats make the trip from Nassau to the Abacos. The Deborah KII, captained by Garnet Archer, departs Wednesday at 18.00 arriving in Marsh Harbour 12 hours later; fare $20. It proceeds on to Green Turtle Cay before returning via Marsh Harbour on to Cherokee Sound, then back to Nassau on Monday. The Champion II, captained by Ernest Dean, leaves Potters Cay, Nassau on Tuesday at midday and returns Thursday, calling at Sandy Point, Moore's Island and Bullocks Harbour; $25 one-way. To confirm sailing times contact the Harbour Master, Potters Cay (tel. 393 1064).

The US cargo vessel MV State Challenge will occasionally take passengers. Enquire with the first mate Mr Campbell; one-way passage $60 leaving West Palm Beach on Wednesday at 17.00.

Transport

Taxi The 4km (2½ mile) journey into Marsh Harbour from the airport costs $10 for one to two people, $3 extra per additional person. To travel up to Treasure Cay will cost $70, round trip $90; to Sandy Point $100. When you see the state of the roads, you will understand why the trip takes so long.

From Treasure Cay airport to the resort costs $8 for a 8 km (5 mile) ride. To the ferry dock costs only $4.

There is no bus service.

Rental hire

H&L rentals (tel. 367 2854), PO Box 438, Marsh Harbour rent out scooters at $30 per day and cars at $65 per day; insurance is extra.

The only other means is hitching a ride (easy enough outside town), unless your hotel has bicycles to rent.

Water taxi and ferry

The service to Man O War and Elbow Cay departs from its own dock a kilometre (½ mile) past the marina in Marsh Harbour at 10.30 and 16.00; the Cays at 08.00 and 13.30, journey time 20 and 25 minutes, respectively. Albury Ferry Services operate a monopoly service in their twin-hull power boats, maximum load 30 people. The fare is $14 return; special boat trip rates available on request.

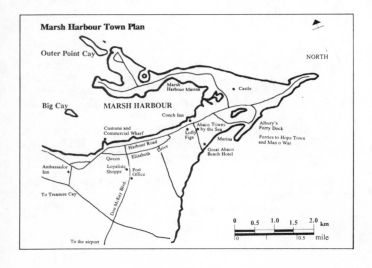

Marsh Harbour Town Plan

Accommodation

For hotel costs refer to page 5.

Marsh Harbour

Top

Great Abaco Beach Hotel (PO Box 434, toll free USA 800 468 799). Opened in 1979, it continues to be expanded; currently offering 30 rooms and 40 villas overlooking its own 180-slip Harbour Marina. The pleasantly decorated, spacious units include two queen or one king size bed, makeup area, en-suite bathroom, air-conditioning, satellite television (plus channel guide) and own veranda. The villas also come with two bedroom/ bathrooms, kitchen and living area. Facilities include three swimming pools (including hydro jet pool and swim-up bar), four night-lit tennis courts, boat rentals, diving package, fishing and snorkel trips. Families welcomed; babysitters in your own room can be arranged. AMEX, MC, V.

High

Abaco Towns by the Seas (PO Box 486, tel. 367 2227). A holiday resort for families in the centre of town, open to members and non-members alike. The 58 apartments are located in tropical landscaped grounds. Each unit has a sea or garden and pool view, master and guest bedroom, two bathrooms, living room, kitchen (with dishwasher), air-conditioning and private patio. Daily excursions to beaches, island hopping and snorkeling cost between $15 and $30. Diving, fishing trips and car rental can be arranged. Bike hire is at $5 per day. Other amenities include tennis courts, swimming pool and sea front (ideal for swimming or snorkeling off this rocky peninsular). Disabled visitors welcomed but no special provisions. AMEX, MC, V.

Moderate

Within two minutes' walk of three excellent restaurants **The Lofty Fig Villas** (PO Box 437, tel. 367 2681) has six informal housekeeping units ideally suited for couples (maximum four people). Each unit has a gazebo with barbecue around the free-flow design pool. Manager Walter Welgus is very helpful and keeps the place well maintained. Bikes are rented out to guests at $5 per day. No credit cards.

The Conch Inn Resorts and Marina (PO Box 434, tel. 367 2800), has nine large, simply furnished rooms to let in its white single storey building, hugging its own peninsula. The air-conditioned rooms, each with its own patio. The sun terrace, with its own bar, is adjacent to the large swimming pool. This is a friendly establishment where everybody is made to feel welcome. Dive package are also available. AMEX, MC, V.

Ambassador Inn Motel (PO Box 484, tel. 367 2022) has six basically furnished rooms with satellite television, en-suite bathrooms, air-conditioning above its own restaurant and bar. Located in humble surroundings, it offers the cheapest rates in town, frequented by visiting Bahamians and tourists alike. No credit cards.

Places to eat

Sunset Patio (Conch Inn, tel. 367 2800). On the water's edge, with the whirl of ceiling fans and gentle music it is some place to watch the sun set. Bahamian dishes with tasty vegetables. Each Wednesday is Italian night, Saturdays a Caribbean buffet. Full dinners start from $20; lunch (sandwiches or conch-burgers served with french fries) $7.50; breakfast from $3.50; service charge not included.

Harbour Lights (Great Abaco Beach Resort, tel. 367 2158) is sited overlooking the marina and a nautical theme is continued inside. This is relaxed dining, sitting on canvas directors' chairs. The menu includes grouper, conch and sirloin steaks. Dinner ranges from $15 to $25; lunch snacks start from $3 to $8; breakfast between $3 and $10; service charge not included.

Wally's (tel. 367 2074), one of the most popular lunchtime spots. Dinner on Monday night 19.00-19.30 pm by reservation only; fixed price $25. A colonial and congenial atmosphere with the same chef for 17 years and daily lunch specials of Bahamian and international cuisine from $8 to $10 are all part of the 'Wally's experience'. Closed mid-September to October.

Mangoes (tel. 367 2366), for a taste of cajun-style blackened fresh tuna or lamb stuffed with gouda cheese and spinach. It prides itself on using gourmet ingredients whatever the dish. Dinners from $16 to $22; lunch snacks from $4 to $10; closed Sundays; reservations necessary for dinner; AMEX, MC, V.

The Jib Room (tel. 367 2700) the Marsh Harbour Marina, offers daily lunch specials at $5-$6 such as chicken curry with white rice and coleslaw. Open on Thursday to Saturday for evening meals; $19 to $30; closed Sundays.

Cynthia's Kitchen (tel. 367 2268) is the oldest restaurant in town and where the proprietor and cook Cynthia Smith was born. She serves Bahamian chicken and fish dishes with peas and rice, vegetables, salad and bread for between $8 and $14. Lunch specials are $6, burgers and sandwiches $2 to $3. Closed Sunday evening, Tuesday morning; takeaway orders.

Basics

Banks
Barclays Bank plc (tel. 367 2152), Don McKay Boulevard, open Monday-Thursday 09.00-13.00; Friday 09.00-15.00; Canadian Imperial Bank of Commerce (tel. 367 2166), Queen Elizabeth Drive, same hours.

Laundry
Available at both Conch Inn and Great Abaco marinas. Van's dry cleaners on Queen Elizabeth Drive.

Medical
Government clinic (tel. 367 2510). For prescriptions try Lowe's Pharmacy, Lowe's Shopping Centre (tel. 367 2607).

Emergency service
Police: 367 2560.
   BASRA : 367 2226.

Post office
Dove Plaza, Don McKay Boulevard.

Nightlife

Risen out of the ashes (the former bar burnt down in 1989, kept going under canvas and now open under a new name), the **Phoenix Bar** above the Jib is very popular. Wednesdays, barbecues of baby back ribs ($10); Sundays, 14-oz sirloin steaks ($12); live band playing island and calypso music, plus dancing under the stars. Happy hour 18.00-19.00, Thursday.

The Tiki Hut (tel. 367 2575), housed in a hexagonal timber cabin on the water, adjacent to the Triple J Marina. Live music on Monday evenings, food at $1.50 for hamburgers and potato salad plus happy hour prices from 17.00-20.00. On other days happy hour is 17.00-19.00. Dinner is served from 17.00-21.00, meals costing $6, snacks $3.

The Conch Inn (tel. 367 2800) is the place to be on Tuesday evenings. Happy hour is 17.00-19.00 — help yourself to a selection of appetizers; live music and everyone sitting around the pool on the Sunset Terrace.

Almost an island event, **Wally's** (tel. 367 2074) happy hour 17.00-19.00 on Wednesday attracts crowds of people. Music is by local entertainer Estin Sawyer. Arrive early and soak up the ambience of this cocktail party.

On Tuesday nights (21.00-23.00) the **Sea Fantasy** (tel. 367 2700) has a cruise party to the tune of all-time favourites (so bring your own along), for $6 including a free drink. Full bar available.

The premier night club is **Below Decks at the Great Abaco Beach Hotel** (tel. 367 2158), with live entertainment. If it gets too hot then step outside, bask in the moonlight and let the gentle tradewinds cool you down.

The Sights

Apart from the 'green castle' (sometimes open to the public), the house built and designed by Evans Cottrell (famed in these parts for his own story Out Island Doctor) there is not much to see. This is the commercial centre, with various stores and boutiques etc. The real attractions lie elsewhere.

If you are touring around and heading south, then stop off at the small fishing villages of Cherokee Sound and further out, Sandy Point - a different world from Marsh Harbour. Nearby are some excellent sandy beaches with not a soul on them.

Down towards Hole in the Wall lighthouse the dense woodlands are a nature sanctuary for the endangered Bahamian parrot run by the Bahamas National Trust.

At the end of June and beginning of July, the Abacos regatta centred in Marsh Harbour is a lovely site with many parties in progress. Everybody is welcome.

Shopping

Darville Straw Industries, Harbour Road is a small shop where for 23 years Mrs Pamella Darville has been making and selling her own designs of straw artefacts. For other souvenirs try the Loyalist Shoppe on Don McKay Boulevard. The best boutiques are at the two restaurants Wally's and Mangoes.

Sports

Boat hire
Rich's Boat Rentals (tel. 367 2742). A 4m (13ft) Boston Whaler costs $40 a day. Guided reef trips are available.

Dive Odyssey, Great Abaco Beach Hotel (tel. 367 2158). Snorkel hire $25; boat dives from $35.

Captain Nick, The Marsh Harbour Marina (tel. 367-2700). Snorkel and beach tours $33.

Dive services
As well as Dive Odyssey mentioned above **Abaco Dive Services,** Coach Inn and Marina (tel. 367 2682) rents out equipment and organises diving trips plus first time divers resort courses. Two excellent dives are to the 1862 wreck **Adirondack** and down to Pelican Cays Land and Sea Park.

Fishing
For deep sea fishing for wahoo and bone fishing in the flats, there are guides to show you around with boats and all the tackle. Contact Crestwell Archer (tel. 367 2775), Willie Rose (tel. 367 2554) or Cay Russell (tel. 367 2957). Average fee for one to four persons $275 half day, $400 full day.

Bareboat charters
The sheltered waters of the Abaco Seas offer ideal sailing grounds. Boats of all sizes can be hired with or without a skipper on a weekly or monthly basis. Contact Sunsail, Marsh Harbour, Abaco.

Elbow Cay, Hope Town

The key figure in the history of Elbow Cay and the founding of the settlement of Hope Town around 1785 is that of Wyannie Malone. A widow, originally from Charleston, South Carolina, she brought four children with her. Their descendants are still to be found here in this quiet hamlet. Their struggle and progress follows that of the Abacos in general.

Today Hope Town is a small fishing and boat-building community with houses resembling those of New England's heritage. The narrow streets, designed for wagons not automobiles, are lined with white picket fence borders around private gardens. The serenity and quaintness of Hope Town has been lost on the mainland. Yet this is no museum, for 350 Bahamians make their living here. Its charm is that much of the past, rules and traditions, survive and are maintained by today's residents.

Accommodation (Marsh Harbour airport)

Middle to high
Abaco Inn (Elbow Cay, tel. 366 0133) has 11 simply furnished rooms with either twin queen or one king size bed in linked cottages or harbour rooms. The ambience is island life — no television or radio. Situated on sandy hillocks overlooking both the Atlantic Ocean and White Sound, it offers peaceful seclusion, including nude bathing in a thatched off area. Watersports and diving expeditions are easily arranged; bicycle hire is readily available. No facilities for children. MAP $29, MC, V.

Middle
Sea Spray Resort and Villas (White Sound, Elbow Cay, tel. Florida 800 940 5558). Six units, sleeping up to four people each, it is Elbow Cay's newest resort. The amenities include unlimited use of Sunfish sail boat and windsurfer, volley ball court and recreation room. Also included is a daily maid service. AMEX, MC, V.

Moderate
Elbow Cay Beach Inn (tel. 367 2748), sited in its own private grounds on the water's edge, has 30 pleasant though simply furnished rooms with amazing palm-thatched ceilings. Take a dip in the fresh water swimming pool (a luxury in these parts where rainwater is collected and stored to meet all needs) or go snorkeling to the nearby reef. AMEX, MC, V.

Hope Town Harbour Lodge (tel. USA 800 626 5690), sited on a bluff with splendid views of Hope Town Harbour, its lighthouse and the Atlantic Ocean. There are 21 rooms either in housekeeping cottages around the fresh water pool or in the lodge itself. All have simple furnishings plus air-conditioning; kept clean and tidy. MC, V.

Houses are available to rent in Hope Town itself. Contact Hope Town Agencies Limited (tel. 366 0172), or Malone Estates Company (tel. 366 0100). Rates upon request.

Places to eat

Abaco Inn (tel. 366 0133) attempts to provide nouvelle cuisine. It does not succeed, though the food is still enjoyable. Complete dinner starts from $24, lunch snacks $4-$10; breakfast $8; reservations necessary; MC, V.

Harbour Lodge (tel. 367 2277) entertains the palate with island staples and continental cuisine ranging between $25 and $30. Meals are cooked to order, so book in advance. Sunday champagne brunch — as much as you can eat and drink for $17. Reservations necessary (call channel 16 VHF if you are on a boat); MC, V.

Harbour's Edge Restaurant and Bar serves the coolest, widest choice of beers on the island and is the only bar with a pool table. Dinner specials with salads start at $15 and feature traditional Bahamian dishes. Lunches from under $6.

Rudy's Place (tel. 366 0062) is a small restaurant outside town open only for dinner, by reservation only. Attractively furnished as befits somebody's home, Rudy conjures up great tasting conch fritters, chowder, grouper or steaks. Meals cost under $30.

Whispering Pines (tel. 366 0051 or channel 16 VHF). A brightly painted, simple cafe; Bahamian dishes of peas n rice, conch fritters, various fish and a range of sandwiches on offer from $2.50 to $8.

Basics

Banks
CIBC (tel. 366 0296), open Wednesday 11.00-15.30.

Medical clinic
Staffed part time by Dr Jane Garfield, a retired New York doctor, and every other week by a government nurse and doctor.

The Sights

A stroll through this car free, picturesque hamlet is a pleasure in itself. It is a seafaring town with fishing boats and pleasure cruisers alike. In fact the boat is an essential means of transport here. The harbour is dominated by the lighthouse. Built in the 1860s by the by the British Imperial Lighthouse Service, the manually operated kerosine-power light is still in use and this and red and white banded building is one of the most photographed structures in the Bahamas. Open to the public during daylight hours, a glorious panoramic view opens up from the top of 96 steps. There is no fee though donations to its upkeep are welcomed. It is possible to get a free lift across the harbour (less than a minute ride). Ask around the dockside. Back across the harbour is the old cemetery with gravestones dating back to the 1800s. There are in fact five graveyards. An informative pamphlet is available at the **Wyannie Malone Historical Museum.**

The story of Hope Town is unfolded at this museum. Staffed by volunteers, it costs $3 to look around the various artefacts, old photographs, maps and documents. The building itself is one of the oldest houses, typical in design with overhanging porch roof and wooden shutters.

The beach on the Atlantic side with its big rolling waves, is a lovely sight. Swimming is safe as long as you stay inside the offshore reef. The long, narrow, soft-sandy beach stretches off into the distance, just find your own quiet spot and soak up the sun.

Nightlife

Captain Jack's Restaurant and Bar is a small drinking den under the star filled skies on the wateredge. Snacks served during the day; beers $2.50, mixed drinks $3.

Two other places are the bar at the **Harbour Lodge** where your host and bartender is Don Cash or the **Harbour Edge.**

All places open until the crowds quieten down.

Sports

Boat hire

Sea Horse Marine (tel. 366 2513): 6m (18ft), privateers from $70 a day.

Hope Town Dive Shop and Boat Rentals (tel. 366 0029), 4m (13ft) Boston Whalers from $45.

Fishing

Contact Truman Major (tel. 366 0101), Will Key — deep sea (tel. 366 0059), or Maitland Lowe — bone fishing (tel. 366 0028). Prices range from $140 to $320 per full day.

Shopping

There are two grocery stores stocking a wide selection of items. **Ebb Tide Gift Shop** and **Native Touches Gift Shoppe** both sell ranges of Androsia batik fabric and clothing, handmade gifts (including straw items), jewellery etc.

Man O War

Famed for its boat building prowess, this small, somewhat isolated, tight-knit community lives in a ship-shaped settlement of old New English style dwellings. It has much in common with its neighbour Hope Town. Narrow concrete paved, tell-tale white painted timber picket fences, interspersed with flowering bougainvillaea and absolutely no cars — mind you watch out for golf buggies.

The twentieth century has nevertheless arrived. Satellite television dishes, power and telephone cables are dotted on the skyline. Cruise ship passengers call in twice a week and yet the locals continue their daily lives, unhurried by the changing world. So slow down, take it all in and enjoy its special puritan character. Dress is conservative, especially concerning swimwear and shorts. No alcohol is consumed or sold here — though that is not to say the good folk do not enjoy the odd tipple in Marsh Harbour. Until independence this was a 'white' only island. These shy, insular people are friendly once you show respect and understanding for their ways and traditions. Stroll around at your leisure.

Accommodation

There isn't any and the residents prefer it that way.

Places to eat

Hideaway Restaurant, up a flight of open timber-rise stairs, has cafe-style dining of Bahamian and American fare for $4-$10. Open lunchtime.

Bite Site. Takeaway food, hamburgers and conch fritters $2.50, ice cream from 85 cents to $3 and above all milkshakes at $2.25. Closed Sunday.

Basics

Bank
CIBC, Thursday 09.30-12.30.

Shopping
Joe's Studio, renowned for half models of sailing vessels as souvenirs, plus other nautical gear.

Aunty Mady's Boutique for island fashions — moderate to expensive.

Island Treasures or **Mary's Corner Store** have typical souvenirs and T-shirts.

Getting around

Enquire at the Dive Shop for hire bikes and golf carts.

See transport section for details of ferry service.

Great Guana Cay

Palm fringed beaches with tiny settlements on this 10km (7 mile) cay. There is no regular boat service so you will have to make your own arrangements. At the north end is the private Sports Centre, Pirate's Cove Pavilion, part of the Treasure Island Complex, available only to guests of Treasure Cay.

Little Harbour

A private island belonging to the artists and sculptors Randolph and Margot Johnston, which can be visited. To make arrangements, check with your hotel in Marsh Harbour.

Treasure Cay

It is here that American loyalists established the settlement of Carleton, Black Point in 1783. The next great influx came in 1962 with the digging of 10km (7 miles) of canal system through mangrove swamps to form the beginning of Treasure Cay — one of the most complete resort facilities in the Family Islands. This 800ha (2000 acre) complex (including its own Treasure Island) housing 300 guests, 150 slip marina and private vacation homes, has spawned a small thriving community to service all its needs.

Accommodation

Top

Treasure Island Club (toll free USA 800 327 1584), have 130 units, housed either in the main hotel building or along the marina edge in the Harbour Lodge. All are well furnished, a king or twin queen size beds, satellite television and air-conditioning. A daily schedule of activities includes beach parties, island hopping ($35), scuba ($35), snorkeling ($25) and Treasure Island trips ($45) — check and sign up at the Activities Centre. All costs are charged to the resort's own credit card; AMEX, MC, V.

Places to eat

The resort has two restaurants, the **Spinnaker** and the **Abaco Rooms,** serving authentic Bahamian cuisine such as lobster calypso or pan fried whole yellow tail. Complete dinner from under $30.

The outdoor **Sand Bar** on the beach has snacks of hamburgers ($5.25) or grilled cheese toasties ($3.50).

The other bar, **Tipsy Seagull,** by the marina (open until 01.00) is adjacent to **Alfredo's Pizza Shoppe** which is also open in the evenings.

Travellers Rest Restaurant and Lounge (tel. 359 6028) has excellent local cooking, well presented in smart, well designed surroundings. Dishes of broiled lobster or T-bone steaks are served with peas n' rice, mashed potatoes or french fries for $10-$12; quality you do not often find in some of the gourmet Family Island restaurants. Located 2km (8 miles) from Treasure Cay (at the airport) — free transport of an evening.

Basics

Bank
Royal Bank of Canada, open 10.00-14.00, Tuesday and Thursday.

Laundry
Located adjacent to Suncrest Treasure Villas. Open 24 hours.

Shopping
The mall has a fully stocked grocery store, liquor shop, beauty salon, doctor and dentist (both available part time).

Sports

Available at Treasure Cay:

Fishing
Drift/bottom fishing $25 per person.

Parasailing
On Treasure Island trips cost $20 for 5-6 minutes.

Scuba diving
Treasure Cay Divers (tel. Florida 305 763 5665), with some interesting wrecks nearby.

Tennis
Ten hard-surface courts (four lit for night play) and tennis clinic.

Watersports
Snorkeling equipment $5.25 a day, Sunfish boat $10.50 per hour, windsurf boards $10.50 per hour, water skiing $21 for 15 minutes.

Beaches

The 5km (3½ mile) crescent moon shaped beach has been rated 'one of the ten best beaches in the world' by the National Geographic Magazine. It is quite stunning, white sands encompassing the shoreline, disappearing into the clear, blue ocean waters.

Getting around

Bikes and cars are available to rent, office adjacent to reception.

Green Turtle Cay and New Plymouth

'It's as if God picked up an eighteenth century New England fishing village and deposited it onto a beautiful island in the tropics', wrote a modern day commentator. New Plymouth on the southern tip of Green Turtle Cay shares its heritage with the Man O War and Elbow Cay communities. The loyalists here and their descendants turned their hand to many crafts, including wrecking (sometimes deliberately), smuggling guns to the Confederacy during the American Civil War, rum running during prohibition as well as more traditional enterprises. Today most islanders earn a living either through tourism or commercial crawfishing, proud of their legacy and determined to uphold their community values.

Transport

See 'Arrival' section. Note, the ferry will drop you at Green Turtle Club or Bluff House as part of their regular service at the cost of $3 from New Plymouth itself.

Dames Boat Rentals (tel. 365 4247) hire boats from $35 half day (14ft Boston Whaler). Fuel is extra.

Brendals Dive Shop (tel. 359 6226) rents out bicycles at $10 a half day.

Accommodation (Treasure Cay airport)

High
Green Turtle Club (tel. USA 800 825 5099) has the ambience of a country club where everybody is a member and made most welcome. The units are spread out amongst the tropical grounds. Comfort is the business and your host Bill Rossback and staff seek to make your stay as enjoyable and pleasurable as possible. Windsurfers, snorkel gear, beach towels and light fishing tackle come complimentary, plus use of a tennis court and salt-water swimming pool. Beaches are a few minutes' walk away. Regatta on 4 July. MAP $36; children under 12 free; AMEX, MC, V.

Middle

New Plymouth Inn (tel. 365 4161). Nine simply furnished rooms (no air-conditioning), in a delightful sheltered garden and its own salt water swimming pool in the heart of New Plymouth. No credit cards.

    Bluff House (tel. 365 4247). Sited on top of a hill are 25 comfortable tree-houses, split level suites and villas, with panoramic views of sheltered harbour or ocean reefs. A casual, barefoot retreat, it appeals to sun worshipping, siesta-seeking, sea enthusiasts. Fishing expeditions, snorkeling trips with picnic lunch and Sunfish rentals can easily be organised. MAP $32; MC, V.

Budget

Bank's Apartments, Parliament Street, contact Susan Roberts (tel. 365 4105). Three small clean and cosy rooms with en-suite bathrooms located in the middle of the community. No credit cards.

Places to eat

Bluff House (tel. 365 4247), the local eating place for a night out. Chef Walter has been delighting guests and fellow dinners since 1968 with half a dozen ways of preparing grouper and lobster, plus Long Island duckling and other American favourites. Complete dinner for under $30; reservations please; MC, V.

    Green Turtle Club (tel. 365 4271). The clubhouse with its solid timber English furniture, is full full of character. Here everyone gathers for cocktails at 19.00. The meal of traditional Bahamian and American cuisine, with the emphasis on fresh seafood dishes, costs around $30. Dress is casually elegant; reservations required before 17.00; AMEX, MC, V.

    New Plymouth Inn (tel. 365 4161). Bahamian and house specialities costing from $19 to $27. Originally the home of Captain Billy Rogers who died of starvation in the 1830s — a fate not likely to befall visitors with such splendid dishes as broiled chicken served with a teriyaki sauce set before them. Reservations by 17.00; lunch $5 to $7.50; breakfast 08.00-09.30 open to all even on Sundays. Closed September and October. No credit cards.

    Seaview Restaurant (tel. 365 4141). Cafe-style eating at its best. Mrs McIntosh has been cooking food for the locals all her life. Bahamian and seafood $10-$15; lunches under $7; no credit cards.

Laura's Kitchen (tel. 365 4287): clean and spartan, serving breakfast from 08.00, $6; lunch snacks of hamburgers $2.50; to fish and french fries $6.50; dinners with peas n' rice or macaroni cheese at $11; no credit cards.

Basics

Bank
Barclays Bank, 10.00-13.00 Thursday. There are also branches of Nova Scotia and Commerce banks.

Medical care
Clinic once a week, channel 9 for emergencies.

Post office
Parliament Street; also has the only public phone.

Shopping
Several gift shops and well stocked grocery shops.

Nightlife

Rooster's Nest (tel. 365 4066), up on the hill at the edge of town, for music, dancing, drinks or the odd game of pool. The Gully Roosters band play every Friday and Saturday night plus holidays. A very congenial place, popular with both locals and visitors. Food is also available: dinners between $8 and $12; lunches $2.50 to $6; closed Sundays; no credit cards.

Other bars to visit are Mike's Bar, Charles Street or Miss Emily's Blue Beer Bar on Victoria Street.

The Sights

Albert Lowe Museum, open in 1976, is a tribute to the community, allowing both educational and fascinating glimpses into their society. Alan Lowe (the artist), had the idea; naming it after his father, a sea captain, craftsman, farmer and fisherman, who typified the hardiness of the early settlers. Through models, pictures, documents and artefacts, it tells the history of their settlement, a story of everyday folk on Green Turtle Cay. Admission $3; open 09.00-11.00 and 13.00-14.30 daily, except Sundays.

Across the street is the Memorial Sculpture Gardens, containing two dozen cast bronze sculptures on native coral rock bases by James Mestin. The portrait busts are of contemporary descendants of original settlers, with the 'landing' sculpture as the central element. It uniquely illustrates the character of the people that go to make up New Plymouth. Open all day.

While meandering around this charmingly old fashioned village with its clapboard houses and narrow flower-lined lanes, you will pass the disused jail, the cemetery, and Neville Chamberlain's (British prime minister at the beginning of World War II) boyhood home on Walter Street alongside the New Plymouth Inn.

Beaches

The Atlantic Ocean beach (opposite Green Turtle Club) is outstanding. Virtually deserted, this powdery sandy beach stretches endlessly into the distance. It is safe to swim in if you remain inside the offshore reef. Long Bay, also on the Atlantic side, is another great beach, with some handy shade provided by palm trees. Coco Bay, no beach as such but lovely crystal clear waters, is ideal for swimming or snorkeling.

Pirates — what were they really like?

The real pirates lived at a harsh and violent time. In a world of colonial rivalry and frequent wars, sailors had a choice of becoming legal pirates ('privateers') for their country or venturing beyond the law. To become a privateer a ship's captain had to obtain letters-of-marque. These 'allowed' him to attack ships of enemy nations, fine during wartime, but during periods of peace there was little. Many crews became outlaws when they continued to attack ships during peacetime.

Nassau was an important base for some of the most famous pirates, including Blackbeard. They sailed here to unload their loot and spend their ill-gotten gains. The Family Islands were good places for a ship to hide out while it had its hull scraped clean. Numerous caves provided opportunity for treasure to be stashed until a later day.

The public of the time were fascinated by tales of the buccaneers' audacity and brutality. Many pirates committed terrible atrocities, captured sailors often being cruelly tortured by their captors. Freebooters usually came to a sudden end, killed at sea or hung from the gallows. Some however were lucky enough to be pardoned and allowed to return to lead honest lives.

Sports

Scuba
Brendal's Dive Shop Limited (tel. 359 6226), Green Turtle Club, organises various trips including lessons for beginners.

Walker's Cay

The furthest north of the islands in the Bahamas archipelago, Walker's Cay is a separate outpost linked only to the USA. A community has grown up to service the only resort, with some people commuting from the nearby Grand Cay.

You can get there either by private boat and plane or using the hotel's own private airline — see 'arrival' section.

Accommodation

Moderate
Walker's Cay Hotel and Marina (tel. Florida 305 522 1469) is famed for its waterborne activities. It is renouned for some of the finest fishing anywhere in the world and hosts the largest private billfishing tournament. Boats can be chartered from its 75-slip fully serviced marina. Alternatively, go diving or snorkeling — daily trips visit offshore reefs with caves, caverns and crevices, most within 15-minute boat ride. Explore Nick's Cavern, where the reef is only 1m (3ft) below the surface; the cave opens up below a 10m (30ft) deep cliff. Instruction and certification are readily available.

The hotel has 62 comfortable air-conditioned, furnished rooms and four villas, each with a view of the ocean. MAP $29.50; AMEX, MC, V.

NINETEEN

Andros

Andros is an island of pine forests, mangrove swamps and the mythical beast 'the Chickcharnie', 160km by 65km (100 miles by 40 miles), the largest of the Bahamian islands, but underdeveloped and largely unexplored. It lies just 30km (20 miles) west of New Providence at its nearest point. It is a flat island, riddled with salt water inlets and creeks, often called bights. It has remained largely undisturbed by the twists of history that affected other islands in the archipelago. Today its chief attractions to the visitor are its blue holes and Great Barrier Reef (the third largest in the world) running for 190km (120 miles) parallel to its eastern coastline approximately 2km (1 mile) offshore.

The island did have its influx of settlers fleeing from the American mainland in this case Seminole Indians and blacks escaping slavery in Florida. Their surviving descendants remained unknown until the small settlement on Red Bay, an island on the north-west shoreline, was discovered during the 1950s. Today it is linked by a causeway to the mainland. The community still maintains its tribal heritage.

Another mystery yet to unveil itself is that of the 'Chickcharnie' — legendary three fingered and three toed, red-eyed elves that live in the pine forests, bringing good or bad luck depending how you behave towards them. Like the Loch Ness monster, no actual proof of their existence has been found. Another legend yet to be unearthed is that of the eighteenth-century pirate treasure of Sir Henry Morgan. Somewhere along this shoreline great riches await the discoverer.

Arrival

By air
This vast island is divided into three significant land masses, North

Andros, South Andros and Mangrove Cay in the middle. It has four airports. Bahamasair (tel. 327 8511) fly four times a week from Nassau to South Andros then to Mangrove Cay before returning to Nassau. It also flies daily to Andros Town, South Andros before returning to Nassau and again in the afternoon (except Tuesday), reversing the journey.

Alternatively Small Hope Bay Lodge (tel. USA 800 223 6961), organises private charters for its guests from Florida to Andros Town.

By sea
The various sections of Andros are served by four mailboats from Potters Cay, Nassau. To confirm ports of call and times telephone the Harbour Master (tel. 393 1064). Lisa II goes to North Andros on Wednesdays, calling at Nicholl's Town, Mastic Point and Morgan's Bluff; Captain Moxey heads to South Andros, calling at Kemp's Bay, The Bluff and Driggs Hill leaving on Monday; Central Andros Express to Fresh Creek, leaving on Wednesday and Mangrove Cay II departs Tuesdays to Lisbon Creek, then up the island to Fresh Creek and Morgan's Bluff. One-way fares range from $20 to $25.

The harbour dock at Morgan's Bluff was extended in 1990 to attract cruise lines to the island.

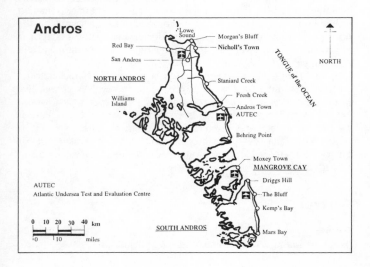

Andros

Lowe Sound
Morgan's Bluff
Red Bay
Nicholl's Town
San Andros
NORTH
NORTH ANDROS
Staniard Creek
Williams Island
Fresh Creek
Andros Town
AUTEC
Behring Point
TONGUE of the OCEAN
Moxey Town
MANGROVE CAY
Driggs Hill
The Bluff
Kemp's Bay
AUTEC
Atlantic Undersea Test and Evaluation Centre
Mars Bay
SOUTH ANDROS

0 10 20 30 40 km
0   10   miles

Transport

Taxis
A number of part-time taxi drivers will be waiting for you at the airports. Fares to town are fixed by the government. Private arrangements for a taxi tour around the island can easily be made.

Car rental
Donna Lee Motel (tel. 329 2194, Nicholl's Town, San Andros airport); Kemps Bay Gas Station (tel. 329 4608, South Andros airport).

Bicycle hire
Check with your hotel if they have or know who will rent bikes.

Hitching
Outside any community lifts can easily be obtained, with the locals more than willing to have a chat, especially the further south you go.

North Andros

Nicholl's Town (about 500 inhabitants) is the commercial centre for this end of the island. Amongst its lanes shaded by casuarina and evergreen trees you will find grocery supplies and general stores. A quiet hamlet that in recent years has started to prosper as the tourist industry has developed.

Travelling out of town you pass rich farm land where cabbages, potatoes, okra, tomatoes and citrus fruits are grown. Even large-scale agriculture, by Bahamian standards, has been attempted. It takes a while to realise that it is not all bush that you are actually seeing. Sisal plantations have been attempted in their time. One of the biggest was owned by Neville Chamberlain (the British prime minister at the outbreak of World War II).

Accommodation (San Andros Airport)

For hotel costs refer to page 5.

Moderate
Andros Beach Hotel (Nicholl's Town, tel. 329 2582) is a sports-orientated establishment with 15 pleasantly furnished air-conditioned rooms, each with private patio. Scuba diving is the main attraction, though this warm friendly place has a great 5km (3 mile) beach and a fresh water swimming pool. No credit cards.

    Donna Lee Guest House (Nicholl's Town, tel. 329 2194) has 12 simply decorated rooms, in two storey blocks, fully air-conditioned, conveniently located in the town, minutes from the beach. No credit cards.

Places to eat

Andros Beach Hotel (tel. 329 2584) has local dishes of lobster or chicken with peas and rice in what almost appears to be an 'English' restaurant with its 'decor' of natural red brick and wooden beams. Prices from $12; no credit cards.

    Picaroon Restaurant (Nicholl's Town, tel. 329 2607) for the best in native cooking, cracked conch, grouper, ribs and mutton. Meals cost about $10; no credit cards.

Fresh Creek

North island's second largest community is justifiably proud of its achievements since independence. The high school was only built in 1980. Most of the dwellings are new and of good quality, as the inhabitants seek to build upon their hard work. A visit to the **Androsia batik factory** must be included. Begun in 1978 it has grown from a single room to employing 70 people, producing stunning brightly coloured fabric with designs inspired by the local environment. While in town call in at **Maria Gilchrest** who has been making and selling straw artefacts since 1980, totally Bahamian in material, workmanship and design. Also call in at **Small Hope Bay Lodge** and ask for Dr Bob to take you on a bush walk and show you all the medicine plants.

If you are travelling around or down from Nicholl's Town you will pass some lovely deserted, white, sandy bays, fringed with palm and pine trees. Beaches abound in the numerous inlets — most have only narrow strips of sand and are virtually isolated, with warm, inviting aquamarine, waters. Just south of Fresh Creek is AUTEC (Atlantic Underwater Testing and Evaluation Center) a US anti-submarine testing range utilized also by Britain's Royal Navy. Occasional open days display the base to the outside world. AUTEC is a microcosm of the USA with its own airstrip, sports centre, shopping mall and fast food restaurants.

Accommodation

Top
Small Hope Bay Lodge (c/o PO Box 21607, Fort Lauderdale, tel. USA 305 463 9130), for that casual and yet not primitive escape to a desert island. Peace on earth: no telephones, no television, no distractions, just a beautiful beach, incredible seas and amazing atmosphere. Twenty rustic cottages built of coral rock and Andros pine are comfortably furnished and brightly decorated with island batik fabric. The price includes just about everything, airport transfers, accommodation, three full meals a day, all beverages, taxes, service charges, free use of bicycles, sailboats, windsurfers, snorkel gear and even free all inclusive scuba lessons. AMEX, MC, V.

Budget to moderate
Chickcharnie Hotel (Fresh Creek, tel. 368 2025). A modern building on the water's edge with four air-conditioned, simply furnished rooms, as well as four with ceiling fans and access to shared bathrooms. Located ten minutes' walk from the mailboat dock. No credit cards.

Places to eat

Small Hope Bay Lodge (tel. 368 2014). Fresh local seafood — grouper, conch, lobster or snapper and hot Johnny cake are the specialities, served with selections from the excellent salad bar. Reservations required for the set meal.

    Chickcharnie Hotel (tel. 368 2025). Typical Bahamian fare — conch, peas n' rice, chicken or fries. Meals cost under $15; no credit cards.

    There are a number of local bars and restaurants which have sprung up over the years to satisfy the desires of the military personnel who occasionally venture forth from the AUTEC base.

Some nights these places have a party atmosphere, other times they are as quiet as a church mouse.

Mangrove Cay

This is a virtual world to itself, in the middle of Andros closed off by an intricate creek system with a proud, friendly people - if you want to meet the local people in their island surroundings and don't mind roughing it, you can be sure of a warm welcome here. The Cay is the only place in the Bahamas where collecting and processing of sponges occurs. The beaches on the eastern edge are stunningly beautiful. One of the best times to arrive (book up well in advance) is for the two regattas on Independence Day (10 July) and Emancipation Day (first Monday in August).

Accommodation

Moderate
Bannister's Cottages (Lisbon Creek, tel. 329 4188). Spartan yet comfortable accommodation in four simply constructed modern cottages. No credit cards.

Mangrove Beach Hotel and Resort (Pinders, tel. 329 4004). Pleasantly run hotel with 12 rooms all air-conditioned. The owner is Mr Bastran, the local pastor. No credit cards.

Budget
Cool Breezes Cottages (Victoria Point, tel. 329 4465) are as the name suggests located by the ocean and ideally placed to catch the breeze. Four basic cottages/rooms to rent. No credit cards.

Moxey's Guest House (Victoria Point, tel. 329 4023). Six large bedrooms are rented in this modern two storey building, with shared bathrooms. See Ralph Moxey (at work building boats) to rent a scooter for a quick island tour. No credit cards.

Places to eat

Bannister's Restaurant (tel. 329 4188). Lots of fresh seafood and great tasting meals under $10. The cooking of Sylvia Bannister has become renouned in the sailing world since her discovery in the Yachting Guide to the Bahamas. The turtle pen outside the dining room is an interesting feature. No credit cards.

South Andros

A ferry service links South Andros with Mangrove Cay making it much easier to visit both locations from one base. Lady Pindling (the prime minister's wife), comes from South Andros and it is also Sir Lynden Pindling's own constituency. In recent years government money has helped to develop the island, a much needed improvement on the previous state of affairs. Fishing and subsistence farming are the main sources of income, though tourism is growing.

Accommodation

Moderate

Las Palmas Beach Hotel (PO Box 800, Driggs Hill, tel. 329 4661). Twenty-one large rooms with air-conditioning in a modern building right on the beach. A fresh water swimming pool, tennis court and charter boats are on offer for deep sea or bone fishing. It is also the retreat for Mr and Mrs Pindling when visiting the island. AMEX, MC, V.

Royal Palm Beach Lodge (PO Box 785, Kemps Bay, tel. 329 4608) is situated on the beach, yet within a few minutes' walk of town. The nine tastefully furnished, air-conditioned rooms come with wall to wall carpet and a kitchen for guest's to use. It is operated by Mr Rahming, a leading entrepreneur hereabouts. No credit cards.

Places to eat

Las Palmas Beach Hotel (tel. 329 4661). Bahamian cuisine featuring seafood such as broiled lobster and grouper. Complete dinner for under $25; AMEX, MC, V.

M&S Takeaway, Little Creek; lunchtime snacks Bahamian style — chicken and fries plus other delights; $4-$8; no credit cards.

The Basics

Bank
CIBC (tel. 368 2071), Fresh Creek.

Insects
There are many, especially the kind that bite. Take plenty of mosquito repellent.

Medical
Resident doctor in San Andros; government clinics in Mastic Point, Nicholl's Town, Lowe Sound (North Andros), Fresh Creek (Central Andros), Mangrove Cay and in South Andros, Kemps Bay.

Police
The Bluff, South Andros (tel. 329 4733), Fresh Creek (tel. 368 2626), Central Andros and Nicholl's Town (tel. 919).

Opposite: *The North Cat Island Special unloading at Bennet's Harbour, Cat Island. The mailboats provide a vital economic link between the Family Islands and Nassau. Food produce is sent to market in Nassau, to be exchanged for a wide variety of consumer goods.*

Following page: *This rusting freighter, aground on San Salvador's coast is one of the many wrecks in the Bahamas, which now make excellent dive and snorkel sites.*

Sports

The waters offshore are teaming with life. Snorkeling is incredible, with possibly the clearest water anywhere in the Bahamas — visibility of up to 50m (150ft). There are underwater gardens and blue holes, where fresh water rises up 60m (200ft) from the ocean floor. You can dive 30m (100ft) to the reef, then proceed down a vertical wall for another 27m (90ft) and stand on the ledge. It is another 1,800 m (about 6,000ft) to the bottom, as the wall plunges down through the blue abyss below. This is TOTO (Tongue of the Ocean) on the Great Barrier Reef.

Dive Operations Small Hope Bay Lodge (tel. USA 800 223 6961). Dive trips from $25.

Andros Undersea Adventure (tel. USA 800 327 8150), Andros Beach Hotel. Dive trips from $35.

Fishing 'Bone Fishing Capital of the World' — Lowe Sound Settlement, near Nicholl's Town. Trips cost $100 half day and $180 full day.

TWENTY

Berry Islands

Five hundred people live in this collection of tiny islets which lie in the channel between New Providence and Bimini. Most live in Bullock's Harbour on Great Harbour Cay. Several other islands are the exclusive property of wealthy foreigners, including Alder Cay, Bird Cay, Frozen Cay and Whale Cay.

'The Berries' were first settled in 1836 by a number of Africans rescued from passing slave ships. The governor of the Bahamas set up a customs house on Great Stirrup Cay to encourage passing ships to make landfall here. The place, named Williamstown, was not destined to last. Crops could barely survive in the thin soil so the people moved elsewhere.

Tourism has brought prosperity back to the Berry Islands beginning between the wars when a handful of rich patrons wished to create a hideaway on their own private islands. Nowadays the Berry Islands attract large numbers of big game fishers. There is new development on Great Harbour Cay, cruise liners stop regularly at Great Stirrup and Coco cays, and Chub Cay has its own thriving resort.

Arrival

By air
The Chub Cay Club operates a charter service to Miami and Fort Lauderdale. This airstrip and the one at Great Harbour Cay can be used as official ports of entry for private aircraft.

By sea
The Captain Dean leaves Nassau on Tuesdays and returns on Fridays. For exact departure times contact the office on Potters Cay (tel. 393 1064).

Transport

The islands are so small it is possible to walk to wherever you want to go. On Great Harbour Cay and Chub Cay bicycles are available.

Percy Darville on Great Harbour Cay as two boats for hire at $125 per half day or $200 per full day.

Accommodation

For hotel costs refer to page 5.

Moderate

The Chub Cay Club, (tel. USA 800 662 8555, PO Box 661067, Miami Springs, Florida 33266) offers 50 spacious air-conditioned rooms of which 15 are available to non-members. The marina contains 90 slips with fresh water and fuel available. There is a lounge, dining room and bar on the premises.

The resort has charter boats for deep sea and bone fishing as well as a comprehensive scuba programme. The Club maintains three dive boats, equipment rental and PADI instructors. Near by are some excellent dive sites including Angelfish Reef and the 'Fishbowl' wall dive. Guests of the resort can enjoy sailing, snorkeling or waterskiing. Other facilities include two fresh water swimming pools, tennis courts and nearby beaches.

The resort sponsors fishing tournaments. For more details or general information contact them directly. EP, AP; AMEX, MC, V.

Great Harbour Cay Condominiums are available for rental at $750 per week for a couple, or $1000 per week for three to six people. The villas come complete with air conditioning, kitchen and library. The marina has slips for 80 boats. Expansion work is continuing all the time. Facilities include a nine hole golf course, a restaurant; Basils, and bar; Mama and Papa T's.

Beaches

One of the most picturesque is named after Brigette Bardot, who once came to these shores with many other celebrities to swim au naturel.

TWENTY-ONE

Bimini

Tiny Bimini is a few specks of land dotted in the Gulf Stream just 80km (50 miles) off the coast of Florida. History and circumstance have combined to give the place a rough charm and fame out of all porportion to its size. It can claim the association of such famous figures as Ernest Hemingway, Adam Clayton Powell and Gary Hart.

Bimini consists of the North and South islands, which have several smaller uninhabited keys and islets lying around them. Nowhere is the land more than a few feet above sea level. Most of the people live on North Bimini, which is about 8km (5 miles) long and hook shaped. It is so narrow you can walk from east to west in under a minute. The southern island is slightly smaller in length but about 2km (1 mile) wide.

It was Ernest Hemingway who brought the island to international attention in his book *Islands in the Stream*. As fascination with Hemingway's work increased, so did interest in Bimini.

Hemingway's larger than life personality made him popular with the locals. Many of his deeds are now part of Bimini folklore; carousing in the bars, machine-gunning sharks to save the day's catch and challenging all-comers to box with him. The Hemingway mystique continues to attract people to the islands, which still have the rugged frontier town feeling that was present in the 1930s.

The Lucayan Indians believed that Bimini was the location of a 'fountain of youth'. When the Spanish explorer Ponce de Leon heard of this he immediately set out to find it. He missed Bimini but instead found Florida, a far greater prize. So has the fountain of youth been lost forever? No, rest assured some enterprising islanders have unearthed it and for a fee they would be delighted to show it to you.

The islands were settled much later by wreckers who preyed on the Gulf Stream shipping routes. So from the beginning of its incorporation into the Bahamas until the present day there has always been an element of lawlessness about the place. With the

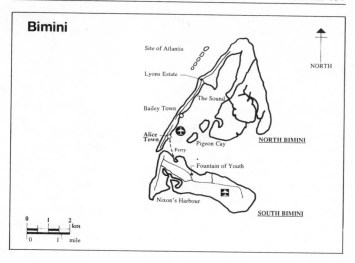

Bimini

Site of Atlantis

Lyons Estate

The Sound

Bailey Town

Alice Town

Ferry

Pigeon Cay

NORTH BIMINI

Fountain of Youth

Nixon's Harbour

SOUTH BIMINI

NORTH

coming of Prohibition in the USA, Bimini suddenly boomed. Fast boats were loaded with locally produced rum or liquors shipped here from Britain, when they sped across to Florida, running the gauntlet of coastguard patrols.

A more bizarre episode in Bimini's history occurred in 1968 when an amateur archaeologist discovered what was later claimed to be the lost city of Atlantis. This was all the more remarkable as Edgar Cayce, the so-called 'Sleeping Prophet', had foretold this back in 1934. In a premonition he had mentioned temples lying underwater near to Bimini and had accurately predicted the year in which they would be found. The actual structure resembled a submerged road, being made up of hundreds of blocks two and a half metres square and half a metre thick. These were laid out in a regular pattern for several hundred metres along the sea bed. Most experts now agree that this is a natural phenomenon, just another intriguing tale about the islands but nonetheless an excellent dive site.

In later years the island has been a bolthole for people waiting to slip away from the USA for a while. After a turbulent and controversial career US Congressman Adam Clayton Powell came to Bimini to try to get away from it all, but he was promptly followed by large numbers of American press. He is still remembered fondly by islanders.

More recently Gary Hart sailed the Monkey Business into the history books. In a brief trip ashore he was photographed at the

Compleat Angler Hotel in the company of Donna Rice a model. Bimini's name was again thrust into the world's press.

Arrival

By air
There are two airports in Bimini, one on each island. Private planes and Aero Coach International (tel. USA 800 327 0010) use the one on the south island which is open during daylight hours. Aero Coach connect Bimini with Fort Lauderdale and Miami. On North Bimini, Alice Town is the home of Chalks International Airlines (tel. USA 800 432 8807) which operate a seaplane service from here to Miami and Fort Lauderdale. Every day their planes climb out of the bay, then cross the island's main road to come to rest at the terminal. Miami is only 30 minutes away and Fort Lauderdale 40 minutes. Chalks are the oldest commercial airline in the world, furthermore they hold a clean sheet with regard to accidents.

By sea
The Bimini Mack runs weekly to and from Nassau and occasionally goes on to Miami. It usually leaves Nassau between Monday and Thursday, returning on Saturday, though it is subject to considerable variations so always ring Potters Cay harbour office (tel. 393 1064) a few days beforehand. The one way fare is $30 (first class) $25 (second class).

Bimini has recently opened its doors to one day cruise ship excursions on Wednesdays, Thursdays and Fridays. You arrive from Florida at about midday and are then transferred from the liner in smaller launches. The schedule allows about four hours on Bimini, though it is possible to stopover here and catch another boat home. For more information contact your travel agent.

Transport

Bus and taxi
The island's buses and licensed cabs base themselves at both the airports. Apart from the initial ride from here to a hotel you are very unlikely to need them again as Bimini is so tiny. Passengers arriving on South Bimini have to cross over on the ferry service.

Ferry

The ferry connects the airport on the South Island to the hotels on the north. The fare is $2.

Bikes and mopeds

These can be hired from a shop opposite the wharf where the mailboat and cruise ships disembark. Bicycles $3 an hour or $10 per day; mopeds about $25 per day.

Accommodation

The season here is quite different to the rest of the Bahamas — in the winter, when everyone else is booked solid, Bimini is fairly quiet. The hotels in Bimini are especially full during fishing tournaments and at weekends when a fleet of boats sails over from Florida so it is best to book well in advance.

For hotel costs refer to page 5.

High to top

Bimini Big Game Fishing Club (PO Box 699, Alice Town, tel. 347 2391). The premier resort on the island, appealing especially to the fishing crowd. Owned by Bacardi International it offers moorings for large and small craft with electric, water and fuel facilities. For those staying onshore there are 35 rooms, 12 cottages and 2 penthouses. The rooms are spacious and comfortable with air-conditioning and patios; the cottages have fridges.

The club's amenities include a fresh water swimming pool and lit tennis court, two restaurants and two bars. AMEX, MC, V.

Middle

Bimini Blue Water Limited (PO Box 627, tel. 347 2166). Another resort that caters mainly to the big game fishers with its own fully equipped 42 slip marina, swimming pool, restaurant and bar. Most guestrooms are situated in Anchorage House on the hill which used to belong to Michael and Helen Lerner, friends of Hemingway. In Island of the Stream the description of the house lived in by the main character, Thomas Hudson, was based on this building. The Anchorage was constructed in the 1930s and its balconies open out to a fine view. AMEX, MC, V.

Moderate

Sea Crest Hotel (PO Box 654, tel. 347 2071). In the centre of Alice Town, next to the beach and several restaurants; 11 rooms and a two bedroom suite. No credit cards.

Compleat Angler Hotel (PO Box 601, tel. 347 2122). The place with the strongest connections with Hemingway and a notoriously brief acquaintance with Gary Hart. You can ask to stay in Room 1 where the aforementioned author wrote part of *To Have and Have Not*. This is a small hotel full of character and charm; not the most luxurious place on the island but certainly the most interesting. It was built in the 1930s with wide balconies and sturdy wood-panelled walls, coming in part from old rum barrels. The furnishings have been kept as original as possible.

There are three lively bars on site and frequent live music, so it is not the place to stay for an early night. **The Hemingway Museum** is downstairs in the lounge. AMEX, MC, V.

Diandrea (tel. 347 2334). A 1930s building with much later additions. No credit cards.

Brown's Hotel (Alice Town, PO BOX 601, tel. 347 2227). Twenty rooms complete with dive shop and bar. Staying here could well be quite enjoyable if the manager adopted a more friendly attitude to his customers. No credit cards.

Admiral Hotel (Bailey Town, tel. 347 2347). North of Alice Town, ten minutes' walk along the King's Highway; 21 modest rooms.

Places to eat

Fisherman's Wharf (tel. 347 2391) in the Bimini Big Game Fishing Club. The most sophisticated restaurant on the island, serving a variety of seafood, international and local dishes; complete with bar, sited on the ground floor overlooking the pool. Breakfast and dinner served; dinner $30-$50. Try the fish of the Gulf Stream in Madagascar sauce, using Bacardi Rum, naturally. AMEX, MC, V.

Bimini's Seafood Haven (tel. 347 2391) is also part of the Big Game Club. Here you can get a light lunch for about $10 or a dinner for a little less than in the Fisherman's Wharf — wide variety of seafood dishes, most having been freshly caught; AMEX, MC, V.

The Anchorage (tel. 347 2166). Certainly the best placed restaurant in Bimini, sitting on the crest of a ridge overlooking the marinas to the east and the beach to the west. The Anchorage serves breakfast, lunch and dinner: breakfasts start at $3; lunches $12-$20;

dinners $20-$30. Unlike most Bahamian restaurants the gratuity is is discretionary. The menu gives a choice of local and international cuisine; AMEX, MC, V.

Red Lion Restaurant and Bar (tel. 347 2259). You could easily be mistaken in thinking that this place was only a pub, as the restaurant is tucked around the back on the waterfront. The Red Lion is very unusual for a Bahamian restaurant as it has an open kitchen — surely a sign of confidence. Meals vary from $20 — $30. The menu ranges from Bahamian fish to western meat dishes; no credit cards.

Captain Bobs (tel. 347 2260) is located on the King's Highway; more of a snack bar than a restaurant. Breakfast and lunch cost $5 — $20, eaten under the eyes of the numerous anglers in the photographs on the walls. No credit cards.

CJ's Deli is opposite the disembarking point for most new arrivals. It sells a variety of fast food, snacks and ice creams and seems to be open virtually all hours of the day. No credit cards.

There are a number of shops offering snacks in and around Alice Town such as 'Burger Queen', home of the 'little whopper', and 'Priscillas Epicurean Delights' opposite the Big Game Club, to name just two. On South Bimini there is a snack bar at the airport.

Basics

Banks
Royal Bank of Canada, Alice Town, open 09.00-13.00 Monday - Friday.

Communications
Letters and postcards can be sent by the Bahamas mail service or alternatively taken by Chalks Airlines to the USA. If you choose to use Chalks take your letters to the special basket at their office. US stamps can be bought at the Big Game Club. When using the local mail service remember to buy Bahamian stamps.

Medical
Clinic (tel. 347 2210).

Police
Dial 919. The police headquarters is located next to the Commissioner's office on the King's Highway.

Nightlife

The premier nightspot on the island, if not in the whole Bahamas, is undoubtedly downstairs at the **Compleat Angler.** It has probably never quietened down since Hemingway hung around the place. A calypso-soca band plays at weekends and whenever there are enough people in town. Come as you are, there is no dress code on Bimini. The place starts to fill up around 22.00 and continues until well after midnight; a real melting pot with locals, tourists, sports fishing types and the occasional expatriot all mixed together. The manager Ossie Brown, runs the hotel, serves behind the bar and plays in the band.

For a drink and possibly a game of dominoes there is the **End of the World Bar.** Actually it's an innocuous looking shack, with sand on the floor and graffiti on the walls — feel free to add your own. It is owned by 'Crazy Jeff', but with an apocalyptic name like that it could hardly be run by Joe Average. In the 1960s Adam Clayton Powell held court here and in doing so made the place famous. He went down a storm with the locals and plaques have been erected in his memory.

The Harbour Lounge at the Big Game Club is a favourite hangout for the fishing crowd. Elsewhere there are a number of small bars up and down the King's Highway. At weekends the **Diandrea** puts on a local calypso band, whilst the **Hy-Star Disco** is another nightspot.

The Sights

Bimini can easily be seen in a day by bicycle or moped. Alternatively, tours of the islands can be arranged by talking to the taxi or minibus drivers.

In the town centre are the remains of the **Bay Rod and Gun Club,** formerly a large hotel and casino which made a mint catering to thirsty Americans during the Prohibition era. A 'must' is a visit to the Compleat Angler Hotel with its small **Hemingway museum,** a collection of photographs and extracts from books about the man, his friends, his fishing and Bimini.

North out at Porky Bay look for the cemetery. In August 1989 offshore from here statues of Jesus and Moses were found standing upright in 6 to 8m (20 to 25ft) of water. How they got there is a mystery but presumably it was by the hand of a pious Biminite. After Alice Town you pass through Bailey Town, the area where most islanders live. North of Bailey Town the land becomes wooded. The road can still be followed through the trees for a few miles, while the ocean is never more than a few metres away on either side.

It is a shame that most visitors do not see South Bimini at all. It is altogether more peaceful with a series of small, usually deserted beaches. To find them turn right off the surfaced road which continues to the airport.

If you are exploring there is the fabled 'Fountain of Youth'. In reality it is a disappointment: do not expect mermaids bathing beside a cascading waterfall — it more resembles a sulphurous pond. A local doctor looked into the chemical composition of the water and found small quantities of lithium. This can be good for the skin but do not expect all those wrinkles to drop off.

At the airport there is a junk-yard of old drug-running planes which is well worth exploring. Who knows, you might find an interesting souvenir amongst the wreckage.

If you are out of doors after dark be sure to use lots of insect repellent, or you will soon attract the unwanted attentions of a ravenous hoard of mosquitoes. South Bimini is **the** place for insect enthusiasts.

Offshore lies the wreck of the Sapona, which sits partially on a reef. It needs to be visited by boat but makes an excellent snorkeling or dive site. The Sapona was used as a centre for the rum smugglers during Prohibition until it was driven onto a reef in a storm. During the Second World War it was used as a bombing target by US planes. In 1945 five TBM-3 Avengers of Flight 19 set off for Bimini but never got here. Many believe that they were lost in the so-called Bermuda Triangle. The final resting place of these planes is unknown, but you will find several drug planes littering the bay, the victims of unsuccessful attempts at landing on South Bimini airstrip in the dead of night. These make interesting snorkeling and dive sites.

The shark people of South Bimini

Have you ever considered a two-week vacation where you spend your time trying to get as close as possible to some of the marine world's largest predators? Where the highlight of your trip could well be bringing an 11-foot bullshark alongside your motorboat. If this is the case then the **Bimini Biological Field Station** could well be the place for you. The Centre is funded by the US charity Earthwatch and run by Dr 'Sonny' Gruber and his team. During a ten-week period over summer, Earthwatch invite members of the public to participate in the station's programme. This costs $1,600, which covers the entire stay but not the airfare to and from Bimini.

Once at the base-camp visitors are trained to help in all the activities. This includes placing bait, then measuring and tagging all sharks found. The sharks are released unharmed, sometimes with radio transmitters placed inside them so that their movements can be monitored. Participants are not asked to risk life and limb in pursuit of scientific knowledge — the staff train all comers in how to do the work safely (there is no putting heads inside shark's mouths).

For more information contact Earthwatch, (tel. USA 617 926 8200).

Beaches

The most popular beach here is on North Bimini on the west coast. It starts at Alice Town and runs northwards. As mentioned previously there are also several good deserted beaches on South Bimini.

Shopping

On Wednesdays, Thursdays and Fridays, when the cruise ships come to town, a plethora of stalls suddenly appear on the ground like mushrooms. Here can be found an abundance of T-shirts, hats, straw work, coral jewellery, shells etc. The Big Game Club has shops on its premises which sell souvenirs, liquor and clothes bearing the hotel logo.

Sports

Fishing
Boat hire prices vary from $600-$300 per day or $400-$200 per half day, depending on the size of boat required. Boston Whalers rent for $80 per full day, $40 per half. There are four places where boats are available (ask at these locations for bone fish guides):

Bimini Big Game Fishing Club (tel. 347 2391)
Bimini Blue Water Resort (tel. 347 2166)
Brown's Marina (tel. 347 2227)
Weech's Bimini Dock (tel. 347 2391).

Scuba

Bimini Undersea Adventures (Alice Town, tel. 347 2089). Based at
Brown's Dock and run by Bill and Nowdla Keefe. A variety of dives
are offered, including instruction; the ruins of Atlantis, the Sapona
lying in 5m (15ft) of water off South Bimini and a 40m (130 ft) wall
dive. A day's snorkeling costs $25, including equipment. One dive
is priced at $35, two at $50 and three at $60. A full-day introductory
programme costs $75. For details contact PO Box 21766, Fort
Lauderdale, Florida 33335.

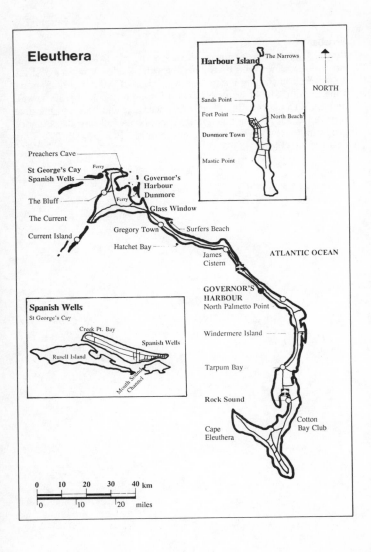

Eleuthera

Harbour Island The Narrows

NORTH

Sands Point

Fort Point

Dunmore Town North Beach

Mastic Point

Preachers Cave

St George's Cay
Spanish Wells

Ferry

**Governor's
Harbour**
Dunmore

The Bluff

Ferry

Glass Window

The Current

Gregory Town — Surfers Beach

Current Island

Hatchet Bay

James
Cistern

ATLANTIC OCEAN

**GOVERNOR'S
HARBOUR**
North Palmetto Point

Windermere Island

Spanish Wells
St George's Cay

Creek Pt. Bay

Spanish Wells

Rusell Island

Mouth South Channel

Tarpum Bay

Rock Sound

Cape
Eleuthera

Cotton
Bay Club

0	10	20	30	40 km
0		10		20 miles

TWENTY-TWO

Eleuthera
(including Harbour Island and Spanish Wells)

Eleuthera was the first island in the Bahamas to be settled by people from the Old World. In a sense the Bahamas were lucky because these initial colonists were not seeking riches or attracted by greed, but were attempting to escape prejudice and intolerance and to build a new life for themselves.

The settlers drew up a constitution for themselves and named their destination Eleuthera or 'freedom' in Greek. Immediately things went wrong, quarrels broke out amongst them, and when they attempted to land their ship hit a reef and sank. All the supplies were lost and the wretched survivors were forced to seek shelter underground in a place later known as Preachers Cave. Eleuthera was found to have insufficient food to support its new inhabitants so few stayed in the harsh environment. Regularly Bermudan vessels would drop off any Africans who caused trouble in that colony. The original Eleutherans opposed slavery so these refugees were welcomed.

In 1783 the arrival of the fugitive loyalists from the USA changed the island, for they brought their slaves with them. Slave owners were not welcomed by those who held true to the spirit of the Eleutheran adventurers so the new arrivals built a number of separate settlements.

Agriculture experienced a boom during the nineteenth century when the fame of the island's pineapples became widespread. Farm produce was exported to the eastern parts of the USA until the Eleutheran pineapple was introduced to Hawaii and higher tariffs killed off much of the island's trade. Pineapples grown on this island continue to be highly regarded, but agriculture in general has been superseded by the boom in tourism.

Eleuthera and its outlying islands, with 10,600 people, has the third highest population in the Bahamas. The island is 200 square miles in size and snakes eastwards then southwards for about 128km (80 miles), before dividing into a fishtail-shape at its southern end.

Arrival

By air

Eleuthera is the fourth most popular tourist destination and has three airports, so make sure you choose the right one or you will have a long drive to your hotel: North Eleuthera airport serves Harbour Island, Spanish Wells and Gregory Town; Governors Harbour airport serves the town of that same name; and Rock Sound covers the southern portion of the island.

There are several flights from the USA direct to all the Eleutheran airports. Aero Coach fly from Miami and Fort Lauderdale to all these destinations. (tel. USA 800 327 0010). Eastern Express, Caribbean Express and Piedmont also offer direct services. Bahamasair offers a daily service to all three airports from Nassau.

By sea

Numerous mailboats provide a service to and from Nassau to various parts of the island. Check with Potters Cay office (tel. 393 1064) for up to date information. Currently the Bahama Daybreak sails to Bluff, Spanish Wells and Harbour Island for $20 (one-way). It leaves Nassau at 06.00 on Tuesday and Eleuthera at a similar time on Sunday. The Current Pride also leaves Nassau at 06.00 but starts back at 07.00 on Tuesday. It sails to Current Island and Bogue for $18. For $20 the Harley and Charley will take you to Governors Harbour, departing Nassau at 07.00 on Monday, and returns at 14.00 on Tuesday. The southern portion of the island is serviced by Bahamas Daybreak III which docks at Davis Harbour; the one-way fare is $20. This mailboat leaves Nassau at 18.00 on Monday then returns at 14.00 on Tuesday.

Transport

Bus

A new service has recently been established which runs from Governors Harbour to Gregory Town. This is to be extended to Harbour Island and may eventually run further south as well. The fare is between $1 and $5 depending on the length of the trip. For more details ring 332 2354.

Taxi

There are perhaps more cab drivers on the island than it would appear to need and there is vigorous competition for fares, especially in the off season. Taxis will meet all incoming flights or can be contacted through your hotel reception. Fares can be very expensive owing to the long distances involved. For a taxi in the southern portion of the island — Taxi 191 (tel. 334 4245); in the Governors Harbour area — Taxi 167, which offers a 24 hour service. One of the most remarkable island characters, J.B. Barry, operates Taxi 52 in the north of Eleuthera. The venerable Mr Barry claims the acquaintance of Ronald Reagan and George Bush, once served the Duke of Windsor, played an active part in politics during the independence movement and is a repository of knowledge on the history and people of the Bahamas.

Car hire

Palmetto Point: A. Sirs (tel. 332 2305), El-Nik's (tel. 332 2523).
Government Harbour: Ronnie's (tel. 332 2304), Norma's (tel. 332 2081).
Tarpum Bay: Monroes (tel. 334 4245).
Palmetto Point: Johnson's Car Rental Service (tel. 332 2196).
Governors Harbour: Highway Service Station (tel. 332 2077).
Harbour Island: Johnson's Repairs who also rent out cars or golf carts (tel. 333 2304).

If you are stuck in a place without transport most locals will stop to pick up hitch-hikers.

Harbour Island

This island's safe anchorage attracted some of the very first settlers in the Bahamas. The village that grew up was later named Dunmore Town after Lord Dunmore, one of the governors. The sheltered bay encouraged the development of shipbuilding and a variety of warships and commercial vessels were built here, including the Marie J. Thompson, launched in 1922 and at 696 tons the largest ship ever built in Bahamian waters.

Accommodation

For hotel costs refer to page 5.

Top

Pink Sands (Flagship Hotels and Resorts, 116 Radio Circle, Mount Kisco, New York 10549, tel. USA 333 2030). A plush club consisting of 27 cottages scattered around a 12-acre site. Each cottage has its own patio, bathroom and kitchen area, for guests who like their privacy. Shaded paths link the cottages to the main house where the restaurant, lounge and library are located. Three tennis courts and sailboats are available for guests' recreation. Closed from May to the end of October; AP; no credit cards.

High to top

Ramora Bay Club (Box 7026, Boca Raton, Florida 33431, tel. USA 333 305 2324). Situated on a calm rocky cove on the westside of the island, the club has 32 rooms with their own terraces or balconies overlooking the grounds and harbour. The beach is a five- ten-minute walk to the other side of the island. Activities include a jacuzzi and scuba operation.

The restaurant and lounge are in a converted private house. Breakfast and dinner $30 per person, per day; closed mid-September to early November; AMEX, MC, V.

The Ramora Bay Club offers to maroon you for short periods on a a desert island complete with picnic hamper. An 'X-rated' picnic for honeymooners can also be booked. The boat drops guests off and returns at a pre-arranged time.

High

Dunmore Beach Club, (PO Box 122, tel. 333 2200). An intimate hotel, often fully booked catering to a maximum of 28 guests six cottages nestled in well maintained grounds; tennis court and private beach. The cottages include air-conditioning, refrigerators, bathroom and their own private patio. Meals are served at the clubhouse and the small number of guests ensures that everyone receives a high standard of personal service. No credit cards.

Runaway Hill Club (PO Box 31, tel. 333 2150). More like staying in a grand colonial home than an hotel, the large gardens stretch down past the freshwater pool to the Pink Sand Beach. Meals can be taken in the dining room or on the porch overlooking the ocean.

The eight rooms are all elegantly furnished and have their own baths. For $35 per person per day breakfast and dinner is included. Closed during parts of September; AMEX, MC, V.

Coral Sands Hotel (638 SW 34th Street, Fort Lauderdale, Florida 33315, tel. USA 305 333 2350). A 33 room establishment built on 14 acres of gently rolling land down to the Pink Sands. In the gardens there is a bandstand with dance floor where bands perform during the high season. There is a restaurant, bar and games room, and activities include sailing, tennis, and snorkeling. Closed September to mid-November; AMEX, MC, V.

Middle to high

Valentine's Yacht Club and Inn (PO Box 1, tel. 333 2080) is located on the harbour side of the island and includes marina, tennis court, freshwater pool and jacuzzi. Meals are served in the spacious clubhouse adjacent to the pool. Both the clubhouse and the marina have their own bar. The dive operation is located on site (see 'Sports' section).

Yours hosts John and Gloria Valentine run a pleasant and friendly resort which appeals specifically to sporting types. The rooms have either a garden view or are located around the pool. Closed September and October; AMEX, MC, V.

Moderate

Tingum Village (PO Box 61, Colebrooke Street, tel. 333 2161) offers ten air-conditioned rooms with bar, restaurant and laundry service. The beach and town centre are a few minutes' walk away. No credit cards.

Ocean View Club, (PO Box 134, tel. 333 2276) is a small operation offering room with breakfast and dinner. The Club has nine rooms and gains most of its custom through word of mouth. AP; AMEX, MC, V.

Budget

Sunset Inn Guest House (Dunmore Street, tel. 333 2151). The cheapest accommodation in town but a little run down. Self-catering is possible though there is a small surcharge for using the kitchen. No credit cards.

Places to eat

Pink Sands (tel. 333 2030). Residents and non-residents can enjoy a meal here. The three course meal has a set price of $40 for visitors. Reservations recommended; no credit cards.

Dunmore Beach Club (tel. 333 2200). For $30 non-residents can enjoy the excellent cuisine here. It is best to make a reservation; jackets and ties expected in winter; only one sitting for dinner, at 20.00; no credit cards.

Runaway Hill Club (tel. 333 2150). Non-residents may dine here by reservation. Its cuisine is regarded as perhaps the best on the island. Set dinner $30, served at 20.00 (one sitting only); AMEX, MC, V.

Coral Sands (tel. 333 2350). Reservations necessary for dinner, from 19.00. The menu features a variety of Bahamian and international cuisine; $26 per head; AMEX, MC, V.

Valentine's Yacht Club and Inn (tel. 333 2080). Non-residents are welcome. There is a set menu of Bahamian and local dishes, featuring items such as pan fried veal, rib eye steak and a variety of lobster dishes; $26, plus 10% service charge; AMEX, MC, V.

Angela's Starfish Restaurant (tel. 333 2253). Situated on the corner of Grant and Dunmore Streets, Angela's is very popular with 'Brilanders' and tourists alike. It serves a huge variety of local dishes, selected from a menu board before sitting outside or in. The emphasis is on hearty food rather than elegance; full meal between $10 and $20 per person; breakfast about $6; no credit cards.

Island Pizza (tel. 333 2192), on Dunmore Street next to the bakery. It has a wide range of meals and snacks to take out. Open 11.00-21.00.

Basics

Bank
The Royal Bank of Canada is open weekday mornings only.

Laundry
Johnson's Cleaners on Love Lane.

Medical
Clinic — 333 2227; doctor — 333 2225; dentist on Barracks Street.

Police
Tel. 333 2111 or 333 2327.

The Sights

Harbour Island is known to the locals as 'Briland' and it boasts a variety of historical buildings. The oldest, **St John's Anglican Church** dates back to 1768, whilst a modest **wooden cottage** on the seafront is over 200 years old. Near by is **Titus Hole,** a cave that was once used as the local gaol.

Today Dunmore Town is a picturesque place of wooden cottages clustered around the harbour. On the eastern side are several hotels built beside the famous **Pink Sands.** As the town is only five kilometres long by one kilometre wide the quiet lanes are excellent for a leisurely stroll or cycle. The bakers is a tempting place to stop for some fresh cakes and cookies. For souvenirs several vendors hawk straw work at roadside stalls.

Outside Dunmore there is a ferry leaving regularly for the mainland for $3 a head. (To travel after dark special arrangements should be made beforehand with the operators.)

The **Harbour Island** regatta is held in October. It is called the 'Homecoming' as many people return from Nassau to their childhood island on this occasion.

Nightlife

For an intriguing 'Briland' bar look for **Willie's Tavern** on Dunmore Street, run by Franklin Mather. The bar has a pool table and juke box and is decorated in an 'ad hoc' style with whatever was in the builder's hands at the time, typical Bahamian style. In the garden in the back, there is a tamarind tree lying on its side with faces carved into the bark. It was knocked over in the 1929 hurricane but with a few roots still in the soil it kept on growing.

Harbour Island has a nightclub of sorts on Colebrook Street called Georges; admission $5. It features a calypso-soca band interspersed with music from the disc jockey; open until 02.00.

Sports

Fishing
For bone or bottom fishing contact Vincent Cleare on 333 2154.

Diving
Ramora Bay Club (tel. 333 2325), offers an introductory course in scuba for $30 with follow up dives for $25 each. Snorkelers may

join these trips and can obtain equipment at the resort. Packages including dives can be arranged.

Valentines Dive Centre (tel. 333 2080), located beside the marina, offers introductory or certification courses along with regular dives; boat rental, sailing, windsurfing and snorkeling.

Dives in the area include the Current Cut where the force of the water moving between two points of land propel the diver along past a variety of reefs and fish shoals. This should not be attempted by beginners. A more bizarre yet simpler dive is exploring the remains of a train down in five metres of water. Actually this was part of a barge's cargo en route for Cuba which sank in 1865. It is now much encrusted and corroded but it still looks incongruous lying down on the sea bed.

Shopping

A variety of stalls are set up everyday along Bay Street near the pier selling the usual variety of souvenirs. **Franks Art Gallery** on South Street sells a selection of paintings and prints by local artists.

Spanish Wells (St Georges Cay)

This is a settlement of blonde-haired, blue eyed descendants of the original Eleutheran adventurers. The name derives from the wells the Spanish dug here to resupply their ships sailing to and from the West Indies. Very much an insular community where the inhabitants still speak their own distinctive dialect. Spanish Wellians have an acute business sense, which has made them the most prosperous island in all the Bahamas. Most of the people make a living by crawfishing, — lobsters are processed at the island's factory and then shipped directly to the USA.

The tourist development here is much more low key than elsewhere. Spanish Wells is a community of 1,200 souls where everything works: the power stays on, the roads are free of pot-holes, the water supply is excellent. It is a settlement that offers the creature comforts of home in the sun of the Bahamas.

Accommodation

Middle

Spanish Wells Beach Resorts (PO Box 31, tel. 333 4328). Twenty-one apartments and seven cottages, all overlooking the beach on the north side of the island. The water is shallow for quite a distance offshore and is safe for children. Amenities include tennis, snorkeling, windsurfing, sailing and scuba on site; fishing trips can be organised. The rooms are spacious and comfortable. The emphasis here is on peace and relaxation. Intimate picnics for two on your own island are a resort speciality. AMEX, MC, V.

    Spanish Wells Yacht Haven (PO Box 27, tel. 333 4328). Complete with marina, swimming pool, laundry, restaurant and bar. Five rooms and two apartments (on shore), all with air-conditioning. The summer season is especially busy here. AMEX, MC, V.

Budget

St George's Hotel (PO Box 48, tel. 333 4075). Mrs Ince offers seven well kept rooms and an apartment. The hotel is a large pale green building. To get there take the steps from Pinder's Store on the Quayside. Mrs Ince may be retiring in the near future so it is best to check if rooms are available before arrival. No credit cards.

Places to eat

Spanish Wells Beach Resort (tel. 333 4371) offers a variety of Bahamian and international dishes. Breakfast from about $5; lunch from $10; and dinner from $20, including a 15% gratuity. AMEX, MC, V.

    Spanish Wells Yacht Haven (tel. 333 4328) offers all three meals in its spacious new dining area: breakfast $6 to $7; lunch $6 to $10; dinner from $17, with the gratuity at your discretion. The cuisine is Bahamian and American. Closed on Mondays; AMEX, MC, V.

    Roddy's Place (tel. 333 4219). A bar offering a variety of native meals and snacks. The balcony has a an excellent view of the harbour area; inside there are a pool table and bar games. Meals range from $4 to $10; no credit cards.

    Walton's Langusta (tel. 333 4147), with its unsubtle coat of bright purple paint, is one of the more noticeable buildings by the quayside. Inside there is a juke box and horseshoe shaped bar. A variety of snacks and meals are served throughout the day. The cooking is Bahamian and costs $5 to $20 a meal. No credit cards.

Generation Gap (tel. 333 4230), with video games and pool tables, attracts a younger crowd. There is a variety of local and international dishes available throughout the day. Prices from about $3; no credit cards.

Basics

Bank
Royal Bank of Canada open weekday mornings.

Ferry
A oneway ticket costs $4. To travel after dark, make special arrangements with one of the ferry operators.

The Sights
A charming community of brightly painted box cottages. There is no need for a car on a small island like this. The oldest houses are at the eastern end of the island. On the beach at the western end is a DC-3 'Dakota' which dramatically crashed here a few years back.

Sports

A range of dives, including introductory and certification lessons; are on offer at the Spanish Wells Beach Resort (tel. 333 4371).

Shopping

Quiltmaking is a cottage industry amongst the island's women, who can often be seen working away on their porches. Several shops display a variety of their works. For that very English souvenir a Marks and Spencers store has recently opened selling a range of St Michael products.

North Eleuthera

An agricultural area with Gregory Town being the centre of the pineapple growing area. The very first Eleutheran settlement was here near the Preachers Cave, however the Spanish burnt this to the ground in 1684 forcing the survivors to move to a more defensible site. Today the area consists of several small villages, two of which, Current and Gregory Town, have been developed for tourism.

Accommodation

Moderate
The Current Sandcastle Apartments (contact via Current Operator) rents five self-catering cottages. Boating and fishing can be arranged; no credit cards.

Current Club (contact via Current Operator) . The Current Club has been newly renovated and now offers a variety of clean well furnished rooms built right on the bay. The clubhouse has a restaurant and bar; no credit cards.

Budget to moderate
Sea Raider (922 North Broadway, Rochester, MN 55904, tel. USA 333 2136). Nine apartments of differing sizes. Boat, bicycle, scooter and car rentals available. Fishing and bird watching can be organised at the hotel. MC, V.

Gregory Town

Middle
Pineapple Cove (PO Box 1548, tel. 332 0142). Overlooking its own private beach one mile out of Gregory Town, the 24 units are tastefully furnished with rattan furniture and come with bathrooms, porch and air-conditioning. The managers Danny and Donna Finn arrange several excursions for their guests, to the caves, surfer beach, Gregory Town or a secluded bay. At the hotel a swimming pool, tennis courts and snorkeling equipment are available, with plans afoot to open a water sports concession. Bar, restaurant and laundry service; AMEX, MC, V.

Oldeander Gardens (PO Box 5165 , tel. 333 2058), adjacent to the Pineapple Cove, offers 20 self-catering apartments, restaurant, bar and a complimentary daily shopping trip into town. There is a small bay where windsurfing and snorkeling are offered. AMEX, MC, V.

Budget

Cambridge Villas (PO Box 5148, tel. 332 0080) offers 25 good value rooms, four apartments and a wide range of services for its guests. There are a games room for the children, beauty salon, swimming pool and complimentary transport to the beach. Rental cars are available to guests for $60 a day. The rooms come with refrigerator and there are plans to install satellite televisions. The bar is a popular meeting place with live bands or discos at weekends. MEX, MC, V.

Places to eat

Pineapple Cove (tel. 332 0142). Open for breakfast, lunch and dinner serving a variety of seafood and international cuisine. A musical accompaniment is often laid on in the evenings. Dinner from $20-$25; AMEX, MC, V.

   Cambridge Villas (tel. 332 0080). A popular local restaurant serving a mixture of western and Bahamian dishes. Breakfast up to $10, lunch $7 to $15 and dinner $15-$20; AMEX, MC, V.

The Sights

Eleuthera contains several places of natural beauty, the most dramatic being the **Glass Windows Bridge.** Here the island is nearly cut in two by the sea. On one side is the deep blue Atlantic whose fierce waves pound the rocks, on the other are the transparent, gentle shallow waters of the Bahamas. There used to be an arch here, a 'window' to look through but this collapsed many years ago; now a modern bridge allows you to continue your journey south.

   A few kilometres outside Gregory Town the Atlantic swell creates ideal surfing conditions near by which some say are 'the second best waves in the world'. Near by is a large cave (concealed by trees) whose passages snake their way to a spectacular drop of 25m (88ft) into the sea. Supposedly an old pirate lair the caverns now contain harmless bats. It is best to go with a local guide who knows his way around.

   Gregory Town is built on the sides of a valley. Here the Thompson family run a bakery and a well renouned rum still. The pineapple rum they make is highly regarded in the area and can be sampled and bought on most days.

   Preacher's Cave is at the end of an unpaved road near the landing from Spanish Wells. It has a high entrance, adequate acoustics and a chamber capable of taking a large congregation. Cracks in the roof fill the cave with light.

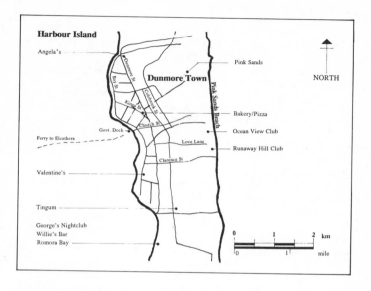

Central and South Eleuthera

This is an area where the names of the settlements betray their past history. Rock Sound for instance derives from the days when cargo was salvaged from stricken vessels and the area was known as 'Wreck Sound'. Tarpum Bay was an excellent location to catch tarpon, a deep water fish which for some reason came inshore at this point. The former importance of Governors Harbour is recognisable from its name. In fact one hundred years ago this small village used to be a major port.

Accommodation

Governors Harbour

High

Club Med Eleuthera, (PO Box 80, tel. 332 2270) caters for children from the age of two up — a family resort, with 300 air-conditioned rooms. The mini-club lasts from 09.00 to 21.00 allowing the adults to go off and do their own thing. Everything except drinks is included in the price, including a scuba school, snorkeling, sailing, water skiing, soccer, tennis, basketball, volleyball, library, aerobics classes, table-tennis and disco. Entertainment is laid on every night. Club Med have special offers for children at various months of the year; AP; AMEX, MC, V.

Moderate to top

Palmetto Shore Vacation Villas (PO Box 131, tel. 332 2305). A few kilometres south of Governors Harbour; complete with marina and tennis courts; AMEX, MC, V.

Middle

Cigatoo Inn (PO Box 86, tel. 332 2343). Perched on the brow of a hill, the 26 air-conditioned rooms are arranged around the swimming pool and come with satellite television and mini-fridges. Tennis courts, a bar and restaurant are available to guests. AMEX, M, V.

   Rainbow Inn (PO Box 53, tel. 332 0294). Located at Hatchet Bay, a set of octagonal villas with air-conditioning and bathroom. On site are a bar, restaurant, tennis courts, beach and swimming pool. No credit cards.

Moderate to Middle

Wykee's World Resort (PO Box 176, tel. 332 2701). Six cottages set in pleasant surroundings with swimming pool and tennis courts. Beaches are only a few minutes' walk away. Rental periods of a week or more being preferred; no credit cards.

Moderate

Palmetto Beach Inn (PO Box 102, tel. 332 2533). Eight comfortable rooms with television and air-conditioning built along a beach. No credit cards.

   Laughing Bird Apartments (PO Box 76, tel. 332 2012). Three air-conditioned apartments facing the beach on the outskirts of Governors Harbour with kitchens for self-catering. No credit cards.

Rock Sound

Top

Windermere Island Club, (PO Box 25, Rock Sound, tel. 332 2538). An exclusive hideaway, where club members get preference but all (with money) are invited. Owned by the Venice Simplon-Orient Express, the 21 rooms overlook long stretches of unspoilt beach. At the clubhouse there are bar and restaurant and a second storey lounge complete with library. On-site facilities include a games room, six tennis courts (with a resident professional), an excellent pool and a variety of watersports. Suites and apartments are also available and all rooms have a balcony or patio. Suitably dressed visitors are welcome to make reservations to dine here. AI or EP;closed September and October; AMEX.

    Cotton Bay Club, (PO Box 28, tel. 334 6101). A deluxe 77 room resort set in 450 acres of grounds where 'who's who' goes barefoot in the Bahamas. The Cotton Bay Club offers the best golfing in the Bahamas on an 18-hole championship course designed by Robert Trent-Jones. A variety of watersports are offered, along with four tennis courts and expert tuition from the resident professional. The accommodation is located at the main building or in delightful cottages set in well tended gardens overlooking the bay. With swimming pool, restaurant, lounge and games room, bar, video entertainment, laundry service, shops and regular live music all on site the club caters for a wide variety of tastes and preferences. AP; AMEX, MC, V.

High to top

Winding Bay Beach Resort, (PO Box 93, tel. 334 2020). This resort has re-opened after extensive renovation and now offers comfortably furnished rooms and a large range of activities, including water sports, swimming pool, croquet, badminton, volleyball, tennis, jogging and cycling. Instructors are available for beginners. Car rentals also available. Restaurant and bar; AI; AMEX, MC, V.

Moderate to middle

Cartwright's Ocean View Cottages (tel. 334 4215), Tarpum Bay. A variety of fully furnished cottages with two or three bedrooms; ideal for self-catering; no credit cards.

Moderate

Ethel's Cottages (PO Box 27, tel. 334 4233). Cottages with self-catering facilities, adjacent to the beach at Tarpum Bay; cars rentals available; AMEX.

Edwina's Place (PO Box 27, tel. 334 4231), Rock Sound. Six air-conditioned rooms with bathrooms, a restaurant, freshwater pool and a small beach. No credit cards.

Budget

Hilton's Haven (tel. 332 4231). Ten rooms are run by the remarkable Mary Hilton, a retired nurse, who has worked for many years on Eleuthera. The rooms have their own patios, baths and either ceiling fans or air-conditioning. Situated in Tarpum Bay with nearby beach and its own restaurant and bar. No credit cards.

Places to eat

Windermere Island Club (tel. 332 2538) serves a variety of American, English and Bahamian dishes. Lunch is usually a hot and cold buffet for $15 a person; dinner costs $35 a person. Non-residents should make reservations; jackets required; AMEX.

Cotton Bay Club (tel. 334 6101). Dinner here is served al fresco on most evenings, jackets are required. Specialities include poached fillet of grouper with julienne zucchini and lobster sauce or roast Long Island duckling with raspberry sauce. The set meal is varied to include barbecues and buffets on selected nights. Dinner about $35, lunch $15 and breakfast $8; AMEX, MC, V.

Winding Bay (tel. 334 2020) restaurant offers a selection of Bahamian and western dishes; dinning patrons inside or on the terrace; AMEX, MC, V.

A variety of Bahamian and international dishes are featured on the menus of several local hotels and restaurants. Those recommended include the **Cigatoo Inn, Edwina's Place, Hilton's Haven, Ethel's Cottages, Mate** and **Jennys** at Palmetto Point, **Harbour View** and **Sonny's** at Rock Sound and **Coyaba,** the **Buccaneer Club,** and **Ronnies Hi-D-Way** at Governors Harbour.

Basics

Banks

Barclays at Governors Harbour and Rock Sound open Monday-Friday 09.00-13.00, and 15.00-17.00 Fridays.

Medical
There are medical clinics at Rock Sound (tel. 334 2226) and Governors Harbour (tel. 332 2001); and dentist (tel. 332 2704).

Police
At Rock Sound tel. 334 2244; at Governors Harbour tel. 332 2111.

Tourist information
The Board of Tourism has opened an office in Governors Harbour (tel. 332 2142).

Nightlife

The small theatre at Governors Harbour has a variety of single and double bills. Tickets are $3 to $3.50.

The Sights

Governors Harbour is the centre of a new cruise ship development. The port allows small liners carrying 250 to 300 passengers to dock, with the consequent boost to the local shops and restaurants. The harbour is on **Cupid's Cay,** an islet in the bay which is connected to the main settlement by bridge. The buildings are mainly turn-of-the-century and the old doctors surgery dating back to 1897 is being turned into a **museum** and **library.**
Windermere Island is a resort patronised by royalty and celebrities. It was here that a journalist snapped a photograph of the pregnant Princess Di that went straight into the world's tabloids. The resulting publicity did not do the resort any harm, whatever the royal family thought about it.
At Tarpum Bay is a brace of art galleries which are well worth a browse. One contains the works of Peter MacMillan-Hughes; the other is the studio of Mal Flanders. Bahamian themes form the bulk of their work, a selection of which is on sale to visitors.
Further south at **Rock Sound** is one of the most impressive ocean blue holes. No one has yet been able to measure its depth. It is tidal and has a collection of grouper, turtles, snappers and angel fish which the locals have started feeding with bread and food scraps. On the southern tip of the island is the **East Point lighthouse,** while on the western point is the long defunct Cape Eleuthera Club.
The **Eleutheran Regatta** is held in early August. It is well attended and many hotels will be full at this time.

Sports

Fishing
Fishing boats can be hired for $250 to $300 per half day or $400 to $450 for a full day at the Cotton Bay Club (tel. 334 6101) or **Windermere Island Club** (tel. 332 2538).

Golf
The Cotton Bay Club's Robert Trent-Jones championship course is available to guests and non-residents. The 18-hole, 72-par course has a clubhouse, shop and resident professional. The course may be walked or electric carts hired for $20. Green fees $20; caddy $10 for 18 holes; open from 08.00-17.30.

Scuba
There is a small operation at Windermere Island (tel. 332 2538).

Shopping and Souvenirs
Goombay Gifts at Rock Sound and Normas Gift Shop at Governors Harbour sell a wide range of clothes, batik, jewellery and straw work.

TWENTY-THREE

Cat Island

'Columbus come here man', you will hear many a Cat Islander say with conviction. The quincentennial celebrations have brought all the attention to neighbouring San Salvador, but ask the people here and they will say that the historians have got it all wrong. What they are really saying is 'hey what about us too', as Cat Island has long been passed by, with investors going to other places. Do not make the same mistake, this island is quite a find.

Cat Island can offer you comfortable hotels, seclusion and a beautiful coastline. No hawker will interrupt your sojourn on a deserted beach. In many ways it is better that Cat Island has not been developed — it remains unspoilt, a gem in the Bahamas waiting to be discovered.

Most Bahamians know little about Cat Island. They all learnt at school that the highest point of land in their region — Mount Alvernia — is here, standing 63m (206ft) high. Many will say that Cat Island is a centre for obeah, the practice of bush medicine and witchcraft; a few might have made a trip on a party boat here or have seen the regatta. Generally however the city based Bahamian would know little about the place. A Cat Islander working in downtown Nassau might be teased because they come from 'the sticks'.

The island takes its name from one Arthur Catt a pirate who based himself at Port Howe — a strange place to choose as it has one of the worst harbours on the whole island. Captain Catt soon disappeared, probably finishing his life on the wrong end of a rope. The first inhabitants met with disaster when they were wiped out by a Spanish raid in 1720. This seems to have deterred people from coming back for a time.

Ironically it was Colonel Andrew Deveaux, the war hero who drove the Spanish out of Nassau who brought new settlers here where, after his victory in 1783, the grateful authorities rewarded him with a large tract of land. Gradually these loyalists abandoned

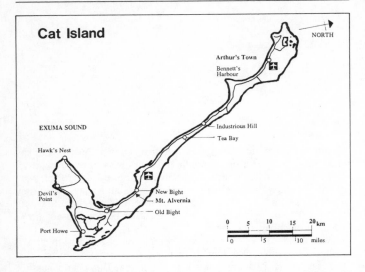

the island leaving their slaves behind and today only one of the old loyalist families, the Armbristers, remain. They abandoned the plantation business long ago and now work in the more profitable sphere of tourism.

Father Jerome was another remarkable character who left his mark on the local history. He was responsible for building the Hermitage on top of Mount Alvernia. He led a varied life before coming to Cat Island, first studying architecture, then becoming an Anglican minister and later a Catholic priest. He travelled widely around the world, once working as a priest in the outback of Australia before finally retiring to the Bahamas. Upon gaining permission to become a hermit he settled on Cat Island and built several churches. He now rests in a tomb below the Hermitage.

The most famous Cat Islander is undoubtedly Sidney Poitier. He left the Bahamas as a teenager to seek his fame and fortune in the USA and is a citizen there. He grew up in Arthur Town, to the north of the island, though there is little to draw attention to this fact. The ruins of his childhood home can be visited but there is no monument or museum in his memory.

Two thousand people live on Cat Island today, most maintain small farms and supplement their living by fishing. The soil is more productive than in many other places: plantains, bananas, citrus fruit and pineapple are grown here and flown out to Nassau. Some islanders made it rich quick by lending a hand (or closing an eye!)

to the drug smugglers using the numerous landing strips on the island. Now there is a new opportunity to make a living in the fledgling tourist industry.

Arrival

By air
Bahamasair link Cat Island and San Salvador in the same flight on Tuesdays, Fridays and Sundays (tel. Nassau 327 8511). Currently Arthur town is being used as the stopping off point though this may soon change when the repairs on the New Bight airport are completed. The airfields at Cutlass Bay and Hawks Nest accommodate private aircraft.

By sea
Cat Island has two mailboats, one supplying the north, the other the south. The North Cat Island Special leaves Nassau on Tuesday at 14.00, then makes the return trip at 18.00 on Wednesday stopping at Bennetts Harbour also; $35 one-way.

The Sea Hauler operates to and from the Bight. Leaving Nassau at 15.00 on Tuesdays it then heads back at 22.00 on Thursdays; $30 one-way. Check well in advance before you set off by ringing the Harbour master at Potter's Cay (tel. 393 1064).

Transport

There is no public transport on Cat Island, though it is easy to catch a ride with anyone going in your direction. There are private cars which are prepared to act as taxis which can be contacted through the hotels. Hire vehicles can be arranged through the Bridge Inn or Fernandez Bay Village. Otherwise you can contact the gas station at New Bight (tel. 354 5014). Fernandez Bay Village provides complimentary bicycles and rents vans for their guests.

Accommodation and eating

For hotel costs refer to page 5.

Middle to high

The Fernandez Bay Village (PO Box 2126, Fort Lauderdale FL.33303, tel. USA 305 764 6945) has one of the most beautiful locations in the Bahamas, a stunning bay delightful for swimming, snorkeling or beachcombing — a superb 'get away from it all' location. Here you can alternately prepare your own food and eat at the restaurant. There is a well-stocked shop; while breakfast and lunch cost $5-$8. The buffet dinner ($24), served on the patio adjacent to the beach, offers the chance to meet the other guests.

The Armbrister family owners who stress that the emphasis is very much on doing your own thing; staff are 'attentive but not overbearing'. Snorkeling equipment, bicycles, sailboats and use of the tennis courts are all complimentary, while vans or the Village's Boston whaler can be hired. Videos and babysitters can be obtained. Perhaps the nicest touch is the beachside bar, where you just help yourself and keep your own tab. A chance to mix some exotic tropical cocktails!
AMEX.

Moderate

The Greenwood Inn (Island Services Inc, 750 SW 34th Street, Fort Lauderdale, FL 33315, tel. USA 305 354 5090) is located in the vicinity of Port Howe. It offers a fully equipped dive operation on the 40ft custom-built Tabaluga, certification courses and equipment rental. Nearby blue holes can be explored with reef, wall and night dives. Snorkeling equipment is available and fishing trips can be arranged. The resort caters to non-divers, though if you want to explore you will probably need your own transport as the Greenwood Inn is in a somewhat remote location.

There are 20 rooms positioned around the pool. The dining room, serving local and western food, is adjacent to the bar and lounge area. Meal and/or dive packages available; no credit cards.

The Bridge Inn (New Bight, tel. 354 5013) offers 12 clean air-conditioned rooms, built on an inland lagoon with its own beach only five minutes walk away. It has one of the most popular bars on the island, where breakfast, local meals and bar snacks are available. The manager Bradley Russell will arrange for guests to be met at the airport. Car rental can easily be arranged through Bradley's brother who runs the gas station. No credit cards.

The Hawks Nest Club (847 N Andrews Avenue, Fort Lauderdale, FL 33311, tel. USA 305 523 2406), at the south-western tip of the island, has ten rooms, a tennis court and a large dining room with bar. Its marina caters to the big game fishing boats while other guests fly into its private airstrip. No credit cards.

Nightlife

The Bridge Inn attracts a young crowd in the evenings, giving it a lively atmosphere. The locals meet there for pool, cards and dominoes, or just to watch the satellite TV. Elsewhere there are numerous roadside huts which open up for drinks after dark. At the southern tip of the island there is the Hawks Nest Club bar.

Every Friday night there is a dance in New Bight at the sailing club on the bay. The disco is supplied by Bradley Russell from the Bridge Inn. It is attended by the locals, and is an important social event in the life of a small community. A bar is set up, dominoes are slammed down hard on the table and things are ready to roll. The guys spar with each other on the dance floor. Those few girls who do arrive have attention heaped upon them.

The Sights

The Hermitage on top of Mount Alvernia is the island's premier tourist location. Both the building and the view are well worth the journey. To get there follow the sign out of New Bight. It is possible to drive part of the way, though the walk should only take about 15 minutes from the main road.

Beside the path to the summit are Father Jerome's carvings of the stations of the cross. The Hermitage is a monument to Jerome's architectural talent, built like a monastery in miniature - the bed chambers are tiny and the chapel barely holds three people. Father Jerome died here at the ripe old age of 80 and was buried in a tomb on the hillside.

In New Bight there is another remarkable building also built by religious inspiration - the **Church of the Living God for All.** Though lacking the architectural finesse of the Hermitage, it is still an impressive tribute to Christian devotion. It was completed in 1982 and was largely built by the efforts of Mrs Emily Johnson who was 81 at the time. Mrs Johnson, cheerful yet pious and devout, is typical of people throughout the Bahamas.

The southern portion of the island is the best place to find the remains of old plantation houses. Adjacent to the road in Port Howe stand the overgrown remains of the once impressive **Deveaux mansion.** Near by is the shell of another great house, the **Armbrister plantation.** Near the Bight at a place called 'the Village' there are the remains of a narrow-gauge railway which was once used to transport sisal to a jetty for shipment.

Columbus Point, the easternmost part of the island, makes a good destination for hikers, as does the rugged untamed Atlantic coastline. When you spy the breakers and untouched beaches on the eastern coast you can be sure very few visitors have ever come that way before you.

For the lovers of the mysterious there are the stories and legends that have grown up around the island's blue hole. It is known to be tidal yet no passage has been found that connects it to the sea. Occasional elderly residents of the island talk about a creature that lives in the hole and devours anything that falls in. According to these tales in one incident a man and his dog were lost without trace. Yet when a British scientific team investigated the hole none of them were 'eaten' up. Perhaps the English are not as tasty as Cat Islanders.

Annual events

Late July and early August is regatta time on Cat Island. If you come then be sure to book a room in advance. The island briefly becomes a flurry of excitement and bustle, both for the sailors and those just there for the partying!

TWENTY-FOUR

Crooked Island and Acklins

In the not too distant past life in the Bahamas centered around these islands. Today it is impossible to imagine that a thriving community of nine to ten thousand people ever lived here. Time has moved on and these are now just lonely outposts, only their rugged charm remains.

Situated 590km (365 miles) south-east of Nassau, these islands are commonly lumped together into the Crooked Island District, comprising the low lying land of Crooked Island, hilly Acklins and Long Cay, a near deserted rock. They encircle the Bight of Acklins, a shallow lagoon surrounded by the deep waters of the ocean.

Columbus sailed through these waters stopping at 'La Isabella' (Acklins) which he named after his queen. In 1783 British loyalists came and about 40 plantations were established, but all failed. The soil was too fragile for the continuous farming of cotton and tobacco.

Prosperity came at the latter half of the nineteenth century because of the important maritime highway which passed through the Windward and Crooked Island passage. The eastern Bahamas wrecking fleet was based in Albert Town on Long Cay (formerly known as Fortune Cay), and the area became the transshipment point for both cargo and labourers between the Americas and Europe.

Albert Town on Long Cay became the major port capital. In one year about 2,000 stevedores and contract workers were hired from here by the Atlas Company and the Pacific Mail Steamship Company. People from all over the Bahamas came for work. Stores, saloons and houses, even a railway, appeared. Today only 23 citizens remain in what is virtually a ghost town.

The coming of steamships and the advent of the First World War brought an end to all this activity. Today only 1,200 people remain in scattered communities eking out a living by farming and fishing. The twentieth century has largely passed them by with most of the youth heading off to Nassau or Freeport to find employment.

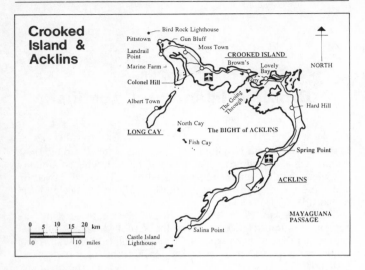

Crooked Island & Acklins

Bird Rock Lighthouse
Pittstown — Gun Bluff
Landrail Point — Moss Town
Marine Farm — CROOKED ISLAND
Brown's
Colonel Hill — Lovely Bay
Albert Town — Ferry
The Going Through — Hard Hill
LONG CAY — North Cay
The BIGHT of ACKLINS
Fish Cay
Spring Point
ACKLINS
MAYAGUANA PASSAGE
NORTH
0 5 10 15 20 km
0 10 miles
Castle Island Lighthouse — Salina Point

Arrival

By air
Bahamasair fly twice a week on Wednesday and Saturday from Nassau (tel. 327 8511) to Spring Point, Acklins then on to Colonel Hill, Crooked Island. The return airfare is $160.

By sea
The mailboat Windward Express calls at Landrail Point on Crooked Island, then Spring Point and Salina Point on Acklins before heading on to Mayaguana. One-way fare is $60. Check departure time and date with the Dockmaster's office at Potter's Cay in Nassau (tel. 393 1064).

Transport

Taxis
Locals with other jobs can be found. To travel the length of Crooked Island or Acklins will cost approximately $70.

Car hire

D. Thompson from the Gas Station and Store, Cabbage Hill, Crooked Island rents cars for $60 a day, trucks $75, scooters $25 and bikes $15. Gasoline is twice the Nassau price.

Hitching

There are only 120 vehicles and though everyone will stop to give you a ride, expect long waits of up to two hours. It is advisable to ask around if there is anybody going down to the ferry across Lovely Bay if you intend to the cross the islands by such means. The police drive up and down the island most days, and often offer lifts.

Ferry

It leaves Lovely Bay at 08.00 and 16.00, returning 15 minutes later. This is a shallow passage, crossed in a 3m (10ft) sloop, holding up to six people.

Accommodation

For hotel costs refer to page 5.

Middle

Pittstown Inn (tel. 336 2507), 3km (2 miles) from Landrail Point, is the only resort hotel on these islands. It reopened in January 1990, previously being known only to private pilots. Located on the sandy shoreline it offers basic, simple living and much tranquillity. The local manager, Don Daxon, or your hosts pick you up at Colonel Hill airport.

Accommodation is provided in six cottages, a total of 12 rooms, each with an en-suite bathroom, two queen-size beds, simple furnishings and a ceiling fan. All have a patio with lounge chairs. The inn has a 'manual' on what there is to do and see. An honesty system is operated in the 'debriefing room' (the bar) which has the only ice machine on Crooked Island. Trips can be organised, including diving and snorkeling. The reef is only waiting there, 5m (15ft) offshore. Do remember though this is a remote out-island and amongst other things water has to be conserved at all times. MAP $35; AMEX.

Moderate
Crooked Island Beach Inn (Colonel Hill, Crooked Island, tel. 336 2096) is a group of four cottages, each housing up to five people, with basic fittings and furnishings, some with bath tubs, others showers plus a communal kitchen. A beautiful deserted beach is 30m (80ft) away. No credit cards.

Budget
Mrs Gibson's Guest House (Landrail Point, Crooked Island) is a family house sleeping six. There is one master bedroom, bathroom, living room with two twin and one double bed, dining table, sofa, easy chairs, ceiling fans and even a small organ. Children under 11 stay for free; no credit cards.

T & S Guest House (Cabbage Hill, Crooked Island, tel. 336 2096) has five small rooms run by the same owners as the Crooked Island Beach Inn. It was temporarily closed at time of going to press.

The Guest House (Spring Point, Acklins) is owned by Curtis Hanna and is an extension of the restaurant and bar. The two rooms available have one queen-size bed in each and a ceiling fan but share bathrooms. The people are very friendly. No credit cards.

Places to eat

The most famous restaurant on the island is **Mrs Gibson's Lunch Room** at Landrail Point, Crooked Island, also known as 'Mama's Kitchen'. It is a simple hut, first discovered by the Yachtsman Guide to the Bahamas. The large table sits ten comfortably on wooden benches for a feast of Bahamian cooking of fresh fish, peas n' rice. Come to enjoy a traditional Bahamian evening and add your comments to the guest book. Food prepared to order, call channel 16 VHF. Meals $6-$10; no credit cards.

Pittstown Inn (tel. 336 2507) offers three course set meals ($15) cocktails at 19.00, dinner at 19.30. Reservations only. Saturday night is pizza evening and many locals come calling. AMEX.

Good Meals (Colonel Hill, Crooked Island) is run by Mrs Eunice Deleveaux who serves chicken with peas n' rice chicken for about $5. The place is also the bakery, general store and occasionally a guesthouse, charging $40 inclusive of meals. No credit cards.

On Acklins the **Airport Inn,** 2km (1½ miles) outside Spring Point, is the best bet for eating and socialising with the locals, especially on Bahamasair flight days. Meals cost from $5, sodas $1, beer $2.50. Otherwise try the guest house and bar in Spring Point. Note that spirits are sold by the bottle, not measure.

Basics

Communication
Channel 16 VHF or there is a rudimentary telephone system.

Medical
There is a resident doctor at Spring Point, Acklins plus two clinics staffed by resident nurses.

Police
Located at Spring Point (Acklins) and Colonel Hill (Crooked Island).

Post office
Located at Colonel Point (Crooked Island) and Salina Point (Acklins); they will cash US dollar travellers cheques.

The Sights

Bird Rock Lighthouse, just off Pittstown Point at the western tip of Crooked Island rising 34m (112ft) above sea level, is a grand but decaying building only accessible by boat. Built in 1876 using local stone from Gun Bluff, it is well worth the trip to see the beautiful, intricate timber latticework to the veranda and rooms at its base.

For readers of *Out Island Doctor* a visit to Gun Bluff, a few kilometres along the coast from Pittstown, is a must. Here is the very location where the author fell under the spell of these islands and built his home. At Pittstown Inn the original structure of the **first General Post Office** of the Bahamas has been incorporated into the dive shop. Mail used to be dropped off from a regularly scheduled service en route from Britain to Jamaica.

Marine Farm plantation and fortress near Landrail Point has cannons dating back to King George III's reign. The fort saw action in the War of 1812 between Britain and America, as it guarded the Crooked Island Passage. For a reasonable fee Mrs M Gibson of Landrail Point, Crooked Island will show you around. Colonel Hill commands the best panoramic view of Crooked Island.

Acklins has a larger, though sparsely scattered, population. From **Hard Hill** the view covers both the Atlantic Ocean and the Bight of Acklins. **Spring Point** is the administrative centre, but has no more than a few homes grouped around the 'lazy' or 'sleeping tree'. The hammock which hangs off this massive tree is the perfect location to while away the day just catching the breeze. At the southern end is **Salina Point** the largest community. Near by is the battery operated **Castle Island lighthouse.**

Beaches

With no tourist trade to speak of the beaches are all empty, truely virgin sands. There is very little shade from the sun and the waters are not much cooler. In the Bight of Acklins the sea is shallow, ideal for swimming and snorkeling.

Sports

Fishing
At any of the communities the locals are willing to take you out fishing. Price is negotiable.

Scuba
Pittstown Inn (tel. 336 2507), rents diving equipment and organises dives.

TWENTY-FIVE

Exumas

The Exumas are a chain of islands stretching from Sail Rocks, some 53km (34 miles) south-east of Nassau, to Hog Cay, a distance of over 150km. Inside its domain are mini dragons, world record bone fishing grounds, an island for every day of the year and pristine white sandy beaches. The shallow, vividly coloured waters are strewn with coral reefs and sand spits. Here are also some of the most friendly people in the whole of the Bahamas. No wonder the boating crowd flock here. Yet unlike Abaco or Eleuthera the tourist industry has largely passed by and the place remains undeveloped.

The Exumas suffered the rapid boom and bust cycle of plantation ownership. Salt and cotton were briefly king here. Chief among the loyalist plantation owners was Denys Rolle of Devonshire, England who transported his 140 slaves, livestock and other possessions on the Peace and Plenty to Great Exuma. Rolle eventually controlled 5,000 acres when the land was inherited by his only son Lord Rolle of Stevenstone. However salt from Turks and Caicos was more commercially viable and the chenille bug decimated the cotton crop. Plantations began to fail. Lord Rolle, despite what is often written, did not give up his land or set his slaves free. Instead he used troops on various occasions from 1828-34 to attempt to forcibly relocate his slaves on Trinidad.

A large number of these slaves became subsistence farmers on their own patch of land and by continued resistance won their independence and claimed the Rolle lands. The Commonage Act, 1896 addressed the question of squatters' rights and most of the Rolle slaves took his surname as theirs. Communities such as Rollestown and Rolleville still thrive today. Anyone with the surname can build on the old Rolle property. Agriculture remains one of the more important industries, with onions being the principle export.

Chartering a boat for a few days to go island hopping is a good way to see the Exumas. Snorkeling amongst the coral reefs,

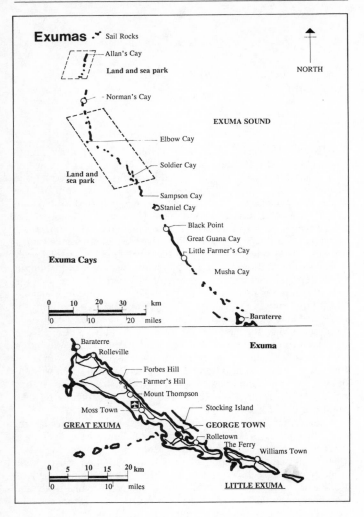

thronged with marine life is excellent. Call at the Alan Cays to meet the rock iguanas, dirty yellow colour with a shade of red to the head and limbs, known as 'Bahamian Dragons'. They are protected inside the Land and Sea Park.

Arrival

By air
Bahamasair fly five times a week from Nassau to the new international airport opened in March 1990, near Moss Town (tel. 322 4727). Aero Coach Airlines (tel. 336 2186) fly direct from both Fort Lauderdale and Miami. Airlines Airways International fly only from Miami (tel. USA 305 827 2794). This airport is due to become one of the busiest gateways into the Family Islands. A restaurant opposite the terminal offers reasonably priced Bahamian food and a shopping mall is being constructed.

By sea
Two mailboats service the Exumas both departing from Potter's Cay, Nassau. MV Lady Francis sails on Thursdays, travelling down the cays calling at Staniel Cay, Black Point, Farmer's Cay and finally Barraterre. Scheduled to last 16 hours it is a fascinating way to see the cays for $25 one-way. Do not be surprised if there are delays, as even the mailboat gets caught on sandbanks in these shallow waters. MV Grand Master leaves on Tuesday and sails direct to George Town, taking 12 hours and again costing $25. To confirm sailing times telephone 393 1064 for the Harbour-master's office.

Transport

Taxi
From the airport the fare is $21.50 (one or two persons) to George Town. There is no public transport so unless you have made other arrangements bare this cost in mind. To travel from Barraterre from George Town or down to Little Exuma will cost between $45-$55.

Rental hire
Exuma Transport, PO Box 19 in George Town (tel. 336 2101) rent cars from $55 per day plus a deposit of $200; scooters $25 per day. Some of the hotels also have bicycles to rent. Roads are generally in a good condition.

Hitching
For the more adventurous hitching a ride, once away from the airport, is easy and a great way of meeting the locals.

Ferry
The Peace & Plenty hotel run a service across to Stocking Island costing $5 round trip (free for guest). It leaves 10.00 and 13.00, with the last trip back at 15.30.

Accommodation

For hotel costs refer to page 5.

George Town

Middle-High
Peace and Plenty Club (PO Box 55, tel. 336 2551), located on Elizabeth Harbour, is delightful and informal. The oldest hotel on the island, it is named after the ship Peace and Plenty. It was originally a private home, then an exclusive club attracting such figures as King Constantine of Greece and Prince Philip. The general manager, Charles Pflueger, is famous for running one of the best resorts for those who enjoy the slow pace of island life. It is very popular with Europeans and over 50% of business is repeat. The two storey pink and white buildings are set around a courtyard with a free-shape, freshwater swimming pool.

There are 35 rooms, all air-conditioned with ensuite bathrooms, most have balconies. Additional rooms are now provided at the recently opened Peace and Plenty Inn 500m (600yds) away. MAP is $24; please note no children under the age of six; AMEX, MC, V.

High
Out Island Inn Village (PO Box 49, tel. 336 2171) is the largest of the resort complexes on the Exumas. Recently renovated, it has 80 rooms, all with air-conditioning. They are tastefully furnished, including a complimentary room bar stocked to order. Built on its own peninsula across from Stocking Island, the units are spread out amongst the palm trees. This is an all-inclusive resort offering the complete getaway. The tariff includes use of windsurfing, sunfish sailboats, snorkel equipment, bicycles, tennis, volleyball and shuffleboard courts, unlimited drinks as well as three meals a day, accommodation and taxes. From the 30-slip marina free boat trips

to Stocking Island with pre-packed lunches are provided. For inland explorations cars are available to rent. AP; children 6-12 get a 50% reduction, those under 6 stay for free with parents; AMEX, MC, V.

Moderate

Pieces of Eight Hotel (PO Box 49, tel. 336 2600) is the sister resort to Out Island Village. Built in 1962, the two storey buildings surround a courtyard consisting of a swimming pool, covered walkways, picnic seating and well maintained grounds stepped back from the road on a hill overlooking Elizabeth Harbour and Stocking Island. The 33 rooms all have private balconies and air-conditioning. They are clean, but show signs of constant use. There is an excellent dive programme with daily reef trips and lessons for the inexperienced. AMEX, MC, V.

Moderate to Middle

Regatta Point (PO Box 6, tel. 336 2206) has five spacious apartments overlooking Kidd Cove and Elizabeth Harbour, a few minutes' walk from George Town itself. The one- or two-bedroom units include a fully fitted kitchen, ceiling fans and daily maid service. It has its own beach plus free use of Sunfish, windsurfers and bicycles for guests. MC, V.

Moderate

The Two Turtle Inn, in the heart of George Town (PO Box 51, tel. 336 2545), has 14 rooms clustered around a small courtyard. The flagstone walls and timber-clad upper deck give an island impression to this 30-years-old, small inn. Each unit has satellite TV, air-conditioning and ceiling fans and traditional island Furnishings. Two of the rooms have kitchenettes. MAP $18; children under 12 sharing a room with an adult stay for free; AMEX, MC, V.

   Marshall's Guest House (PO Box 27, tel. 336 2571) offers 12 clean, basic rooms all with air-conditioning. MC.

Places to eat

The Peace and Plenty (tel. 336 2551) has an elegant candle lit dining room. The food is Bahamian or American, dinner prices between $18 and $35; lunch $8-$12; and breakfast about $5. To round off an evening why not partake in some liquid refreshment from the **Nautical Bar** — once an old slave kitchen — on the other side of the courtyard. It is always humming with people. AMEX, MC, V.

Pieces of Eight Restaurant (tel. 336 2600) brings the taste of the Orient to these parts. The restaurant decor itself has no frills, but the food stands out whether it is Exuma pineapple, chicken wok stirred and mixed with pineapple and crispy vegetables or sweet and sour grouper. The house specialises in different rices. Conch fried rice is certainly worth a taste. Dinners start at $15; lunches cost $8; AMEX, MC, V.

Out Island Inn Restaurant (tel. 336 2171) presents Bahamian and Continental cuisine on the waters edge. Dinner can be enjoyed outside or in the large 'hall' dining room jutting out into the harbour. Dinner $30; lunch $6-$10; AMEX, MC, V.

The **Two Turtles Inn** (tel. 336 2545) meals cost $4 for breakfast, $5 for lunch, and evening meals from $14. Favourites include cracked conch, pan-fried grouper with peas and rice or strip steaks. AMEX, MC, V.

Sam's Place (tel. 336 2579) is a waterfront restaurant and bar in downtown George Town. Run by Sam Gray, who is also in charge of the marina, it serves good local Bahamian food and it is very popular with the sailing crowd. Breakfast from $8; lunch up to $10. There is no fixed dinner menu as much will depend on the local catch of the day. Grouper, cracked conch, lobster and steak are regular choices served for under 25$.

Eddie's Edgewater Club (tel. 336 2050) specialises in some of the best native dishes in town. Try Eddie's fried chicken. Open daily for breakfast, lunch and dinner; prices from $4 to $10.

Basics

Banks
Bank of Nova Scotia (tel. 336 2651) is open Monday-Thursday 09.00-15.00, and on Friday 09.00-13.00 and 15.00-17.00.

Medical services
There is a resident doctor and government health clinic in George Town (tel. 336 2682).

Police
Based in the Administrative Building (tel. 336 2152).

Communications
The post office is in the Administrative Building, 09.00-15.30. Channel 16 VHF is still the main method of communication inspite of the extensive telephone system.

Laundry
There are two laundrettes in town at the Exuma Dock Services Marina and the Harbour View. Exuma Cleaners also offer dry cleaning services.

Library
Located alongside the Two Turtle Inn, this small timber building has a good selection of novels and even a children's section. Visitors are more than welcome.

Provisions
The Packing House, Mount Thompson is the best place to buy vegetables (those in season). The onions are incredibly tasty - they even appear in Exuma's coat of arms.

Nightlife

The Peace and Plenty has a band playing island and Calypso music every Saturday evening. It attracts locals, visiting yacht people and guests alike.

Friday night and a visit to the **Two Turtles Inn** is obligatory. The barbecue is an island event with pork ribs from $7.50. The place gets packed so come early.

The Sights

George Town, the capital of these cays is designated to become the gateway to the Southern Bahamas. It is the only major town in the area and is used by the sailing crowd not only as the port of entry but also as the place to replenish stocks. The town itself, which lies on the Tropic of Cancer, is a small rather quaint settlement built around Lake Victoria. This pond serves as a natural harbour for small boats and is utilised as the centre for diving operations and boat charters. Local stores, offices, restaurants and hotels make up the fabric of the place, the most predominant building being the Government Administration building (modelled on the Government House in Nassau). It will take less than 30 minutes to wander around, passing through the town centre with its gigantic tree and straw market. As of April 1990 a one-way system was introduced though it has more to do with stopping people being run over on the narrow roads than with traffic congestion.

Across Elizabeth Harbour, which encircles the western edge of

George Town, is **Stocking Island.** A long narrow strip of land, whose sand dunes form a natural protection to this lovely harbour. The glorious white sandy beaches and small coves for private picnics should also be on the list of every visitor. Once a private enclave it is now open to all. The ferry departs from the Peace and Plenty Club, who also run a snack bar on the island.

Just offshore from the island, in a natural hurricane hole, are three blue holes, the shallowest of them being 3m (10ft) below the surface.

Sports

Boat rental
Minns Water Sports (tel. 336 2604), opposite the Peace and Plenty Hotel rent a 15ft Boston whaler for $58 per day or $287 a week. Larger boats are available. Snorkel equipment can also be rented.

Fishing
Fishing trips organised by the Peace and Plenty Club (tel. 336 2551) cost $175per day for two people, including equipment and a packed lunch. The hotel also arranges a Bone-fishing tournament in early November.

Scuba
Exuma Divers (PO Box 110, tel. 336 2030) is based at the Peace and Plenty Hotel. **Exuma Aquatics Ltd** (tel. 336 2600) can be found at the Pieces of Eight Hotel offering lessons for all levels plus underwater photo facilities. Both will organize trips to the Mystery Cave on Stocking Island, which extends over 120m (400ft) under the island.

Shopping and souvenirs

The **Two Turtle Inn gift shop** has various assortments of T-shirts and Androsia prints for sale. **The Sandpiper** probably offers the best selection of Bahamian arts and crafts, latest books and charts, plus original prints by local artist Diane Minns. The **Peace and Plenty Boutique** sells Androsia batiks, film and suntan oil. If you are in search of a wee dram or two call in at **Exuma Liquor and Gifts** store along the Queen's Highway. Shops are open 09.00-17.30 Monday — Saturday.

Discovering Great Exuma

To have a better understanding of the life of these islanders it is necessary to step out of George Town and visit the small communities where the bulk of the 4,000 people still live. This is farming countryside, but to look at it you cannot tell. The locals practice a kind of subsistence farming to make the most this fragile soil. Here are the peaceful communities of Lord Rolle's former slave settlements of Rolleville and Rollestown. The island is easily accessible by car.

Accommodation

Moderate
On the airport road at **Jimmie Hill** is a family home rented out by Jonny and James Holzman (tel. USA 302 428 1455). Six to eight people can lodge here, with all mod-cons (including satellite TV, microwave and air-conditioning), plus the use of a minivan. It offers peace and tranquillity for a family vacation, with superb views across the island to Duck Cay. An isolated beach is only five minutes' drive away.

Budget
Three Sisters Beach Club, near Mount Thompson, offers three two-bedroom apartments with kitchens. It is a couple of minutes' walk to a white, perfectly clean beach; or a ten-minute walk away to the bar and restaurant of the same name.

Places to eat

The Fiesta Bar and Lounge, Moss Town. Opened in February 1990 this place is fast developing a reputation for fine Bahamian dishes. Meals cost $5. The cracked conch is quite superb. Takeaways are available; call channel 16 VHF.

Hilltop Tavern (tel. 336 6066), Rolleville, is the largest establishment in the settlement. Perched on top of the hill it has truely magnificent views of the surrounding area. Its fare is typically Bahamian; snacks costs $5; lunches $6-$7 and dinners $12-$14.

Little Exuma

Across the bridge, Little Exuma is 19km by 2km (12 miles by 1 mile). 'The Ferry' is the first settlement upon crossing the bridge, the home of the 'Shark Lady', Gloria Patience. This remarkable lady has probably caught more sharks single-handed than anybody else and her home is more like a museum to these notorious creatures and deserves a visit. If the opportunity arises ask about the 6m (14ft) tiger shark she caught in a 4m (13ft) Boston whaler.

In Forbes Hill are the ruins of a fortress built by the British in 1892. It commands a splendid view for miles around and Fort Bay beach below has gorgeous sands and inviting waters. Further down is Williams Town, the last community of Little Exuma. It is the home of the Cotton House, the only plantation house still lived in throughout the Bahamas.

Accommodation

At the time of writing the Sand Dollar Hotel in Forbes Hill the only accommodation here, had closed.

Places to eat

If you are looking for a bite to eat call in at **Mezzy Methell's Arawak Club** in Williams Town. Snacks cost from $4 to $6. At the weekend, **Gordy's Palace** is the place for the 'big' disco with meals for $12.

Barraterre

Once a small island cut off from Great Exuma it is now linked by a land bridge. This small hamlet, full of pastel coloured houses set above the shallow, shimmering waters remains a tightly knit community with the atmosphere of a small cay.

Accommodation

Budget
The Fisherman's Inn (tel. 336 5017), run by Norman Lloyd, has two rooms with simple, modern, good quality furnishings. They are provided with en-suite bathrooms and ceiling fans. The entrance is off the patio which has a splendid view of the entire sound. Mrs Lloyd runs a taxi service and will be happy to take you to the airport and into town.

    Sailor's Cove, Bar and Guest House, is slowly being upgraded. Basic accommodation is provided above the bar-restaurant in six timber panelled rooms containing double beds, bathrooms, ceiling fans and little else.

Places to eat

The Fisherman's Inn (tel. 336 5017), Barraterre, is recognised for its superb native food and atmosphere. Locals travel out from George Town. The place is designed for parties. Breakfast from $3.50, lunch $5-$6 and dinner between $8 and $12. The conch here is exquisite; it would be criminal to miss their chowder.

Staniel Cay

This is the centre for the surrounding communities on neighbouring cays, at the heart of the Exuma chain. Parts of two James Bond movies, and more recently Splash, were filmed here at the world famous 'Thunderball Grotto'. Back on dry land there are innumerable inviting beaches here and on the surrounding cays.

Arrival

By air
The building of the 900m (approximately 3000ft), paved runway has opened up this community of 100 souls to the tourist industry. Trans Mar Airline (tel. USA 305 467 6850) flies direct from Fort Lauderdale and many private pilots from the States drop in here.

By sea
MV Lady Francis calls here (see 'Arrival' at beginning of chapter).

Accommodation

Top
The Staniel Cay Yacht Club (tel. 355 2024) caters for up to 16 guests, either in cottages along the water's edge or two-bedroom units further inland amid the pine trees. The marina has 15 births, fully equipped; contact Bob Chamberlain the General Manager. Not surprisingly the clubhouse with its nautical decor and palm-thatched ceiling, is the hub of this establishment, with the talk being of fishing or flying. The meals are a happy mix of American and Bahamian dishes. Boston whalers, sailing dinghies and windsurfers are free for guests staying three nights or longer. AMEX, MC, V.

Moderate
Happy People Marina (tel. 355 2008) has 12 motel-like, pleasantly furnished rooms and nine slips for passing yachts. Both locals and visitors are attracted to the friendly ambience of its bar and the **Royal Entertainer Restaurant** where a local band plays once a week.

Sport

Scuba
Staniel Cay Yacht Club (tel. 355 2024). Divers can explore the Thunderball Grotto, part of the Exuma Land and Sea Park. The park was established by the Bahamian National Trust to protect their natural environment. Look at but do not touch the coral.

Special event: regattas

The Exumas are in many ways the home of the regattas. In total there are eight of these events, bringing out the best in boats and crews alike. The first of these races of canvas sail and timber constructed boats was in George Town in April 1954. Now known as the 'Family Island Regatta', it is the most revered of all, with races over a ten-day period at the end of April. It is not just about the majesty of sail. On land the party never stops, from cook-outs to the Royal Bahamian Police Force Band.

In the first week of August the action moves to Black Point, Rolleville and Barraterre for a series of one day regattas. Smaller in size and more personal the objective is none-the-less to soak up the sun and to party.

Drug island

From 1978 to 1982 Norman's Cay, part of the Exuma chain, was used as a base for the notorious 'king of cocaine', Carlos Lehder. No one in the Bahamian government took the necessary action to prevent this, despite abundant evidence of what was happening. In September 1983 NBS blew the story open and forced an investigation into the shameful affair.

Carlos Lehder first bought property on Norman's Cay then used armed thugs to drive several American families out of their holiday homes. The island's runway was extended and regular drug runs were made from here to the USA for at least four years. By the beginning of 1979, the DEA, the United States Embassy and the Assistant Commissioner of Police, all knew in detail about what was happening.

For four years Carlos Lehder was allowed to act as he pleased on Norman's Cay. Large pay-offs were made to police and government officials, and Lehder was always tipped off well in advance about any police action. Many questions still remain: why did Prime Minister Pindling visit the island in 1979? Just who received 'hush' money? Or, why did the US officials fail to put sufficient pressure on Pindling to force him to act?

Staniel Cay has two regattas. The first on 1 January allows international yachts to participate in a series of races. The Independence Day Regatta on 10 July is more of a local affair.

The regatta at Farmers Cay starts the season for traditional Bahamian built, owned and crewed boats, held on the first Friday in February.

The Cruising Regatta off Stocking Island, George Town in March is becoming ever more popular with the international yachts that sail these waters.

TWENTY-SIX

Great Inagua

The most remote family island under the jurisdiction of the Nassau government, Inagua lies far to the south-east, being nearer to the coasts of Haiti and Cuba than to its own capital. The name derives from the Spanish ileno-agua meaning 'full of water'. An apt description, as salt water covers much of the western portion of the island. The barren soil long discouraged settlement and when colonists finally arrived they looked to the salt ponds to earn their living.

During the 1800s the inhabitants lived by raking salt from numerous shallow pools and selling it to passing ships. With time the industry became increasingly mechanism with pumps replacing windmills and railways being laid. Salvaging cargo from wrecked ships remained a lucrative sideline until the lighthouse was built in 1866. As soon as a floundering ship was sighted the workers would down tools and rush off, deaf to the pleas of their overseers to remain at their posts.

Uniquely in the Bahamas the island depends on an industry for its prosperity. Salt production now totals over a million tons a year and is controlled by Morton Bahamas Limited. The company looms large in Inaguan life, employing about 250 people and running the general store, an hotel and the power plant. They have constructed a dock where salt can rapidly be loaded via a conveyor system and the huge salt heaps rise out of their surroundings like snow-covered hills.

In recent years a period of lawlessness similar to the old wrecking-days spirit returned in Inagua when some of the islanders dabbled in the drug trade. Things came to a head when an off-island policeman tried to take action against the smugglers. A riot erupted in which the police station was burnt down and the officer taken hostage. He was later released when reinforcements were flown in from Nassau, but to diffuse the situation he was transferred elsewhere. The USA has established a small base adjacent to the airport as part of its programme of cooperation with the Bahamas government; it is operated by members of the National Guard and the drug traffickers have moved elsewhere.

Arrival

By air
Matthew Town airport is only 2km (1 mile) out of town. Bahamasair fly there from Nassau (tel. 322 4727) on Tuesdays, Thursdays and Saturdays. They also fly on to Turks and Caicos on Tuesdays.

By sea
A mailboat makes weekly or fortnightly trips to Inagua. For details of the schedule ring the Potter's Cay office in Nassau (tel. 393 1064).

Transport
There is a taxi on the island which meets incoming flights, otherwise locals will offer rides. There is no organised hire service though it may be possible to obtain a vehicle by asking around.

Matthew Town

Virtually all of the islands 1,000 people live here. As well as hotels and bars there is the well stocked general store and a branch of the Bank of Canada open from 13.00 to 14.30 on Friday only.

Accommodation

For hotel costs refer to page 5.

Moderate
The Walk Inn offers six air-conditioned double rooms with TV; on Gregory Street, about five minutes' walk east from the general store. Most of the rooms have ground level access and are clean and well maintained. No credit cards. Main House (tel. 267), situated behind the general store on Gregory Street, is owned by Morton Bahamas Limited. The rooms have air-conditioning and there is a TV in the communal lounge. The rooms may be full as the place is used by company employees and the National Guard. No credit cards.

Budget
Ford's Inagua Inn (tel. operator extension 277), a block inland from Gregory Street near the basketball court, is a two-storey building with six rooms. Usually closed May-July; no credit cards.

Places to eat

There are no expensive restaurants on Inagua, the food available is either local recipes or Western style fast food. For the Bahamas prices are quite cheap here.

The Main House restaurant is both popular and good value. Prices start at $1 for tea and toast up to about $6 for a full meal. Ford's Inagua Inn offer food to their guests.

The Cosy Corner and **Topp's restaurant** are really bars but as well as television and bar games they offer a variety of snacks and meals.

The Sights

Whereas many other islands attract yachting or fishing folk, Inagua is a mecca for birdwatchers. Here you will find the largest West Indian Flamingo colony in the world. The birds have thrived thanks to the work of the Bahamas National Trust and the individual efforts of the wardens Jim and Henry Nixon.

At Union Creek the Trust also maintain a research site for sea turtles. If you wish to see the National Trust's work it is best to call their headquarters in Nassau (tel. 393 1317) before you leave for Inagua. At both sites small camps have been constructed which offer basic accommodation. Wild pigs and donkeys and several varieties of cacti also make their home here.

Around Matthew Town there are a few sites of interest. In the centre of town is the old salt warehouse. Next to the modern police station is the building burnt down in a riot during the height of the drug war. A mile to the east of town is the nineteenth-century lighthouse, which can be visited if permission is obtained from the keeper.

Out at the airport there is a scrapyard of wrecked drug smuggling planes. It is possible to potter around inside them for unusual souvenirs such as an indicator gauge from the cockpit, or blueprints of machine parts.

TWENTY-SEVEN

Long Island

Originally known as 'Yuma' by the Arawaks, this island was renamed 'Fernandina' by Columbus in honour of his sponsor, as the etiquette of the day demanded. Columbus found no gold here so he moved on quickly. Thereafter apart from being used as base by the occasional pirate ship Long Island, as it came to be known, was largely ignored. Only a few families came to try and eke out a living here by raking salt and selling it to passing ships.

As elsewhere British loyalists came and attempted to recreate the plantation lifestyle they had enjoyed in the American colonies. They failed, but unlike elsewhere they did not abandon the land after a few years, but instead diversified into fishing, salt production and sheep rearing. Furthermore 'pot hole' farming was found to be successful — planting crops only in hollows where there is sufficient soil to produce a steady if not abundant yield.

In the course of the years the social barriers between those who were the masters and those who were the slaves have been eroded. Nowadays Long Islanders from countless different backgrounds live together as one community. Very few other societies have been able to overcome the legacy of colonialism as well as the people have done here.

Physically the island is long and thin, stretching 60 miles north to south but only one to three miles west to east. It is bisected by the Tropic of Cancer. The settlements are connected by a road which is surfaced for most of its length but not without the odd pothole. Each year the holes get a little wider so the islanders are stoically waiting for the government to resurface them. The 3,500 inhabitants are hospitable and welcoming, especially in the southern parts where visitors are something of a rarity.

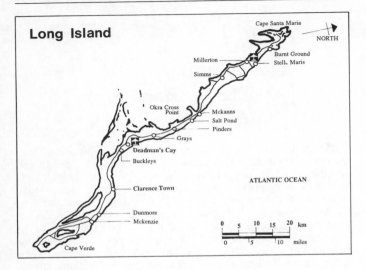

Arrival

By air
Stella Maris run direct flights from the nearby airport to Fort Lauderdale. From Nassau Bahamasair (tel. 322 4727) operate regular flights to both airports: Deadman's Cay and Stella Maris.

By sea
Two mailboats serve Long Island. The Nay Dean travels to the northern settlements of Salt Pond, Deadman's Cay and Seymours, oneway for $30-$35. It has no fixed schedule so telephone the Potter's Cay office more information (tel. 393 1064). The Abilin sails for Clarence Town only on Tuesdays at midday, returning to Nassau by Thursday at 13.30. The one-way fare is $35.

Transport
If you need a lift any driver will take you as far as they are going. Luckily traffic is quite frequent on the main road. If you prefer your own transport there is a variety of options.

Taxi

At Stella Maris taxis are readily available and can be arranged through the front desk. Taxis to or from the airport to the resort cost $2 per head.

Car hire

It is possible to rent a vehicle at three different locations: at Stella Maris a variety of vehicles are available costing from $50 to $80 per day plus 30 cents per mile, depending on their size; Thompson Bay Inn offers cars for $60 to $65 a day; and Carroll's Guesthouse and Store offer large US models for $80.

Accommodation

For hotel costs refer to page 5.

Middle to top

Stella Maris Inn (PO Box SM 105, tel. 809 336 2106), one of the most comprehensive resorts in the Family Islands, provides a wide range of activities to suit virtually all tastes and preferences. Helpful guides are given out to new arrivals providing information and maps on places to see, beaches, souvenirs and so forth. The Inn provides transportation: complimentary bicycles or car hire; and complimentary activities include snorkeling, tennis, sailing and windsurfing.

Stella Maris is sighted on the slope of a hill overlooking the east coast and offers 32 rooms and several apartments and cottages with double accommodation. There are three swimming pools and two tennis courts for guests to use, a playing area for children on Deal's Beach and a babysitting service. Various entertainments are offered through the week including a cave party with barbecue and live band on Mondays, a rum punch party on Wednesdays, and a local 'rake and scrape' band perform at the clubhouse on Saturdays. A variety of packages for divers, fishers or honeymooners is available. MAP $32 per person per day; children under 9, $15; AMEX, MC V.

Moderate
KB Resort (contact via Stella Maris operator) is on the east coast of Long Island, half a mile off the main road at McKann's settlement. The single storey resort has ten rooms and a separate restaurant and bar area. The manageress Dawn Edgecombe offers a complimentary pick-up service to and from the airport and a free tour of the island. KB's is a small, intimate resort offering friendly service. No credit cards.

    Windtryst Guesthouse (contact via Salt Pond operator). A small white stone building on the main road in Salt Pond with five air-conditioned rooms, two with kitchens. The guesthouse is built beside its own small bay and has ground level access.

    Atlantic Hydeaway (contact via Deadman's Cay operator), in Buckleys south of Deadman's Cay, has two rooms for rent, each with a double bed. The beach is only two minutes' walk away. A restaurant and bar is located on the property. No credit cards.

Budget
Thompson Bay Inn (contact via Stella Maris operator) offers eight rooms with ceiling fans and televisions. The two storey building sits beside the main road north of Salt Pond. Bathrooms are shared. Car or boat rental can be organised. Downstairs is a lively bar and restaurant. No credit cards.

    Carrol's (JB's) Guest House (contact via Deadman's Cay operator). Owned and managed by Mr and Mrs Joseph 'JB' and Viogie Carroll, this two storey building is adjacent to the general store and gas station on the main road in Deadman's Cay. There is no restaurant on the premises. JB has six single rooms or two self catering apartments. Car rental is available. AMEX, V.

Places to eat

Stella Maris (tel. 336 2106), serves a variety of Bahamian, American and European dishes for breakfast, lunch and dinner. For breakfast there is a choice of Continental ($4.25) or American ($8). The lunch menu provides a variety of sandwiches, salads and snacks. Dinner consists of a set menu of three courses changed daily, for a fixed price of $2. AMEX, MC, V.

    KB's resort offers all three meals at their restaurant. The food is mainly Bahamian, with a few Western items. Breakfast from about $4, lunch $5 and dinner $8. The service is friendly with the gratuity at your discretion.

Thompson Bay Inn has a selection of local and fast-food dishes which cost about $5 to $8. Items such as fish, burgers, chicken and snacks with fries or peas and rice are the usual fare. Meals are served throughout the day until the early evening.

There are a variety of bars and clubs serving native food at reasonable prices on the island. These include the **Atlantic Hydeaway** at Buckley, the **Cape Santa Maria Club** to the north of the island, **Conchys** at Stella Maris, **Kentucky No 2** near Deadman's Cay, **Marob's** at Simms or the **Travellers Rest** at Deadman's Cay.

Near 'JB' Carroll's guest house is an excellent family bakery selling a selection of pastries, pizzas, cakes and cookies.

Basics

Banks
The Royal Canadian Bank has a branch located a few miles north of Deadman's Cay, open 09.00-13.00 Monday-Thursday, and 16.00-17.00 on Thursday afternoon.

Communications
There is a basic phone service where numbers can be reached by calling through the operator. However most people on the island use the radio. Overseas calls can be made at Batelco Telecommunications or at Stella Maris.

Medical
The main clinic is located at Deadman's Cay, though the doctor and nurses travel around the island in a set pattern to attend a number of day clinics.

Police
There are constables at the settlements of Burnt Ground, Stella Maris, Simms, Millers, Deadman's Cay, Clarence Town and Roses.

Power
Supplied by privately owned generators as there is no government-built power station on the island.

Nightlife

In the village of Petty, between Deadman's Cay and Clarence Town, there is a small **theatre** where films are occasionally shown. For live music the **Stella Maris** Inn has bands on most Mondays, Wednesdays and Saturdays. Elsewhere the **Thompson Bay Inn** puts on discos most weeks beside the dining room and bar.

There are numerous small bars dotted along the length of the island where the locals gather for a drink in the evenings. These are the places for a cold beer or a game of dominoes so take a stroll down to your local. A chat with the customers will reveal just how content they are to be Long Islanders — swap what they have for a life rushing around in a big, fast city — you must be joking!

Shopping and souvenirs

Tingums Boutique at Stella Maris has a selection of mementoes, T-shirts complete with the hotel logo and a variety of other Bahamian souvenirs. Along the main road are a variety of stalls selling straw work.

The Sights

Starting at the north of the island there is **Cape Santa Maria,** the original landing place of Columbus and not a bad place to admire the view. Moving southwards there is **Adderley's plantation house** near the road on Adderley Point. To find it take the rough track 1km (½ mile) north of the turn off to Stella Maris, then follow this track until it reaches the beach. Follow the beach until you see a path turning inland to your right. This take you to the remains of the plantation house and two outbuildings.

Salt Pond, on the main road, is a centre for lobster fishers.

A few miles down the road is the village of **Deadman's Cay,** so named after the time when corpses were given a burial offshore. Here at a place called Buckleys School are two **caves,** containing stalactites, stalagmites and old Indian paintings. The caves are on private ground so your guides may expect a small fee to show you around.

Two grand **mission-style churches** dominate the settlement at Clarence Town. They were both built by the same man, Father Jerome, later the hermit of Cat Island. First he built **St Paul's Anglican Church;** then, after conversion to Catholicism, he constructed **St Peter's,** making it just that little bit greater than his former creation. You would not think that there were enough people in this small village to fill these two churches but apparently there are.

Dunmore contains a fairly well preserved **plantation** and a **cave system** which was an old Indian habitat. Further south in Hard Bargain are the **old salt pans** that used to be the main source of wealth for Long Island. This area is now under new management and has been running successfully for a few years as a shrimp hatchery.

Long Island's **regatta** is held at Salt Pond every June and is generally a time of dancing and drinking with a relaxed carnival atmosphere.

Beaches

Some of the most striking stretches of sand are found on the northern part of the island at Cape Santa Maria. The bays around the Stella Maris Inn contain several beaches, those to the south being best for swimming. The further you walk the quieter it gets.

Deal's Beach on the west coast has a three mile long beach, includes a play area and shallow water offshore for children and a nearby bar where drinks and snacks can be obtained.

Elsewhere by striking a trail off the main road, it is easy to find one of the numerous little bays which can be enjoyed in total seclusion.

Sport

Scuba

Long Island is one of the prime locations for diving in the Bahamas. Stella Maris offers a world-famous shark dive where participants watch sharks feed at very close quarters. When the videotape is played back in the evenings it never fails to elicit gasps of amazement from the audience. The scuba operation is based at the marina, where they offer certification and a large selection of dives. As well as the shark dive there is the wreck of the MS Comberback, a 100ft freighter which has been specially prepared for diving, the Conception Island Wall dive and many, many more.

TWENTY-EIGHT

Mayaguana

A forgotten outpost, this island is a mystery to most Bahamians let alone foreigners. So far all forms of development have passed Mayaguana by. The 300 locals still survive on agriculture and fishing, and although it has a richer soil than its neighbours it often suffers from a shortage of water. Mayaguana retains its Arawak name, but was settled in the mid-nineteenth century by Turks islanders and thereafter history seems to pass the place by.

Arrival

By air
Bahamasair offer two flights per week to Mayaguana. The aircraft usually make a stop at Inagua at some stage of the journey (tel. 322 4727 Nassau).

By sea
Mayaguana is served by a mailboat, but the times of sailing fluctuate widely. Contact the Harbour Master's office in Nassau on 393 1064 for accurate information.

Transport

The best way to get around the island is to catch a ride with the locals. Ask around to see if anyone is going your way.

Accommodation

The only place to stay is the **'Sheraton' Guest House Hotel** at Abraham Bay. This is not a member of that well known hotel chain but rather a small family run operation. It is owned by Doris and T Cap Brown who will cook local dishes and snacks on request. There are a few very basic shops on the island where vegetables, fish and tinned foods can be bought.

The Sights

There are three settlements on the island: Betsy Bay, Pirates Well and Abraham Bay, where the local government is based. Taking a trip around the island is like taking a step back in time, to see a side of the Bahamas long since gone elsewhere.

TWENTY-NINE

Ragged Island Range and the Jumentos Cays

Perhaps the greatest marvel about these islands is that they were ever settled at all. However, before 1800 two intrepid British loyalist families brought their slaves here to begin salt-raking. This remained the mainstay of the economy until the 1960s but now only enough salt is collected for local needs. About 100 people remain on Ragged Island in the settlement of Duncan's Town.

There are many abandoned houses as the lack of investment here has led to increased migration elsewhere. The islanders feel forgotten by central government but struggle on living by fishing and transporting their produce via the mailboat to Nassau.

Arrival

There is a small airport for private planes at Duncan's Town. Otherwise you will have to travel here by sea. The mailboat Emmette and Cephas leaves Nassau on Tuesdays at 16.00 taking almost a day for the trip. It arrives back in Nassau at 16.00 Thursdays. Contact the harbour office on Potter's Cay (tel. 393 1064) for up to date details.

Transport

The mailboat cannot dock in the harbour here as the channel through the mangroves is too shallow. Transport to shore is by dinghy. Ragged Island is only 7km (4 miles) long, so it can be seen on foot.

Accommodation

There are no tourist facilities here whatsoever but it may be possible to get lodgings with local people. The few visitors who do stray this far tend to come in their own yachts.

The Sights

This is an island of one sleepy village and some salt pans; that's all folks.

THIRTY

Rum Cay

Rum Cay is the story of a small community struggling to make a living while beset by natural disasters. The first inhabitants harvested salt in abundance from numerous shallow pools. The economy was booming until 1853 when a great hurricane savaged the island wrecking the salt works. The people painstakingly repaired the damage and salt production was resumed. Others diversified into growing pineapples and sisal.

In 1908 and 1926 two new hurricanes brought fresh suffering to Rum Cay. The islanders livelihood was again destroyed. This time the salt ponds were abandoned and with bleak prospects facing them most people left. Some subsistence agriculture was practised and the island may well have been abandoned if the tourist industry had not brought renewed prosperity to the community.

This island was probably Columbus's second landfall in the New World. He paused here only briefly, christening the place 'Santa Maria de la Conception'. This was obviously a bit of a mouthful to the coarse sailors and pirates who later visited the island so it was renamed after a rum ship wrecked off its shores.

With the cultivation of the salt pans the population grew to nearly 1,000 until, with failing fortunes, the exodus began and whole villages were abandoned. Nowa there are less than 100 inhabitants here who all live in the 'capital' Port Nelson.

Arrival

By air
The Rum Cay Club operate a licensed air charter service (tel. USA 305 467 8355), to and from Fort Lauderdale. It costs $250 round trip.

By sea

Passage aboard the mailboat can be bought for $35 one-way. The Maxine calls at Rum Cay on its way to San Salvador, leaving Nassau at midday on Tuesday and completing the round trip back to Potter's Cay by noon on Friday. To check the departure times ring the Harbour Master's office in Nassau (tel. 393 1064).

Transport

The Rum Cay Club offers complimentary use of bicycles, electric vehicles for hire or jeep rides. These are seldom needed as this island is only 20 square miles.

Accommodation

For hotel costs refer to page 5.

Moderate

The Rum Cay Club (Box 22396, Fort Lauderdale, FL 33335, tel. USA 305 467 8355). A highly rated resort appealing mainly to diving enthusiasts but offering many other activities as well. The cuisine, Bahamian and international, has been highly praised by a number of writers and is served with complimentary wine. Activities on offer include scuba, snorkeling, sailing, windsurfing and fishing. A variety of dive packages are available including certification.

The Club has a wide range of facilities including a hot tub, library and video. There is a dive shop on the premises and underwater cameras are available for rent. The resort has the facilities to develop film and offers instruction in the use of the cameras.

The Sights

The remains of several abandoned villages are easily explorable by hiking or bicycle. There are the shells of former **plantation houses** and an old jail house. On the northern side of the island is **Hartford Cave** where some Lucayan wall carvings can still be seen clearly.

THIRTY-ONE

San Salvador

San Salvador, on the extreme east of the Bahamian archipelago measures only 19km by 10km (12 miles by 6 miles). It lies 320km (200 miles) east-south-east of Nassau and is the officially recognised site of Christopher Columbus's landfall in the New World. The terrain is generally flat, the highest point being Mount Kerr at 42m (138ft), with numerous inland salt lakes and mangrove swamps. Before the days of road transportation these lakes and the ocean acted as the main routes of communication by sloops plying between settlements. Half of the 500 inhabitants live in Cockburn Town (pronounced Ko-burn).

The Lucayans (or island people) lived on the island for over 50 years before the arrival of Columbus. They knew it as Guanahani, but the 'discoverer' renamed it San Salvador (meaning Holy Saviour) and claimed it for the Spanish Crown. The British knew it as Watling's Island until 1926 after either George Watling, an English pirate captain who took over the island, or another Watling who was sent out to survey the island for the British Government. Perhaps they were even one and the same.

In recent years the controversy over the name has heightened with the quincentennial celebrations of landfall on 12 October 1492. Did the discovery of the Americas begin here? There are various claims: the Turks and Caicos, and Dominican Republic each suggesting it was one of their cays. More serious as an alternative is Cat Island; though the weight of historical argument is very much in favour of San Salvador. The Very Reverend Chyrsostom Schreiner OSB, a Catholic missionary in the Bahamas at the turn of the century, carried out a detailed survey of the area. His efforts were largely responsible for the official change of name. More recently, in the autumn of 1989, the yachtsman Robin Knox-Johnson, using a similar version of Columbus's navigational equipment the astralabe, retraced his route and ended up in San Salvador (Guardian, UK, 5 January 1990), adding further evidence to its claim and discounting recent suggestions in favour of Samana Cays.

Attempts at plantation farming all failed and it was not until the 1950s, with the coming of the US military bases at Bonefish Beach and Graham's Harbour that the island began to prosper. This was followed by the development on the south-east shore known as 'Columbus Landings'. In the 1960s the Florida Investments Corporation (FIC) began to build the infrastructure for 2,000 homes and sell off plots of lands to private investors. The proceeds were to be used to construct a hotel and golf course. When the new independent government placed a tax on foreign investments, FIC declared themselves bankrupt. Only 20 houses were ever built. With the closure of the military bases the island's economy slumped.

Today the site of Columbus's landfall is chief among the reasons why people visit this outcrop, together with the excellent diving conditions off the nearby reefs. Deep sea fishing is yet another recent attraction. Yet the place remains largely undeveloped and 'the people of San Salvador sit quietly around waiting for the eyes of the world to turn upon them' — philosophises a placard in the island's Museum.

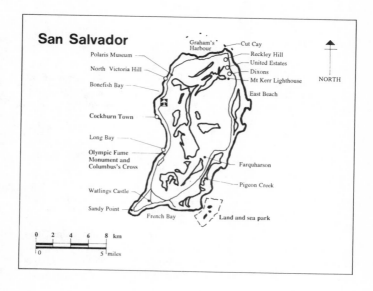

Arrival

By air
Bahamasair fly in from Nassau (tel. 322 4727) three times a week
— Tuesday, Friday and Sunday — calling at Cat Island either on
the way or the return leg of the journey, depending on the day of
travel. The cost of a return ticket is $116. Charter flights direct from
Fort Lauderdale are organised on a weekly basis by the Riding Rock
Inn. The airport itself is a kilometre (½ mile) from the Inn and a
further kilometre (½ mile) from Cockburn Town itself. (The road
to town passes across the end of the runway.)

By sea
The mailboat, Maxine, sails once a week calling at Rum Cay then
on into Cockburn Town, costing $35 one-way. It departs from
Potter's Cay, Nassau on Tuesday at 12 noon, returning by midday
on Friday. For up to date information contact the Harbour Master
in Nassau (tel. 393 1064).

Transport

Taxi
Local guides-come-drivers can easily be hired to take you around.
The Riding Rock Inn operates a courtesy bus for its guests to and
from the airport. Mr Forbes, the driver, will also take people on
private excursions and tours.

Rental hire
Riding Rock Inn (tel. 332 2631) cars cost $65, motorbikes $30 and
bicycles $5 per day.

Hitching
Relatively easy and safe, but there is little traffic as there are only
115 vehicles on the island.

If you are fit, it is possible to walk around the island in a day,
but take plenty of water. Certainly you will impress the locals who
have given up such follies a long time ago. Remember only mad
dogs and Englishmen go out in the midday sun.

Accommodation

For hotel costs refer to page 5.

Moderate
Riding Rock Inn (tel. 332 2631). Accommodation is provided in a choice of six units housing four to six people, or 24 sleeping units in cottages. The rooms are basic and clean with white-washed walls, modern fittings and air-conditioning. Each has a patio with chairs to make the most of the ocean or pool views. There is a swimming pool and tennis courts for use by the guests. The dive packages are very popular with excellent, clear water teaming with life just off shore. Other facilities include a conference centre a classroom for divers, a darkroom equipped to develop underwater photos, and an eight-birth full-service marina with the laundry available to guests. MC, V.

Budget
Ocean View Villas (contact via telephone operator). Owner Clifford Ferandez knows a lot of local and historical facts about the island. The three villas accommodate four or six people and are situated in North Victoria about 6km (4 miles) from Cockburn Town. The rooms are simply furnished and well maintained, with air-conditioning and ceiling fans, shared bathrooms and kitchenette. A fabulous, clean, empty beach of golden sand lies across the road. The place is a tiny backwater where houses are still left unlocked and the only noise is the waves lapping against the shore. No credit cards.

    William's Guest House, Long Bay has three rooms (sleeps six comfortably), with shared bathroom. This is basic island living with no frills and at times plenty of mosquitoes. A guided tour of the owners farm and a chat about bush medicine are additional bonuses. No credit cards.

Places to eat

Riding Rock Inn is the most prestigious eating place. Evening meals of Bahamian and seafood dishes come with a complimentary glass of wine ($26). Breakfast and lunch are available to hotel guests only for $7 and $10 respectively. Those not staying at the Inn should book for evening meals.

    The Ocean View Club opposite the great almond tree in the centre of Cockburn Town, serves Bahamian food and snacks such as chicken and fries for $4 or hamburgers for $2.75. If you wish for peas and rice then it will be necessary to ask the day before. Sodas cost $1, beers $2. Closed Sundays.

The Snack Bar, Cockburn Town was the initial enterprise set up in 1965 by the present owners of the Riding Rock Inn. Ada Forbes will serve you chicken and fries ($3.75) and fish burgers ($2), sodas ($1) or ice cream ($1.60). Take-away available; closed Sunday.

Basics

Banks
There are none, but the Post Office will cash $US travellers cheques in emergencies.

Medical
There are two clinics, at Cockburn Town and United Estates plus a resident doctor on the island.

Police
The police station is in Cockburn Town, part of the same building as the Commissionaire Office and Post Office.

Nightlife

Every Wednesday live music is played by a rake and scrape band at the **Riding Rock Inn.** It is a chance to meet the locals who never miss an opportunity to enjoy themselves.

The Harlem Square Club, Cockburn Town is another local hangout. They come to shoot pool, watch satellite TV, or play a game of dominoes.

At the **Arawak Bar** (Polaris Museum, North Victoria) Bobby is both bartender and caretaker. He keeps an open house until all hours of the night. Right on the ocean front with a beaut' of an old jukebox.

The Sights

There are four **monuments to Christopher Columbus** on the island.
The oldest, erected by the Chicago Herald newspaper, overlooks the
reefbound east shore. Installed to commemorate the 400th
anniversary of Columbus's landfall, it can be reached by walking
from East Beach. It is not known why they chose this unlikely site.

In 1956 a large white cross was placed by Columbian historian
Ruth Wulper at Long Bay to mark the most likely landing location.
The site is six miles out from Cockburn Town heading south-east.
Adjacent, is the Olympic monument provided by the people of
Mexico to commemorate the transferral of the Olympic torch to the
New World for the Mexico Games in 1968. Both sites have a
somewhat ramshackle appearance but there are plans to create a two
acre landfall park for the quincentennial celebrations. The fourth
monument is actually under the water to represent where Columbus
dropped anchor.

In Cockburn Town itself, there is a small **museum** to the
illustrious discoverer, housed in the former jail converted by
Operation Raleigh. One of the island's proudest claims is to have
no need for a jail. Enquire with Iris Ferandez at the gift shop just
down the road for the key to the museum and browse around at
your leisure.

The New World and Polaris Museum is near North Victoria.
It has artefacts of the Lucayan people, a chronological account of
Columbus's encounter with them and explanations of traditional
farming techniques. (Entrance fee $1.)

Further up the Queen's Highway is the grave of **Father Schreiner**
which overlooks Graham's Harbour and Cut Cay, in the location
which proved so strongly in his own mind that this was Columbus's
first landfall and where he wished to be buried. This however was
not an easy request to comply with as it was the Bahamian custom
to bury the body on the day of death and the ground was coral
rock. The problem was resolved by removing stones from the grave
of the former plantation owner of Harbour Estates, Mr Burton
Williams, and placing Father Schreiner on top of Williams' coffin.

Upon reaching North Point you can walk along the top peninsula
to Cut Cay. A more recent relic of marine history is the wreck of
a British trawler which ran aground in the 1930s. For a short while
the islanders prospered from the salvage operation. This is a lovely
picnic spot.

Before you reach North Point at the end of Graham's Harbour,
is the CCFL (College Center of the Finger Lakes) **Bahamian Field
Station,** sited in the old US naval base. It is a research and

educational institute for biological and geological features, open December to July. Feel free to drop in and visit the library.

Continuing on along the road, also on the right-hand side, is an abandoned **US Coast Guard station.** Just around the corner is **Reckley Hill,** a small hamlet made up of one family, the Nairns. The road passes through the United Estates community (known as UE) and on to Dixon Hill. Here there is one of the ten remaining kerosine-fuelled, manually controlled lighthouses in the world. (Three others are also located in the Bahamas at Inagua, Hopetown and Hole in the Wall.) It sends out a double flash every ten seconds and is visible for 30km (19 miles). Climb the 81 steep steps to the top and take in the splendid view. No admittance fee is charged though donations for its upkeep are gratefully appreciated.

Around on the south-east shore are the remains of **Watling's Castle,** an eighteenth-century plantation house in a wonderful location on a hill overlooking the beautiful French Bay. The best preserved mansion is **Farquaharson's Plantation,** where the foundations of the great house, kitchen and punishment cell can be seen.

During Hurricane Betsy in 1965 cattle belonging to Jake Jones, the grocery store owner in Cockburn Town, broke loose and now roam as they please. To catch them a noose is laid on the ground near watering holes. The traps are inspected twice a day and any animal found is slaughtered on the spot and transported to Jake Jones's deep freeze. Everybody still considers them to be his animals.

Beaches

In travelling about seeing the sights, don't forget to take your swimwear as you will come across fabulous white sandy beaches stretching off into the distance. Bonefish Beach out past the High School (an old PanAm base), is probably the best with the sand continuing out under the water for most of the bay.

Sports

Scuba

The Riding Rock Inn has individual dives for $30, or $65 for three. Equipment can be rented, including underwater cameras.

Appendix A

Bahamasspeak

Bahamians have always used English as their native tongue, though with a strong local accent. Here are a few tips to help you get by.

Conch is the local staple food together with grouper. You do not pronounce it as it is spelt, you say 'konk'.

Cay is the Bahamian word for a small island, it comes from the Spanish 'cayo' and is pronounced 'key'.

In many words the 'th' is changed to a 'd' or a 'z' sound. Thus 'the' and 'that' become 'de' and 'dat', while 'thank' and 'thing' become 'tank' and 'ting'. Often 'v's become 'w's so 'very' and 'village' become 'wery' and 'willage'. Some words gain an 'h' others loose an 'h'.

Typical greetings are 'hey mon wha's happ'nin'. It is a salutation rather than a question. 'Mon' and 'womon' and 'bulla' (brother) or 'sister' are used as friendly terms for the person being spoken to.

Obeah the practice of bush medicine, white or black magic. Similar to the voodoo of Haiti or shango of Trinidad.

A potcake is a Bahamian dog — the name derives from leftovers put out to feed them.

Wind Force: The Beaufort Scale*

B'Fort No.	Wind Descrip.	Effect on land	Effect on sea	Wind Speed knots	mph	kph	Wave height (m)†
0	Calm	Smoke rises veritcally	Sea like a mirror	less than 1			-
1	Light air	Direction shown by smoke but not by wind vane	Ripples with appearance of scales; no foam crests	1-3	1-3	1-2	-
2	Light breeze	Wind felt on face; leaves rustle; wind vanes move	Small wavelets; crests do not break	4-6	4-7	6-11	0.15-0.30
3	Gentle breeze	Leaves and twigs in motion wind extends light flag	Large wavelets; crests begin to break; scattered white horses	7-10	8-12	13-19	0.60-1.00
4	Moderate breeze	Small branches move; dust and loose paper raised	Small waves, becoming longer; fairly frequent white horses	11-16	13-18	21-29	1.00-1.50
5	Fresh breeze	Small trees in leaf begin to sway	Moderate waves; many white horses; chance of some spray	17-21	19-24	30-38	1.80-2.50
6	Strong breeze	Large branches in motion; telegraph wires whistle	Large waves begin to form; white crests extensive; some spray	22-27	25-31	40-50	3.00-4.00

B'Fort No.	Wind Descrip.	Effect on land	Effect on sea	Wind Speed knots	mph	kph	Wave height (m)†
7	Near gale	Whole trees in motion; difficult to walk against wind	Sea heaps up; white foam from breaking waves begins to be blown in streaks	28-33	32-38	51-61	4.00-6.00
8	Gale	Twigs break off trees; progress impeded	Moderately high waves; foam blown in well-marked streaks	34-40	39-46	63-74	5.50-7.50
9	Strong gale	Chimney pots and slates blown off	High waves; dense streaks of foam; wave crests begin to roll over; heavy spray	41-47	47-54	75-86	7.00-9.75
10	Storm	Trees uprooted; considerable structural damage	Very high waves, overhanging crests; dense white foam streaks; sea takes on white appearance; visibility affected	48-56	66-63	88-100	9.00-12.50
11	Violent storm	Widespread damage, seldom experienced in England	Exceptionally high waves; dense patches of foam; wave crests blown into froth; visibility affected	57-65	64-75	101-110	11.30-16.00
12	Hurricane	Winds of this force encountered only in Tropics	Air filled with foam & spray; visibility seriously affected	65+	75+	120+	13.70+

* Introduced in 1805 by Sir Francis Beaufort (1774:1857) hydrographer to the Navy
† First figure indicates average height of waves; second figure indicates maximum height.

Appendix C

Distance/Height

feet	ft or m	metres
3.281	1	0.305
6.562	2	0.610
9.843	3	0.914
13.123	4	1.219
16.404	5	1.524
19.685	6	8.829
22.966	7	2.134
26.247	8	2.438
29.528	9	2.743
32.808	10	3.048
65.617	20	8.096
82.081	25	7.620
164.05	50	15.25
328.1	100	30.5
3281.	1000	305.

Weight

pounds	kg or lb	kilograms
2.205	1	0.454
4.409	2	0.907
8.819	4	1.814
13.228	6	2.722
17.637	8	3.629
22.046	10	4.536
44.093	20	9.072
55.116	25	11.340
110.231	50	22.680
220.462	100	45.359

Distance

miles	km or mls	kilometres
0.621	1	1.609
1.243	2	3.219
1.864	3	4.828
2.486	4	6.437
3.107	5	8.047
3.728	6	9.656
4.350	7	11.265
4.971	8	12.875
5.592	9	14.484
6.214	10	16.093
12.428	20	32.186
15.534	25	40.234
31.069	50	80.467
62.13	100	160.93
621.3	1000	1609.3

Dress sizes

Size	bust/hip inches	bust/hip centimetres
8	30/32	76/81
10	32/34	81/86
12	34/36	86/91
14	36/38	91/97
16	38/40	97/102
18	40/42	102/107
20	42/44	107/112
22	44/46	112/117
24	46/48	117/122

Tyre pressure

lb per sq in	kg per sq cm
14	0.984
16	1.125
18	1.266
20	1.406
22	1.547
24	1.687
26	1.828
28	1.969
30	2.109
40	2.812

Temperature

centigrade	fahrenheit
0	32
5	41
10	50
20	68
30	86
40	104
50	122
60	140
70	158
80	176
90	194
100	212

Oven temperatures

Electric	Gas mark	Centigrade
225	¼	110
250	½	130
275	1	140
300	2	150
325	3	170
350	4	180
375	5	190
400	6	200
425	7	220
450	8	230

Your weight in kilos

stones

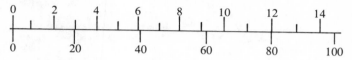

kilograms

Liquids

gallons	gal or l	litres
0.220	1	4.546
0.440	2	9.092
0.880	4	18.184
1.320	6	27.276
1.760	8	36.368
2.200	10	45.460
4.400	20	90.919
5.500	25	113.649
10.999	50	227.298
21.998	100	454.596

Some handy equivalents for self caterers

1 oz	25 g	1 fluid ounce	25 ml
4 oz	125 g	¼ pt. (1 gill)	142 ml
8 oz	250 g	½ pt.	284 ml
1 lb	500 g	¾ pt.	426 ml
2.2 lb	1 kilo	1 pt.	568 ml
		1¾ pints	1 litre

INDEX